Virtue in Business

The virtue approach to business ethics is a topic of increasing importance within the business world. Focusing on Aristotle's theory that the virtues of character, rather than actions, are central to ethics, Edwin M. Hartman introduces readers of this book to the value of applying Aristotle's virtue approach to business. Using numerous real-world examples, he argues that business leaders have good reason to take character seriously when explaining and evaluating individuals in organizations. He demonstrates how the virtue approach can deepen our understanding of business ethics and how it can contribute to contemporary discussions of character, rationality, corporate culture, ethics education, and global ethics. Written by one of the foremost Aristotelian scholars working in the field today, this authoritative introduction to the role of virtue ethics in business is a valuable text for graduate students and academic researchers in business ethics, applied ethics, and philosophy.

EDWIN M. HARTMAN was Visiting Professor of Business Ethics and co-director of the Paduano Seminar in Business Ethics at the Stern School of Business in New York University until his retirement in December 2009. Before joining Stern, he taught for more than twenty years in the business school and the philosophy department at Rutgers University, where he was founding director of the Prudential Business Ethics Center at Rutgers. He is the author of *Substance, Body, and Soul: Aristotelian Investigations, Conceptual Foundations of Organization Theory*, and *Organizational Ethics and the Good Life* (named Book of the Year [2003] by the Social Issues in Management Division of the Academy of Management).

Business, Value Creation, and Society

Series editors

R. Edward Freeman, *University of Virginia*
Jeremy Moon, *Nottingham University*
Mette Morsing, *Copenhagen Business School*

The purpose of this innovative series is to examine, from an international standpoint, the interaction of business and capitalism with society. In the twenty-first century it is more important than ever that business and capitalism come to be seen as social institutions that have a great impact on the welfare of human society around the world. Issues such as globalization, environmentalism, information technology, the triumph of liberalism, corporate governance, and business ethics all have the potential to have major effects on our current models of the corporation and the methods by which value is created, distributed, and sustained among all stakeholders – customers, suppliers, employees, communities, and financiers.

Published titles:

Fort   *Business, Integrity, and Peace*
Gomez and Korine   *Entrepreneurs and Democracy*
Crane, Matten, and Moon   *Corporations and Citizenship*
Painter-Morland   *Business Ethics as Practice*
Yaziji and Doh   *NGOs and Corporations*
Rivera   *Business and Public Policy*
Sachs and Rühli   *Stakeholders Matter*
Mansell   *Capitalism, Corporations and the Social Contract*

Forthcoming titles:

Hemingway   *Corporate Social Entrepreneurship*
Maak and Pless   *Responsible Leadership*
de Bruin   *Ethics in Finance*

Virtue in Business

Conversations with Aristotle

EDWIN M. HARTMAN

CAMBRIDGE
UNIVERSITY PRESS

CAMBRIDGE
UNIVERSITY PRESS

University Printing House, Cambridge CB2 8BS, United Kingdom

Cambridge University Press is part of the University of Cambridge.

It furthers the University's mission by disseminating knowledge in the pursuit of education, learning and research at the highest international levels of excellence.

www.cambridge.org
Information on this title: www.cambridge.org/9781107642300

© Edwin M. Hartman 2013

First published 2013
First paperback edition 2015

A catalogue record for this publication is available from the British Library

Library of Congress Cataloguing in Publication data
Hartman, Edwin, 1941–
Virtue in business : conversations with Aristotle / Edwin M. Hartman.
    pages   cm. – (Business, value creation, and society)
Includes bibliographical references and index.
ISBN 978-1-107-03075-6 (hardback)
1. Business ethics.   2. Virtue.   3. Aristotle.   I. Title.
HF5387.H37324   2013
174´.4 – dc23   2013011345

ISBN 978-1-107-03075-6 Hardback
ISBN 978-1-107-64230-0 Paperback

For M. S. H. and S. M. H.
sine quibus non

Contents

Foreword

Ed Hartman has brought Aristotle to life for the business world of the twenty-first century. This book leaves no doubt about the relevance and importance of Aristotle's wisdom for today's executives and management thinkers. And Hartman shows that it is not just a matter of the importance of virtues and the golden mean. He shows in detail how understanding the strengths and weaknesses of Aristotle's worldview enlightens how we can think about business today.

There is very little certainty in today's business world. There are breathtaking technologies that change everything from life spans to how we see each other. And there seems to be an increasing shortage of "common sense." Hartman navigates these waters with an Aristotelian sense of what is important and what is not. He does not founder on dichotomies such as "normative vs. positive" or "business vs. ethics" or "science vs. philosophy." He shows how a modern-day pragmatist in the spirit of both Dewey and Rorty can read Aristotle as contributing to the theoretical conversation in business ethics, and as yielding practical insights into how organizations need to be managed in this new world.

Hartman brings a career of philosophical training, teaching in business schools, and work as a management consultant to the task. He has studied with some of the best philosophical minds in the world, and has worked with senior executives from industry and education. He has given us a new interpretation of Aristotle that is both philosophically deep and practically relevant.

For instance, in Chapter 4 he makes Aristotle relevant to those behavioral theorists who question our ability to deliberate and improve the kinds of decisions we might make. Chapter 5 has much to say to so-called "new institutionalists" who want to work only at a very abstract level in organizations. Yet Chapter 7 is quite relevant to the policy analysts who want to prescribe how issues such as globalization should unfold with the help of mediating institutions, including businesses.

Aristotle had a remarkably comprehensive view of his own world, and Hartman follows suit, but he is able to make Aristotle speak to others who do not share or even understand Aristotle's worldview. Yet perhaps some of the most remarkable passages in the book are the stories of people from Hartman's own consulting experience. He then goes on to interpret how Aristotle would see these situations, not in terms of the world of Ancient Greece, but in our modern terms. These passages bring Aristotle to life for business in a way that has never been done.

It is a pleasure to publish this book in the series on Business, Value Creation, and Society. The purpose of this series is to stimulate new thinking about value creation and trade, and its role in the world of the twenty-first century. Our old models and ideas simply are not appropriate today. Hartman's interpretation makes Aristotle a citizen and an important voice in this new world. We need more new scholarship like this that builds on the work of our intellectual heroes yet offers the alternative of a world of hope, freedom, and human flourishing.

R. Edward Freeman
University Professor and
Elis and Signe Olsson Professor
The Darden School
University of Virginia
Charlottesville, Virginia, USA

Acknowledgments

Interpreting Aristotle is a humbling task. One stands on the shoulders of giants; occasionally one steps on their toes. The giants include not only the great interpreters of Aristotle but also leading scholars in fields to which Aristotle has something to say: ethics, psychology, sociology, politics, and so on and on. So much has been written about trust, social capital, the commons, individualism, rationality, liberalism, baseball, and much else that it would be difficult for one scholar to encompass them all. For this scholar it is impossible. The most I can reasonably hope is that those whose mastery of these subjects exceeds mine will learn from my work that Aristotle has something interesting to say to them.

Over the years I have learned about Aristotle from many sources. I can no longer recall exactly who taught me what, so I cannot fairly acknowledge all my debts. It will be obvious that, as I have worked on this book in recent years, I have been much influenced by the work of Terence Irwin, Julia Annas, and Daniel Russell on the *Nicomachean Ethics* and that of Fred Miller on the *Politics*. I am sure I also owe thanks to Rosalind Hursthouse, Nancy Sherman, Martha Nussbaum, Sarah Broadie, John Cooper, and others for their work on Aristotle's ethics. I am grateful to John Keaney for a graduate seminar on the *Politics* nearly fifty years ago. My great teachers of the *Metaphysics* were Richard Rorty, Gwilym Owen, Richard Woods, and Terry Penner. Penner, my very patient thesis adviser, gave me a good start on Aristotle's *De Anima*, and David Furley contributed to my further work on it. Gregory Vlastos was my guide to Socrates and Plato. On philosophical issues generally I learned most from Rorty, Antony Kenny, and Donald Davidson. James Ward Smith, Alan Montefiore, and Richard Hare taught me a great deal about ethics. Nick Sturgeon, Don Waterfall, Frank Lewis, Richard Kraut, Hardy Wieting, and Alexander Nehamas were good influences in many areas of philosophy, starting but not ending in graduate school. Where social psychology offers insights to virtue ethics, the great recent influence on my thought has been the work of Jonathan Haidt, though John Doris and Daniel Kahneman are deservedly highlighted here as well. But social psychologists have been working on me since I took an undergraduate class with David Rosenhan.

I had the pleasure of working with Alejo Sison and Joan Fontrodona in editing a special number of *Business Ethics Quarterly* on the virtue approach to business ethics. I learned a great deal from them and from the contributors, and I profited from their encyclopedic knowledge of the literature of the field.

But for the encouragement of Ed Freeman, I might still be in management consulting rather than business ethics. I trust that his efforts have improved both fields. Ed has offered good advice on this book, as on much else that I have written.

Concerning virtue ethics as an approach to business ethics I am, as so many are, most in debt to the late Bob Solomon. Miguel Alzola, Robert Audi, Jerry Cavanagh, Joe DesJardins, Ron Duska, Gabriel Flynn, Kevin Jackson, Daryl Koehn, Domenec Mele, Dennis Moberg, Geoff Moore, Craig Walton, and Gary Weaver have contributed to the virtue approach and to my work. I will add Pat Werhane's name, though it may not have occurred to her that she is a virtue ethicist. Other names deserving of mention appear in the Bibliography. It was my privilege to have Miguel Alzola as a student. I doubt that I have taught him as much as he has taught me.

Many Rutgers colleagues helped me in my years there. I thank Jeff Buechner, Wayne Eastman, Harvey Feder, George Gordon, Candace Hetzner, Nancy Holmstrom, Doug Husak, Jim Livingston, Don McCabe, Brian McLaughlin, Michael Rohr, Mike Stouder, Mike Valdman, Pheroze Wadia, and Danielle Warren. I appreciate the administrative support I received from Annette Allen, George Benson, David Blake, Ivan Brick, Steve Diner, Hal Eastman, Phil Furmanski, David Hosford, Lisa Hull, Barbara Kovach, Art Kraft, Fran Lawrence, Marc Mappen, Rosa Oppenheim, Jerry Rosenberg, Norman Samuels, Glenn Shafer, Jeff Slovak, Cecile Stolbaugh, my late friend Howard Tuckman, and Emilio Venezian.

The Prudential Foundation generously funded the Prudential Business Ethics Center at Rutgers. During my tenure as director, Harold Davis, the guiding spirit of the Center, and Oliver Quinn were Chief Ethics Officers at Prudential and invaluable colleagues.

I thank Rutgers for giving me two leaves of absence to work on this book. In addition the University gave an Academic Excellence Grant to the Prudential Business Ethics Center and the Eagleton Institute of Politics at Rutgers for a project on ethics in New Jersey. It was a pleasure to work with and learn from Ruth Mandel, Don Linky, and others at the Institute.

At Rutgers I was twice a fellow of the Center for the Critical Analysis of Contemporary Culture, an extraordinary laboratory of ideas. I am especially grateful to Andy Abbott, Amanda Anderson, George Levine, Jonathan Loesberg, Candace McCoy, Dennis Patterson, Pat Roos, Renee Weber, and Bruce Wilshire.

At New York University's Stern School of Business I was fortunate to be able to participate in the Paduano Seminar and to converse with some outstanding colleagues, including Bruce Buchanan, Bob Frank, Rex Mixon, Gary Simon, and David Velleman. The Seminar's fellows and guest speakers taught us all a great deal. Tom Cooley and Ingo Walter offered excellent administrative support.

I profited from speaking and listening at California State University at Sacramento, the University of Montreal, Gettysburg College, the University of New Mexico, the Witherspoon Institute, the Eller School at the University of Arizona, IESE Business School of the University of Navarra, and the Wharton School. At the Darden School I taught PhD seminar modules on Aristotle's ethics to some extraordinary students. Dave Schmidtz, the director of the always stimulating Freedom Center at the University of Arizona, made it possible for me to meet Mark LeBar, Dan Russell, and others. I attended the Ruffin Lectures at Darden many times and always came away enlightened and energized.

George Bragues was a helpful editor of the section of the *Handbook of the Philosophical Foundations of Business Ethics* (Springer) to which I contributed. Chapter 4 of this book is a later version of my contribution. Dan Russell edited the *Cambridge Companion to Virtue Ethics* and offered good advice on my piece. James Bailey shepherded a contribution of mine to publication in *Academy of Management Learning and Education*. Some parts of that article reappear in Chapter 6. Al Gini did the same with my contributions to *Business Ethics Quarterly*, and Robert Baum played that role at *Business and Professional Ethics Journal*. Many anonymous reviewers, including some at the *Journal of Business Ethics*, improved my work.

In addition to those I have already mentioned, I am indebted to many in business ethics who have been generous with their ideas: John Boatright, Norm Bowie, George Brenkert, Joanne Ciulla, Daylian Cain, Deb Cohen, Richard DeGeorge, Robbin Derry, John Dienhart, Tom Donaldson, our late friend Tom Dunfee, Ed Epstein, Tim Fort, Bill Frederick, Dan Gilbert, Ken Goodpaster, Stewart Herman, Mike Hoffman, Nien-he Hsieh, Ian Maitland, Joshua Margolis, Dave Messick, Christopher Michaelson, Jennifer Moore, Laura Nash, Lisa Newton, Richard Nielsen, Wayne Norman, Lynn Paine, Bobby Parmar, Rob Phillips, Gordon Sollars, Alan Strudler, Manny Velasquez, and Andy Wicks. I am sure there are others, to whom I apologize.

For insights on a variety of topics I thank the Philosophers of the Oracle Inn.

Mary S. Hartman has been, as always, an invaluable source of intellectual and moral support and immeasurably more. Our son, Sam Hartman, is an inspiration to us both.

Two anonymous reviewers for Cambridge University Press offered encouragement and incisive criticism. They are responsible for having improved this book, but not for any of my errors of omission or commission.

Ed Freeman, Paula Parish, and Claire Poole have been the most conscientious editors imaginable. Ekta Vishnoi guided me ably through the mysteries of indexing. Harry Langford helped make my text readable. I thank them all for their highly professional assistance.

Earlier versions of some claims I make in this book have appeared in these places:

2013. "The virtue approach to business ethics." In D. Russell (Ed.), *Cambridge Companion to Virtue Ethics*, 240–64. New York: Cambridge University Press.

2012. "Aristotle on character formation." In C. Luetge (Ed.), *Handbook of the Philosophical Foundations of Business Ethics*, Vol. 1, 67–88. New York: Springer-Verlag.

2011. "Win-win and the common good." In R. Phillips (Ed.), *Stakeholder Theory: Impact and Prospects*, 76–98. Cheltenham, UK: Edward Elgar Publishing.

2011. "Virtue, profit, and the separation thesis: an Aristotelian view." *Journal of Business Ethics*, 99, 5–17.

2008. "Socratic questions and Aristotelian answers: a virtue-based approach to business ethics." *Journal of Business Ethics*, 78, 313–28.

2008. "Reconciliation in business ethics: some advice from Aristotle." *Business Ethics Quarterly*, 18, 253–65.

2006. "Can we teach character? An Aristotelian answer." *Academy of Management Learning and Education*, 5, 68–81.

2004. "De rerum natura." In R. E. Freeman and P. Werhane (Eds.), *Business, Science, and Ethics*, 201–20. The Ruffin Series No. 4 (a special edition of *Business Ethics Quarterly*).

2001. "Character and leadership." *Business and Professional Ethics Journal*, 20, 3–21.

2001. "An Aristotelian approach to moral imagination." *Professional Ethics*, 8, 58–77.

1998. "The role of character in business ethics." *Business Ethics Quarterly*, 8, 547–59.

1996. *Organizational Ethics and the Good Life*. New York: Oxford University Press.

Introduction to Aristotle, virtue ethics, and this book

An overview of Aristotle's philosophy

Aristotle is widely thought to be the philosopher of common sense *par excellence*. According to Aristotle, what intelligent adults believe about the world is true on the whole, though their opinion needs some refinement, or occasionally some alteration.[1]

Socrates, by conspicuous contrast, has little respect for the opinions of distinguished citizens, or any other opinions for that matter, about ethical issues. His method is to show that people are ignorant where they – unlike Socrates himself – claim to know. Plato goes from there to claim that real knowledge is not about the world of space and time at all. What is truly real, the object of certain knowledge, is the eternal Idea. Here as elsewhere certainty has a powerful grip on philosophers. Throughout much of the history of Western philosophy there have been thinkers who asked how we could have certain knowledge of anything, other than perhaps the contents of our own minds, or mathematics. And if that sort of knowledge was hard to find, it was harder still to find some basis for ethics, some sound answers to the questions "What ought I to do?" and "What reason have I for doing what I ought to do?" These questions seemed beyond the reach of human opinion, even of science. Only philosophers could handle them, according to some philosophers.

Aristotle does not think this way. He does not demand ironclad certainty; he does not worry greatly about our knowledge of the external world, or of ethics. He typically begins his investigations in ethics and elsewhere by looking at some commonsense views that we, or at least the wise among us, share. These he calls *ta koina* – common things. But though he begins with common things, he does not regard our

---

[1] Almost any interpretation of Aristotle will be controversial. My views, which owe something to many commentators, are in the mainstream of recent critical work, I think.

apprehension of them as an immutable foundation on which all knowledge is built. On the contrary, his method tidies up common sense and makes it coherent. His conclusions – his views on form and matter, his definition of the soul, his conception of well-being – are subtle but not radical. For example, his notion of a person of good character sounds right and insightful to us, as it must have to his contemporaries. He does not put forward altogether new conceptions of courage, justice, or friendship. He does not in the least suggest that becoming a good person is a superhuman achievement, though it is neither easy nor very common. The effect of the *Nicomachean Ethics* is not to undermine our ideas about ethics but to sharpen and rationalize them. He also brings his findings on biology and psychology to bear on ethics, as each of his studies builds on what he has learned earlier.

The development of Aristotle's philosophy

First and most basically, Aristotle addresses the idea that there are individual material objects in space and time and that we can have some knowledge of them. That may seem obvious, but Aristotle wants to defend the position against some attacks. Heraclitus challenged it in claiming that everything is changing all the time, with the result that identification and reference are impossible. Plato challenged it from the other direction by arguing that secure identification and reference are indeed possible but require Ideas as their real objects. But it is not clear how Plato's view shows that we can do what we ordinarily want to do: talk meaningfully about an actual river continuing to exist, remaining the same over a period of time, if the water is constantly changing.

Aristotle solves the puzzles by distinguishing between the form (or essence or, occasionally, nature) of a substance and its matter or accidents. A thing may appear to be a combination of form and matter, but it is in fact identical with its form: it always has matter, but not necessarily the same matter permanently. So when we say that a thing has lasted over a period of time, we are in effect saying that its form has lasted, while its matter or some of its accidental characteristics (weight, color, etc.) may have changed. The Ohio River remains the same river even though the water that constitutes it is constantly changing. A tree remains the same tree even as its leaves come and go and it grows new wood. (As it happens, the Greek word *hyle* means both matter and wood.)

Aristotle sometimes uses artificial objects like a discus or a lintel as illustrations. In the former case, the shape is the form; in the latter, the position above a door or window is the form. But artificial objects present hard questions. If over time we replace all the boards in a ship, does it remain the same ship? And if it does, what can we say about the ship that could be constructed out of the discarded boards? Fringe cases of this sort do not worry Aristotle, particularly when they involve artificial things. He believes that one cannot always draw bright lines, but that discourse is not impossible for that reason. In any case, only natural things are true substances.

Substances have primacy over qualities and similar items in the sense that the latter are modifications of substances, and may attach to substances for a time but then go away while the substances persist. These modifications, or properties, of substances depend for their identity and persistence on the substances that they modify. Time and space too are parasitic on substances, according to Aristotle, since he defines both of them by reference to substance, in particular by reference to the movement and change of substances.

One of the capacities of natural substances is the capacity to change, and in particular to grow to maturity. One way of explaining what happens in the world is to note that an animal has the capacity to move (and more), or that an acorn has the capacity to become an oak tree. In this way events in the world are dependent on the substances that participate in them. Thus far Aristotle remains consistent with common sense, for better or worse, though his elaboration and his defense of his position are sophisticated. His task becomes more complicated when he turns to the nature or essence of the human being.

The substance that has a soul

By the time he writes the *Nicomachean Ethics*, Aristotle has in his pocket not only common opinion but some views about substances from the *Metaphysics* and about persons that he has reached in *De Anima* by a dialectical process similar to that used in the mature books of the *Metaphysics*.[2] He also brings some findings from the *Physics;* those support and are supported by his metaphysical work. So

---

[2] About Aristotle's progress I agree largely with the account of Irwin (1988, chapter 1).

Aristotle begins his ethics with a certain view of humankind. A human being is a substance, and what makes a human a substance rather than just a pile of flesh and bones is the set of capacities that we call a soul or mind. What makes a person a person in particular, as opposed to a dumb animal, is the characteristically human ability to reason. You can reason abstractly in sophisticated ways, and even design a life for yourself as a member of a *polis* – what we now call a city-state – and a participant in its governance. From this it is no great leap to the claim that what makes a human being excellent – the word *arête* can be translated as virtue or excellence – involves sociability and, distinctly, rationality. To act accordingly is to live well. The life that you are able to design for yourself should take into appropriate account your own rational capacities. It should also attend to your limitations and your opportunities, including those associated with your being necessarily a sociable creature – a citizen, a friend, and a family member.

Aristotle and Newton: science and persons

So Aristotle embraces the commonsensical rather than the other-worldly and unattainable. But he also embraces the commonsensical rather than the scientific, in our sense of the word, and there will be problems where science and common sense diverge.

Aristotelian science is radically different from, and less successful than, the modern conception of natural science. We need to consider whether Aristotelian ethics is inferior to modern ethics for the same reasons.

Aristotle is not wrong in taking humankind to be a part of nature. It makes sense, too, to explain some events in the world by reference to substances, including persons, actualizing their potential or not. When botanists, of whom Aristotle is one, talk about plants, they seem ready to say on the basis of careful observation what causes this or that species to flourish and what counts as flourishing for the species. Facts about nutrition and growth form the basis of their judgments about which plants are faring well and which are not. McKinnon (2005) discusses this point at length and draws an analogy, as Aristotle does, between the flourishing of plants and animals and that of human beings. One can speak intelligently about whether young Andrea will fulfill her potential, though this does not sound like the sort of language that can support an exact science.

When Aristotle says that one event or one thing is the efficient cause of another, he is not presupposing, as most modern philosophers do, that there is a law of nature linking the first with the second. He does believe in final causes, and therefore in teleological explanations – that is, explanations that indicate the purpose that something serves or the end that it achieves. Teleological explanations make sense in a universe in which there are natural movements of natural objects towards natural final destinations. Aristotelian science, based on neither careful measurement nor highly systematic observation, does not contemplate a universe that works according to universal and immutable laws that support causal claims; still less does it countenance laws linking unobservable entities. Aristotle seems to believe that some relationships hold only most of the time and that, in part for that reason, our understanding is sometimes only approximate.

Newton, improving on Descartes and Leibniz, takes a different view, which on the whole prevails today. Nature is rational just in the sense that it is law-governed. The point of Newtonian science is to use universal scientific principles to explain particular events and states, as opposed to things, and it has been successful in the sense that it can predict future events and states and explain past ones. Aristotelian science has never known that kind of success; so we have reason to infer that the differences between Aristotle and Newton are in Newton's favor.

We may also be inclined to infer that what makes one sort of science better than another would also make one way of thinking about ethics better than another – that ethics too ought to be based on universal principles, that what is primarily right or wrong is a particular act (i.e., an event) according to whether or not it is consistent with a universal ethical principle, rather than a person (i.e., a thing) according to whether the person achieves his or her natural end. In the Newtonian universe things and events do not proceed towards their natural ends. How useful are explanations and justifications of human behavior based on the notion that people proceed in that direction?

The place of persons

The Newtonian view of the universe does pose a problem for us. What place in this universe has the human being, a willing, feeling, creating organism? One answer, offered by Descartes and others, is that the human being is not a merely physical being subject to the laws governing physical beings. A person is primarily mental; the body is a vehicle, a repository for the mind. Some philosophers see the body as something of an encumbrance, since it implicates us in emotion, selfish desire, and all manner of evil. Rationality, the faculty characteristic of the mind as opposed to the body, is good. Moral goodness requires that we overcome the body and its ways.[3]

Some philosophers, including Spinoza (and Democritus, one of Aristotle's predecessors), reduce mental activity to physical activity. They see no special kind of substance of which mental events are made, no exemption from physical laws. According to Kant, the greatest of the Enlightenment philosophers, freedom of the will requires that our rational will, uncaused by physical states and directed only by rationality, causes our actions despite the otherwise law-bound inexorability of nature. Our thoughts should obey the laws of reason, the rule-maker in the realm of the mental, which are even more reliable and inexorable than are the laws of nature. Morality too is based on reason, according to Kant.

Kant and many other Enlightenment philosophers take rationality to be the savior of humankind, with respect to both science and human good. Without it we cannot solve our scientific problems or build anything that requires engineering. Without it we cannot organize our lives. When it is absent or overwhelmed by emotion or desire, we cannot think usefully, together or on our own, about what there is or what we ought to do. We might look to religion for guidance, but not all of us will look to the same religion. We may then be plunged into murderous religious conflicts because we have no rational way of reconciling differing accounts of religious truth or, therefore, of moral truth. That is the lesson that some Enlightenment figures drew from the horrors of the Thirty Years' War (see Toulmin, 1990, especially chapter 2). We may be inclined to think that the philosophers of the Enlightenment were unduly optimistic about the power of reason, but theirs was perhaps an understandable reaction to the spectacle of Christians killing one another *en masse* over transubstantiation.[4] We

---

[3] I shall not try to distinguish morality from ethics. Many different philosophers have drawn the distinction in many different ways.

[4] In truth, in some religious conflicts the combatants are motivated more by hatred of the other than by religious conviction. But the absence of reason is a problem in any case.

might infer that ethics ought to concern itself with reasonable principles applicable to all.[5] In the absence of any detailed conception of the good life, whether based on religion or philosophy, Enlightenment philosophers typically enshrined the individual's autonomous choice in this and other areas.

Positivism: facts and evidence

At the very peak of the modern age, during the brief flowering of positivism in the late nineteenth century and the first half of the twentieth, the reconciliation of science and human values was effected by some no-nonsense philosophers in a way that Descartes and others had resisted: science just took over. All meaningful propositions were, it was argued, logical or empirical propositions, the latter being testable in the court of experience. Propositions about morality were neither. Kant had made a similar distinction between analytic and synthetic propositions – those true or false by virtue of the meaning of the words expressing them and those true or false by virtue of describing the world. "All bachelors are unmarried" is an analytic proposition: the predicate is contained in the subject, and the sentence is an analysis of the concept of bachelor. "All bachelors are happy" is a synthetic proposition, which brings together the notion of bachelor and the logically separable notion of happiness. It purports to tell us something about the world, and it can be tested by reference to experience. The distinction has come under heavy fire, most famously by Quine (1980, chapter 2), who argued that susceptibility to the court of experience is (to oversimplify) a matter of degree, and that meaning proves on inspection to be a slippery notion. Others have joined Quine in rejecting the claim that our empirical knowledge can be built up from immediate acquaintance with foundational bits of knowledge. Today there are few philosophers who will claim that our knowledge starts from a perfectly certain foundation of immediately observable facts, with no implicit or explicit reference to any background, theoretical or otherwise. Far more philosophers hold that our ability to describe what is readily observable, including some mental events, requires us to have learned a public language.

---

[5] But some Enlightenment philosophers, such as Hume and Kant, took virtue seriously.

Positivists typically dealt with mental entities by reducing them to dispositions to act. They did not believe that science left any room for freedom of the will, or therefore for ethics. But no matter: the propositions of ethics, being neither analytic nor synthetic, were nothing more than the expression of emotion, with no truth value. According to a less radical view, since no normative statement could follow from a statement of fact, normative statements were primarily prescriptive rather than descriptive. R. M. Hare, a postpositivist, argued (in Hare, 1952, for example) that "Murder is wrong" does not mean "Yuck! Murder!" but instead entails "Do not murder." But can I not know that some act is wrong and yet encourage you to do it, and do it myself? Not quite, Hare would respond. I shall argue in Chapters 1 and 2 that Aristotle would probably say that anyone for whom a virtue does not have a positive emotional connotation lacks knowledge of that virtue.

Aristotle had seen humankind and human purposes as part of the natural world in part because he had a teleological view of the world. Descartes and Kant had separated humankind from nature in some important ways. The empiricists of the twentieth century readily assimilated humankind to the natural world because they had a reductionist view of human nature, as of ethics, history, and much else. Their views have had a not altogether fortunate impact on social scientists, including scholars of management.

Where we are today

Now we find ourselves in an era that combines some of the characteristics of previous eras. We still regard science as providing outstanding examples of knowledge, but we are no longer sure that the world is quite as ready-made for a unified scientific theory and language as Newtonians believed. We do not believe that all questions worth trying to answer are scientific questions or that all of science, including biology, reduces in any important sense to physics. As Aristotle says, it is a sign of erudition not to demand more precision of a subject matter than it admits of, and ethics does not admit of geometric precision – or, we would add, the kind of precision we now expect of science. In drawing distinctions in ethics we find ourselves asking, "But where do you draw the line?" Sometimes that question is impossible to answer in a straightforward way even when the distinction is worth drawing.

It is conceivable that humans might be subjects for natural science in a sense that Kant would not accept, but there is no present prospect of that. We believe that there are ways of explaining and criticizing human behavior that do not fit the standards of natural science, even less austere natural science as we understand it now. In particular, we have reason to believe that human behavior is explicable by reference to reasons even though humans often act unreasonably, and even though psychology is not strictly a natural science (Davidson, 2001). And while we find psychology and sociology and therefore organization theory and organizational behavior useful, we do not – or at any rate we should not – suppose that either individuals or organizations are suitable subjects for natural science alone. In fact there are moral reasons for avoiding reductive social science.

We do not regard mind and body as separate substances, but that gives us no reason to stop talking about the mind. We believe that mental events and their related actions can be described and explained in ways that do not apply to standard physical events. Aristotle has a similar view: he claims that mental events and physical events are not separable, but are related as form to matter. Recall that the form or essence of something is what makes it what it is; the matter or accidents of the thing may change while the thing persists. The soul is what makes flesh and blood a human being. Aristotle allows that a particular physiological event within a certain context can be a sufficient condition of a psychological event. (For further discussion see Hartman, 1977.)

Many of our explanations of human behavior we state in terms that are to some degree normative. A common sort of explanation for why Jones did something is a reason that Jones had for his action: it indicates what Jones was trying to bring about. In most cases the explanation succeeds only if you understand that the desired outcome was in some way good for Jones. If I tell you that Jones broke into the hardware store because he wanted to drink a can of varnish remover, you will probably think that I have failed to give you a satisfactory explanation.

Virtue vs. principles

We would expect followers of Newton, who believe that the universe runs according to universal laws, to believe that ethical actions are ones done according to universal principles, such as those based on utility, fairness, and rights. We identify some property of an act that makes it right or wrong because (here is the principle) all acts that have that property are right or wrong as well. In Aristotelian science, on the other hand, it is substances that are primary. In Aristotelian ethics, as Chapter 1 details, the good human being is the focus of ethics, what explains and justifies human behavior. A good act is something that a good person does; a good person has a certain character, a set of virtues rather than vices. Virtues are prior to good acts, which they cause.

Aristotle accepts principles as an important part of ethics, but the principles that he contemplates admit of exceptions and are consistent with his emphasis on relationships like friendship and citizenship. Some of them are in effect definitions of virtues. Aristotle focuses on the particular, the specific, as well as on what states and events have in common. So a generous person, for example, must be attuned to the features of a situation that will make an act of assistance more or less appropriate. He sets great store by emotions and habits as well as reason. He takes the context of acts seriously, and stresses our duties to our friends and fellow citizens – obligations following from our sociable nature.

Enlightenment ethics, on the other hand, characteristically values humankind in all times and places. According to Kant, for example, one must act on principles that can be made universal, and must treat humanity in all its forms as an end in itself and not merely as a means to one's own ends or another's. Smith's "impartial spectator" treats humanity in all its forms without favoring any form, or any human.[6] This sort of principle embodies a noble sentiment, but I shall argue that it does not guide our actions any more clearly than does virtue-based advice.

Principle-based theorists can argue that what is wrong with virtue ethics is just what is wrong with Aristotelian science: there are no reliable rules. Virtue ethics does not even aspire to perfect reliability. It demands that we act from virtues like justice and courage, but it seems at first look to offer little help in distinguishing good acts from bad ones, and still less in justifying the basis of the distinction. It seems

---

[6] But Smith is a virtue ethicist, similar in some ways to Aristotle. See Calkins and Werhane (1998) and Werhane (1999).

to offer feeble guidance for action. Do what a good person would do in this situation, Aristotle seems to say. But how do we know what that is, unless we adopt some principle? Hence the point of the old satire *Aristotle on Golf*: "...the virtue of a good golfer is to hit well and according to reason and as the professional would hit." (https://stpeter.im/journal/639.html). I argue in Chapter 2 that virtues can indeed guide actions and help us evaluate them. If someone advises you to be honest or generous in a certain case, you need no translation.

Teleology and the good life

If, as Aristotle claims, a person is a substance with a certain purpose and therefore a certain excellence (an alternative translation of *arête*), it makes sense to advocate a kind of ethics that represents the most that we humans are by nature capable of attaining, given that we cannot demand divine perfection of ourselves. To say that we fulfill our nature in being people of good character implies that we are born with the capacity to be virtuous. This is less daunting than the doctrine of Original Sin and more plausible than Plato's view. Virtue is worldly also in the sense that it is a way of living well in the world – specifically, in a *polis* – rather than forsaking the world and aiming at something beyond it.

Aristotle clearly bases his ethics on a teleological view of science, which includes animate and inanimate entities. There is today no unanimity on the question whether a scientific view of the world can allow even enough teleology to countenance desires and similar states, which do not figure in anything like a scientific theory. Some organization theorists (see, e.g., Pfeffer, 1982) have gone so far as to deny that desires and rationality have any place in the explanation of behavior. Davidson (2001) argues that reasons are causes in a way that is compatible with our scientific view even though reasons are not postulates of any scientific theories. Equally persuasively he argues that we can explain human behavior by reference to rationality even though people are not always rational.

Untroubled by the modern notion of causality, Aristotle sees human beings as rational deliberators according to what his interpreters call the practical syllogism. We begin with premises that express some value (e.g., dry food is good for you), move on to premises that express a particular fact (e.g., the stuff in this bowl is dry food), and conclude by eating what is in the bowl. Thereby we both explain and justify an action. The process depends on our ability to describe states and events correctly – to frame them appropriately, as we now might say. Sometimes we do not.

Many find Aristotle's practical syllogism unconvincing as an account of how we actually think, as I note in Chapter 2. We are not so rational, argue Haidt (2001, 2006, 2012) and others. We have no grounds for postulating states like values and virtues as generating anything like first premises of practical syllogisms, argue Doris (2002) and others. Virtues are fixtures of folk psychology rather than postulates of a rigorous theory for explaining behavior. Behavior is better explained by the agent's immediate situation.

We see in Chapters 2 and 3 that Aristotle is aware of the fragility of our rationality and the weakness of our will that undermines virtue, and yet he invokes rationality and virtue as explaining and even justifying our behavior, much as Davidson does. But he arguably goes too far in claiming that statements about the ends of human beings state scientific facts about them and that what is natural determines what is moral. Most moral philosophers today are skeptical of any claim that some event or state of affairs is right or wrong because it is natural or unnatural. So, for example, even if one believes that homosexuality is unnatural – a claim that is not as easy to prove as it may appear to be – it does not obviously follow that gay sex is morally wrong.[7] Aristotle claims that part of being a flourishing human being is a matter of not only having desires but having natural desires, which in the case of human beings are rational desires. I argue in Chapter 3 that his claim embodies some important insights.

Good and bad desires

Aristotle implies that there is something incomplete about utilitarianism, and standard economic theory as well, insofar as they describe the good life as being about the fulfillment of one's preferences. The good life – flourishing – is instead about the fulfillment of the preferences natural to a rational and sociable creature. It follows that you have good reason, just from your own point of view, to be a virtuous

---

[7] There was a time when psychologists classified homosexuality as a pathology. One can see why the classification was disputed.

person, truly rational and sociable, a good citizen of a good *polis*, and a good friend.

Frankfurt (1981) makes a well-known distinction that applies to Aristotle. Normal people have second-order desires – that is, desires to have certain first-order desires. For example, I may wish that I did not desire fattening foods so much; I may want to become the sort of person who likes going to the opera. If you are a rational person in this sense, Aristotle says, you can develop second-order desires that determine what your first-order desires are; you can come to be the sort of person who wants to eat healthy food, associate with faithful friends, be a good citizen.

It is altogether unrealistic to suppose that one can just decide to have and to act on good desires rather than bad ones. Most of us are born with the potential to lead rational and sociable lives, but you do not achieve a good life without cultivating that potential. I show in Chapter 4 how Aristotle argues that over time, by habituation, you can indeed make progress towards becoming the sort of person who enjoys doing good things – that is, a person of good character. You achieve virtue by developing the correct desires, attitudes, and emotions and then acting accordingly. Your parents have something to do with it, but your community plays a decisive role.

But habituation is not the whole of the process. Once you have generally good habits, you must develop the capacity to reason about how to act with practical wisdom in complex situations. This requires what Aristotle calls dialectic, a process of reasoning aimed at creating a coherent body of principles and intuitions that stand one in good and defensible stead where there are no readily applicable rules.

Aristotle's position raises two questions, both about freedom. First, do we want to say that freedom is just a matter of acting according to approved desires? Can I not freely do something wrong? Second, if I am a creature of my environment, political or otherwise, how am I a free agent?

Freedom and virtue

Consider Jones's decision to break into the hardware store because he wants to drink a can of varnish remover. Unlike Hume and other philosophers who think that rationality is purely a matter of fitness of means to ends, Aristotle would say that Jones is thinking and acting irrationally because he is aiming at something that cannot be part of a good life. For us the claim that Jones was motivated by his desire for a drink of varnish remover would not count as an adequate explanation. Our standard explanations of behavior presuppose some limits on what normal people want. Desires beyond those limits require further explanation, often involving pathologies of some sort. If Enlightenment philosophers and their modern successors believe that human freedom is a matter of doing whatever one wants for whatever motivation, they are wrong.

In particular, when philosophers like Rousseau claim that man is born free but is everywhere in chains – in effect, that humans are first of all individuals who can and should be unfettered by any society – Aristotelians reject this form of radical individualism by replying that the very notion of a human being unconnected to any community and unmotivated by communal considerations makes no sense.

Those who believe that nature does not tell us what ends to pursue argue, against Aristotle, that we are and ought to be free to create whatever lives we prefer to live without abiding by limitations set by what Aristotle or anyone else claims to be our nature. Yet Aristotle speaks to our intuitions. Whatever we may think of teleology, however expansive may be our view of what sort of life one may justifiably live, we think of certain lives as impoverished even if they are enjoyable. We do not envy contented people of very low intelligence. We do not admire those who fail to fulfill their potential. We may believe that the way we are – for example, that we are rational and sociable – at least limits, if it does not determine, what is good for us.

The problem with Aristotle's position, from the point of view of the Enlightenment and of modern libertarianism, is that it seems to make human liberty a matter of living according to some fairly narrow conception of the good life. It is no coincidence that Aristotle does not talk about human rights in the way we do,[8] and that his follower Alasdair MacIntyre (1985) hardly countenances rights. Yet Aristotle holds that tyranny is unjust, and that acting on the basis of one's own rational deliberation is a good thing in itself.

Some philosophers hold that no descriptive statement about a person can imply a normative one. They maintain a sharp distinction

---

[8] But Miller (1995) argues convincingly that Aristotle does have a conception of rights, stated primarily in the language of justice.

between what is the case and what ought to be the case. Just as a matter of logic, the sentence "Jones regularly gives alms to beggars" does not imply that Jones is a generous person or even that he regularly does something morally good, absent a premise linking alms-giving to morality. Putnam (2002, chapter 1) does not agree that we can always cleanly separate is from ought. He argues that this separatist view owes much to the positivists, who had a certain conception of facts: a paradigmatic fact was something immediately observable, with no implicit or explicit reference to any theoretical or other sort of background. So "Jones is brave" and "Jones is a psychopath" may be shown by evidence to be true or false, though some have considered the statements problematic as factual claims. Aristotle does not have that problem with them, nor do many respectable psychologists, especially personality theorists, who postulate functional states and pathologies whose description has a normative element. To call a psychological condition or a desire that it generates a pathology is to say that there is something unhealthy or otherwise wrong with it, and it states a fact.

Autonomy

The discussion so far suggests, and Aristotle believes, that if you are a virtuous person you have considerable control over yourself. You can not only decide where to take your life, you can decide what sort of person you will be. It is natural and appropriate for you to aspire to what reflection, including reflection on your capacities and needs and limitations, leads you to consider the good life to be. That is a life of an autonomous person of good character. That broad notion accommodates a wide range of possible lives – wider, probably, than Aristotle contemplates. Such a degree of control over one's moral development is hard to achieve. It may be more difficult than becoming the sort of person who is motivated primarily by the promise of great wealth, for example.

I have suggested that some are skeptical of Aristotle's view of rational deliberation, which he considers essential to human beings and therefore central to ethics. Newtonian science raises further questions about whether it makes sense to explain human action by reference to rational deliberation. This is a problem for Enlightenment philosophers as well as for Aristotle, and we discuss it in Chapter 4.

In a Newtonian universe events are determined by prior causal conditions. The expression "for the most part," one of Aristotle's favorites, has no place. Nor is there any teleological explanation: ends and purposes have no part in explaining events. According to many philosophers, such a deterministic universe makes free will impossible. How can a decision, whatever sort of event it may be, change the course of nature? Is not a decision itself the result of some causally sufficient conditions? If I know in advance what these conditions are in your case, I can predict what you will decide, because it is determined what you will decide. Your will cannot change things. So goes the argument, which philosophers like Democritus and Lucretius found challenging long before the Enlightenment.

According to this argument, science simply eliminates deliberating and deciding. There is just no point in talking about good or bad or responsible decisions, for a decision that is fully determined by prior conditions is not really a decision at all. A person can be ethical in the sense of acting according to ethical principles (though not voluntarily), but cannot be virtuous in the sense of acting on the basis of rational deliberation.

On the other hand, we might accept universal causality but argue that it has no bearing on the freedom of the will, which we might say is a matter of being able to act on the basis of accurate information and good reasons. Having this ability – which, according to many social psychologists, is not as common as most people think – may be a result of good luck, and it appears to be a matter of degree, but it is compatible with causal determinism. One's practical wisdom is a sufficient causal condition of one's action, other things being equal. Thank God for the preexisting sufficient conditions of my practical wisdom!

If this approach is right, then the problem of free will is still a practical problem, and one of the questions it raises for managers and others is where to find the sufficient conditions of ethical behavior. According to Aristotle, the answer lies in the virtuous or vicious character of the agent. According to some social psychologists, it lies in one's immediate environment.

There is at least one more sense in which Aristotle differs from many modern philosophers, not entirely to his disadvantage. Aristotle is not concerned about epistemological questions.

Cartesian epistemology

Many philosophers since Descartes have supposed that one is immediately aware of the contents of one's own mind – pains, thoughts, sense data, etc. – and that from this sort of knowledge one makes inferences about the world of space and time. It may seem plausible to say, as Descartes did, that you know that your mind exists, hence that you do. Anyone who thinks this way may then find it a bit exasperating that Aristotle ignores the epistemological mystery: how do I get from my (certain) knowledge of my mental contents to my (inferential) knowledge of the surrounding world?[9] Although Aristotle does at times claim that there are facts that we can know without inference, he does not offer these as the basis of all knowledge.

Descartes is an epistemological foundationalist and an individualist, and he probably could not be the first without being the second. Aristotle does not think he has found an entirely firm basis for all empirical knowledge within his own mind. He is neither an epistemological foundationalist nor an individualist in the way Descartes is. Without ever arguing the point, he assumes that the kind of thing the individual can know is just what others in the community can know. Aristotle starts from where *we are* – not where *I am*.

The status of pleasure

If you are a Cartesian in epistemology, you are more likely than is an Aristotelian to assume that the factors motivating your behavior are your individual internal states, such as pain, fear, hunger, desire, and so on. You are also more likely to believe that being well off is a matter of experiencing good feelings and satisfying your desires. According to Cartesian epistemology, we are not immediately aware of external objects; instead we infer on the basis of internal objects of immediate awareness that there are trees and houses and other people around us. According to Cartesian moral psychology – here we must extrapolate a bit – the immediate objects of my enjoyment are my mental states, which in turn may be caused by external objects or states. This too is very different from Aristotle's view. Aristotle

---

[9] Most philosophers today would consider this question a bad one. Our knowledge does not begin with knowing mental states.

appears to believe that pleasure is not always a feeling distinct from the pleasurable experience, and he does not describe the experience itself as taking place purely in one's mind. In fact he takes no great interest in the subjectivity of mental states generally.[10] This idea that pleasure is not purely a mental state in that sense makes it easier for Aristotle to accept the notion that one might take genuine and immediate pleasure in the prosperity of one's community or the success of a friend without inferring that what really pleases one is some internal experience of one's own that is a result of one's noticing that prosperity or success. There is controversy about Aristotle's views on pleasure, but it seems safe to say that he holds that pleasure is not always distinct from the pleasurable activity. So you can directly enjoy a friend's success or your own virtue. (See *Nicomachean Ethics* (hereafter *NE*) II 3 1104b4f. and X 5 1174b32f.)

That very inference is often made by psychological egoists, who characteristically claim that one's own interest is the only motivation of one's deliberate acts. Charitable acts are not counterexamples: the giver of alms who seems to be motivated by the beggar's happiness really craves the warm glow of self-satisfaction that charitable people experience. The evidence for this view is weak, but the theory survives by trivialization: any conceivable counterexample is consistent with the theory. Whatever it is worth, which is not very much, the theory would not have occurred to an Aristotelian philosopher. Aristotle holds that the agent's intentional act is typically, though not always, good for the agent. He even believes that we usually do what gives us pleasure; but since he holds that pleasure is not a state distinct from natural and unimpeded activity, he would not regard the claim as a significant insight about human motivation.

Surely Aristotle's view is a sensible one. When I say that I get great pleasure from gardening, I do not mean that gardening causes me to have sensations of pleasure; I mean, roughly, that gardening is something that I readily do when I can do whatever I want to do and do not have to do anything in particular. We can see why Aristotle does not consider the moral person the one who fights against either pleasure or self-interest generally and in favor of duty, in the way Kant describes. The proper goal – often not achieved, to be sure – is to see

---

[10] See Hartman (1977). I am simplifying Aristotle's view, but the details of it do not affect my immediate point.

to it that interest and duty are on the same side. It does not follow from the Aristotelian position that one's best interests always coincide with the ethically good thing to do, though that is possible and would be desirable, because it would make one a good person.

Aristotle's minimal interest in subjectivity helps explain his conception of flourishing (the Greek is *eudaimonia*, which is usually translated *flourishing*, but sometimes *happiness* or *well-being*) as being a matter of achieving natural human characteristics to the highest degree. Those to whom subjectivity is a critical feature of mental events are more likely to believe that a happy life is one that is full of good feelings, without regard to fulfilling one's potential.

In yet another, related sense Aristotle differs from the Cartesian tradition. Descartes is well known for considering the mind and the body separate but interacting spheres. Aristotle does not regard the soul and the body as separate in that way, as I have noted. The Cartesian separation, perhaps reflecting his Christian education, made it easier to think of the person as an arena of competing forces: the flesh and the spirit, and so on. This un-Aristotelian view goes some further way towards explaining why the Cartesian tradition would not immediately see how self-interested action could encompass morally good action.

Aristotle on business

An Aristotelian approach to business ethics poses a special challenge. Aristotle himself doubts that a businessperson can be truly virtuous, because he believes that businesspeople take money to be an end in itself rather than a means to some good end and that the jobs that most of them have do not grant space for autonomous, virtuous action. Making a lot of money does not amount to living well and according to one's sociable and rational nature. In Chapter 5 we consider MacIntyre's argument that Aristotle's ideas of virtue and the good life are in radical opposition to the whole spirit of business and business-people, whose overriding objective is financial gain. That employees make money and produce goods that meet consumers' demand will not impress an Aristotelian very much. Living well for employees is a matter of enjoying exercising the virtues, not making money. For customers, living well is not a matter of buying a lot of stuff, though it is good not to be poor.

But it is one thing to say that a firm must make a profit; it is quite another to say that making a profit is the overriding purpose of every firm and by extension of every employee. There are other purposes, and there are opportunities to learn and exercise certain virtues and to live well, even in a profitable organization. It is true, however, that not all employees in organizations or stakeholders of organizations have much interest in being virtuous. Not all organizations are good communities; and as Aristotle says, bad communities do not make their citizens good. It is not my purpose to make the case for optimism, but instead to suggest what virtue in business looks like and to argue that it is possible, not that it is probable.

Efficiency vs. virtue

As the industrial revolution was in full swing, Frederick Winslow Taylor and others argued for a kind of scientific management that in effect made people cogs in a machine. The good news for the employees was that they shared in the profitability of efficiency; the bad news was that their work had no value beyond its contribution to corporate and therefore personal profit. Taylorism is no longer the dominant model of management of people, in part because most jobs are different now, but MacIntyre and other critics of capitalism argue that because employees' work is still designed with profit in mind, there is no room for the kind of activity that might be virtuous. Aristotle takes a similar position in arguing that leisure, which farmers and shopkeepers do not have, is necessary for living a good life.

The notion that business ethics is an oxymoron is not hard to understand. I shall not claim that most firms are highly supportive of ethics, but it is not true that just being a firm makes an organization the enemy of virtue. In many businesses, in fact, social capital is supportive of financial success, as therefore is ethics. Aristotle does not believe that most people are entirely virtuous, but he does believe that every person has good reasons for being virtuous. We can extend his argument to businesspeople, in whom ethical excellence and excellence in business may overlap to a significant degree. Unfortunately we cannot ignore the ways in which business sometimes undermines our best values in favor of those related to acquisitiveness.

Teaching business ethics

Among the arguments against the very possibility of teaching business ethics, two stand out. First, as Aristotle himself says, one becomes virtuous over a long time, not overnight. How much can be done, or undone, in one semester, particularly for students who are acquiring a business mentality? Second, according to some social psychologists, we are creatures not only, or even primarily, of our upbringing but of our immediate environment. Your virtues, if they exist at all, have little or no effect when you are in the grip of a powerful corporate culture.

Chapter 6 addresses these questions. A good business ethics course sharpens and improves students' moral intuitions, principally through case studies. These intuitions are not usually pathological ones, for most students have been habituated, as Aristotle would say, reasonably well. What more is needed is, as Aristotle says in his discussion of moral development, a dialectical discussion of these intuitions and the principles that ought to be consistent with them. This will not guarantee future virtue, but the toxic effects of bad cultures can be minimized if students are aware of their susceptibility to them and can thus withstand these effects or take care to avoid such cultures in the first place.

Multinational concerns

Capitalism is spreading globally, and it will be dominant for the foreseeable future. How this fact should lead us to think about business ethics, and the virtue approach in particular, is the subject of Chapter 7. Capitalism's dominance is in some ways good news, and not only from the point of view of prosperity. A kind of justice, too, is served where employees and others are judged by their ability to contribute to the firm and therefore to the economy rather than by their gender or race. But executives will need to come to terms with certain traditional moral views, which are not about what we would call utility and justice so much as about solidarity and purity. Our courses in business ethics should be helping produce globally oriented executives who can contend with that way of thinking about morality.

Here the cosmopolitan morality supported by the Enlightenment would seem at first look to be just what we need, for it takes all of humankind as its subject matter. Traditional views, and even Aristotle's ethics, look partial and parochial by comparison: the emphasis on community makes virtue seem to be what distinguishes Us from Them, the cannibals and other barbarians. How can we in liberal capitalist democracies converse usefully with citizens of nations whose ethical traditions are so different from ours? Aristotle's ethics is not very cosmopolitan, and we must consider whether the virtues that he and we take seriously can be extended to new places and new times, as the scope of Us is broadened.

But Aristotle is no unsubtle traditionalist. His views represent a kind of mean between traditional and modern conceptions of morality. He claims that humans, characteristically rational, can get beyond their habitual ways of thinking when new situations arise. He offers dialectic as an adaptive way in which rational people can address ethical issues. He does not address whether people can participate in dialectical conversations across cultural lines, but what he does say offers some suggestions about how it might be done.

In the end our contemplation of global ethics vindicates Aristotle in at least one important sense. You become morally fitted for a multinational and multicultural world not by learning the great principles that unite all humankind, but by first becoming a good citizen of some smaller community – it could be a firm, or part of a firm – that serves as a necessary mediating institution between you and the rest of the world. Even as we contemplate global ethics, we can profit from Aristotle's claim that the *polis* is the cradle of virtue.

A summary of the argument

- Chapter 1: Aristotle rightly emphasizes the virtues of character in explaining and justifying behavior. A person of good character is rational and sociable, and consistently has appropriate emotions and the ability to recognize crucial details. Principles, especially the utilitarian principles that underlie much of economics and management theory, are of limited help in making ethical decisions. What is required is practical wisdom, which is not reducible to any principles.
- Chapter 2: Talk of virtues can guide action: you may usefully tell me to be courageous or generous. But one can go wrong as a result of weakness of will, which is often a matter of framing one's situation incorrectly. Much the same can be said of strategic decision-making.

Corporate culture may have such a strong effect on one's actions that some psychologists question whether it makes any sense to postulate character, or for that matter rationality, as a cause of behavior. Aristotle tries to account for our lapses in rationality, but arrayed against him are many who doubt that we typically think rationality.

- Chapter 3: Humans are not motivated as the *homo economicus* model and agency theory suggest. Aristotle makes the case that the good life is not about satisfaction of any old preference, as some economists believe, but of preferences of the sort that are worthy of what human beings are: rational and social creatures. We have good reason to try to acquire such preferences, which generate social capital among other goods. Aristotle's views about the good life may seem unduly narrow and based on contestable views of human nature, but even liberal theorists will grant that there are natural limits to what can be considered a good human life.
- Chapter 4: Aristotle argues that virtues are in the first instance habits learned in one's community, and thereby he raises problems about autonomy. Mature virtue requires rationality in preferences and actions; it is rare and difficult to achieve. We make ethical progress by means of dialectic, which seeks to reconcile our principles and our intuitions. Since these may be called into question by new situations, dialectic is an ongoing educational project.
- Chapter 5: Though Aristotle does not admire businesspeople, the virtues that he advocates are supportive of effective organizations and productive markets, contrary to the claims of MacIntyre and others. In particular, the goal of profit does not undermine internal goods any more than the goal of the safety of the *polis* undermines martial courage. Organizations thrive with loyalty to the sort of leadership that encourages social capital, though in some cases loyal organizational citizenship can be exploited. In a similar way, an organization may thrive externally by developing mutually advantageous relationships with those in its supply chain and other stakeholders, though here too it does not always work out that way.
- Chapter 6: The Socratic approach to teaching ethics may make students moral skeptics, but the Aristotelian character-oriented approach may meet some of their concerns about ethics and expose some of the questionable assumptions implicit in the vocabulary that business students typically learn. Teaching business ethics can play a role in character development: students can improve their

moral intuitions, learned early in their lives, through case studies and through reflection on their values. And they can learn to deal with ethical issues through dialectical conversations. They can also learn to recognize the dangers of bad corporate cultures and other threats to their rationality, and to cope with them or avoid them.

- Chapter 7: Multinational business requires managers to deal with a range of issues that reflect serious differences about what is ethical, even about the nature of ethics. Between the modern and traditional views of ethics Aristotle offers a conciliatory position that enriches both views, and his dialectic suggests a way for their proponents to converse usefully about contested issues and about new questions raised by technological progress. Aristotle's emphasis on community as the school of ethics is reflected in the way in which ethics learned in mediating institutions, such as organizations, may eventually cross cultural boundaries.

1 | Virtues and principles

Principles and their problems

Moral philosophers have long held that ethics is about principles that an agent can apply in choice situations to find the right action to perform. A utilitarian, for example, will hold that one ought to act to maximize happiness. A moral philosopher concerned with justice might argue that we ought to act impartially, or in support of a certain sort of equality in the distribution of goods or opportunities. A libertarian will argue that the overriding rule is that we ought to respect people's rights by not interfering with their autonomous actions so long as those do not harm others. A subtle utilitarian might argue that we should act on certain principles of justice and rights because doing so will maximize happiness in the long run, whereas focusing on maximizing happiness in considering each act that we perform will defeat the purpose of utilitarianism. A Kantian will demand that we act on principles whose universal application we can support.

Principles seem to perform better than virtues in telling us how to act, as we may think ethics ought to be able to do.[1] If you tell me to be generous or courageous and to act accordingly, I may wonder exactly what I am supposed to do and whether it is possible for me simply to decide to be courageous or benevolent if I am not already.[2] I might think that I would be better served by advice to follow some moral principle: do not lie; treat people alike unless there is good reason to treat them differently; make people better off.

But there are some problems with the notion that morality is about principles. To begin with, the advocates of principles often too readily presuppose that the world presents itself to us in ways that readily

---

[1] This is not self-evident, however. Annas (2011, pp. 32–34) argues that ethics should not tell adults what to do in any detail. They should work it out for themselves.
[2] These two issues are the topics of Chapters 2 and 4.

accommodate the standard theories. For example, Kantians appear to assume that we can readily identify the maxim of a certain action, the principle on which it is based, but often we cannot. In situations of ethical import there are so many descriptions and therefore possible principles applying to a particular case that it may be difficult to determine which one deserves to be called the maxim. If I lie to the secret police to save a friend, am I acting on the maxim that lying can be universalized, or that lying to the secret police to save a friend can be universalized? In fact Kant himself (1981, p. 3) says that we need "a power of judgment sharpened by experience" to connect maxims to the particular case (Kupperman, 2005, p. 204). Utilitarians are in a similar situation: they often assume that we know which of the probably numerous consequences of an act matter to its moral quality, and how much, and which do not. Koehn (1995, p. 534) notes that standard moral theories slight the context of an act, in part because they focus only on certain of its outcomes and other features.[3]

Critics raise the issue of incommensurability against utilitarians, especially economists, who typically presuppose that goods can readily be compared on some common scale and that therefore calculating benefits and harms presents no serious problems. If morality were like profitability, moral evaluation would in principle be no more difficult than working out how much various employee accomplishments contribute to stockholder wealth – not in itself an easy task. We might then be able to "prove" that the lives of rich people are worth more than those of poor people because rich people regularly pay more than poor people on safety to reduce the probability of their death in auto accidents and elsewhere; so we must presume that poor people themselves hold that their own lives are of less value than those of owners of Volvos rather than compact cars.

We have reason to abandon utilitarian principles in cases that would maximize happiness but violate justice and rights. But if we agree that justice requires us to handle cases similarly if they are similar in relevant respects, how do we decide what the relevant respects are?

We do not make sound moral judgments by beginning with a certain notion of fairness or any other standard and then applying it to business or politics or any area of life, for the notion of fairness has

---

[3] For more along these lines, see Kupperman (1991, especially pp. 74–89 and 115) and Sen and Williams (1982).

little substantive content if it has no connection to any of these areas. Suppose we say, plausibly, that it is unfair to treat people better or worse according to personal characteristics that they cannot help having. Then we would have to agree that talented people should not be paid more than untalented ones. But most of us believe that it is fair to pay employees according to what they contribute to the bottom line, and will therefore reject a conception of justice that rules otherwise, perhaps on utilitarian grounds. On the other hand, those whose talent lets them contribute more to the economy surely do not deserve more votes. We cannot settle these issues by invoking a prior and widely acceptable principle of fairness.

The difficulty of using principles is evident to everyone who begins a business ethics course by talking about various ethical theories that are to be applied to actual or possible situations. Is justice about income distribution at all?[4] How do we decide what rights employees have? How do we – people who are trying to do the right thing, and not just philosophers – choose among the available principles? Should we try to find principles that govern the application of these principles? Then further principles for applying those, and on into infinity?

Application issues aside, we cannot be certain that a consensus on moral principles is possible. Intuitions differ, and there seems to be little prospect of agreement between utilitarians like Peter Singer and libertarians in the mold of Robert Nozick. The easier it is to reach a consensus on a principle, the vaguer and less useful the principle is.

A defender of principles might argue that we have some rough and ready ones that we can use for all practical purposes. But do we? There are few ethical issues interesting enough to merit discussion in a firm or a business ethics class that can be solved by the application of a rough and ready principle. We can sometimes do what Socrates did: we can show that some proffered moral argument suffers from incoherent premises or counterintuitive or appalling consequences.[5] What we cannot do is bring to bear a principle that will both gain universal

---

[4] Matson (2001) argues that justice is about earning and owning, and not about equality. He rejects Rawls's (1971) attempt to split the difference.

[5] In Chapter 4 we introduce dialectic, Aristotle's more elaborate version of Socrates' method. We revisit Socrates in Chapter 6.

acceptance and settle an argument about whether, for example, to make a substantial grease payment.[6]

A comparison with management

These difficulties should come as no surprise to any manager. The relationship between ethical principles and complex reality resembles the relationship between management theories and practical effectiveness.[7] Theoretical work on span of control, for example, is unquestionably valuable. But even if a newly minted Master of Business Administration (MBA) convinces Smith, an experienced manager, that competent research on span of control shows that Jones ought to be able to handle more subordinates, Smith might remind the MBA that Jones is in some relevant respects not a very good manager, or that the subordinates have unusually diverse jobs or are physically separated by a significant distance, or something of the sort not addressed in the literature. MBAs who have not yet discovered the limited applicability of what they learned in business school may be surprised to discover how accurately an experienced manager with no discernible knowledge of theory can predict whether another manager will be successful. MBAs with business experience will understand some of the difficulties of applying the best theories, even as they acknowledge their value.

Virtue ethicists do not claim to make ethics very precise. On the contrary, Aristotle says that ethics is not like geometry. It is more like medicine (at least the medicine of Aristotle's day) or comedy, he says (*NE* IV 8 1028a23–34); and I would add management or performance evaluation. There are rules, but they are not as definite as those of geometry (*NE* I 7 1098a29–34), and they are more difficult to apply to the real world. You have to develop a feeling for it. But this does not imply relativism: that management is unlike geometry clearly does not mean that there are no right or wrong answers to questions about

---

[6] Kohlberg's (1981) famous account of moral development takes universal principles to be the highest stage of morality. He does not consider arguments against principles.

[7] Arguably management theories are easier to apply than ethical principles because many of the latter do not have clear statements of purpose behind them.

management. Nor does it show that there are no useful management principles, no good or bad managers.[8] And so with ethics.

Virtue ethicists do claim that talking about virtues is more useful than talking about right actions. Suppose I am a senior executive looking for a replacement for Smith, who has just left the company. I solicit your view of Jones as a successor. If you say that Jones is a bad manager, I am likely to ask for more information. Is he poor at strategic thinking? Unable to motivate his people? Lazy? Not technically competent? If you respond to questions like this by saying that he fails to add value, you will not be helping me. Similarly, if I ask you whether Jones is a good person, you will not satisfy me by saying that he usually does the right thing, or even that he usually does the productive thing, or that he discriminates only on the basis of relevant attributes. You will be much more helpful if you tell me that he is kind but demanding, courageous, patient but not too patient, level-headed but not unfeeling, and honest.

We might object that virtues are unobservable, but Dyck and Kleysen (2001) argue persuasively that certain virtues are, and that they allow us to classify managers' abilities and behavior usefully. Horvath (1995) makes a similar point. We should be careful not to take the point too far. I can often know by observation that Jones is angry, but Jones can sometimes conceal his anger. But not always; and in any case, it is a mistake to narrow the field of observables to those things and events that can be easily observed without inference or knowledge of background.

Some will find talk about Jones's virtues rather than about his doing the right thing more credible as well. I may be something of a skeptic about morality; so if you tell me that Jones is a moral person, I may wonder whether you and I have the same moral standards, or whether there are any that are solidly enough grounded to guide us all. But you can give actual evidence that when Jones speaks his mind he is motivated by courage rather than by a propensity to make a fuss. Virtue ethics uses normative terms in factual explanations; I see no problem about that. Stalin killed vast numbers of people because he

---

[8] But Pfeffer (1982) and Rosenzweig (2007) are among the management theorists who believe that external events and states determine a company's fate more than does good or bad management.

was evil. That is no more problematic than saying that someone made an egregious mistake because he is stupid or suffers from attention deficit disorder.

The current state of play

Most of what I have said thus far is not very original, for in recent years virtues have again come to the fore in moral philosophy and in business ethics as well. MacIntyre (1985) is perhaps the best known of the virtue ethicists among business ethicists. Anscombe (1997) and Foot (1997) were pioneers. Williams (1981, 1985), Slote (1983, 1992, 2001), Kupperman (1991, 2005), Annas (2011), McDowell (1997), Hursthouse (1999), and Russell (2009) have been influential as well. Solomon (1992), Koehn (1992, 1995, 1998), Weaver (2006), Klein (1995, 1998), Alzola (2008, 2012), Jackson (2012), Sison (2003, 2008), Shaw (1995), Walton (2001), and Moore (2002, 2005a, 2005b, 2008, 2009, 2012) emphasize virtues and character in business ethics, as do some others named in the Bibliography. Audi (1997, 2012) was influential in virtue theory before he began to apply its lessons to business ethics. There have long been professors in Catholic universities (DesJardins, Duska, Moberg, and Cavanagh, for example) who have attended to virtue ethics, thanks in part to the tradition of Aquinas.

These virtue ethicists, often following Aristotle's *Nicomachean Ethics*, argue that ethics is primarily about character, good or bad, and the virtues that constitute it. What matters most, and ought to be the primary subject of moral deliberation and education, is what sort of person one is. Virtue ethicists characteristically believe that right action is defined by reference to the virtues, not vice versa, and not by reference to principles.

What a virtue is

A virtue is, to begin with, a stable disposition to act. A disposition in the sense that I have in mind is not just a tendency to do something under certain circumstances. A virtue is not like brittleness. A virtuous person characteristically prefers to act and usually does act in a way that is in some respects good for others or for the virtuous person. The virtuous person enjoys acting virtuously and wants to be the sort of person who enjoys acting virtuously. So you are a generous person if and only if you characteristically act generously. If you give money to needy people sporadically or reluctantly or because you are trying to impress someone or because you feel guilty, you are not acting from generosity. Generosity and other virtues are able to explain behavior and justify it: virtues cause virtuous acts, and those acts are good because they are virtuous. Virtue requires that you know what you are doing; the decision must be yours and must be for the sake of the action itself;[9] and you must decide what to do on the basis of a psychological state that is firm and unchanging (*NE* II 4 1105a29–33).

Virtues and vices are similar to personality traits, but with ethical significance: a virtue is characteristically part of the good life of an agent who is a contributing member of a good community. Someone who has the personality trait of being mildly compulsive is likely also orderly, dependable, punctual, principled, and detail-oriented. These are virtues, most of them; but in excess some of them are vices, as are their corresponding defects, and the virtues are a mean between them (*NE* II 6–8). Courage is a virtue; recklessness and cowardice are vices. Indifference to the suffering of others is a vice; indifference to the outcome of the World Cup is not. Aristotle considers intelligence a virtue, which he classes as an intellectual virtue, but it is a necessary condition of consistently acting correctly in any sense.

Aristotle does not distinguish virtues from vices on a purely utilitarian basis, though good results characteristically follow from virtuous action. A virtue – *arête* can also be translated as excellence – is part of the fulfillment of the nature of a thing. It is the nature of human beings to be sociable and rational. That means that they naturally, though not reliably, aspire to and should and sometimes can live in a way that fulfills the purpose of human life. That in turn entails having the right goals, including one's own psychological and physical health and the health of the community.

One of the reasons for focusing on virtuous people and how their virtues cause them to think and act, more than on their manifest behavior, is that one can perform an act that, considered purely in itself, would seem to be a morally good one but that is caused by a vice and therefore is not a good act. So, for example, I might work

---

[9] This feature raises complex issues that we shall discuss in several contexts.

overtime without additional pay and thereby benefit my organization but with the intention of gaining the trust of my supervisor in case I need to deceive him/her later on. In that case I am not acting from virtue. One can follow the rules and do the right thing out of hope of gain or in ignorance or in fear of punishment or for some other reason not related to virtue; that is another reason for saying that having a virtue is not a matter of abiding by the rules.

The mean and context

A virtue is a mean between vicious extremes, Aristotle says. So, for example, courage lies at the mean between the vicious extremes of cowardice and foolhardiness. Aristotle infers from this that the courageous person stands firmly against or fears the right things for the right purpose in the right way at the right time (*NE* III 7 1115b17–19). Your emotions are part of your character, for good or ill. They too must be neither excessive nor deficient. That is, they must happen at the right time, be about the right things, relate to the right people, and be focused on the right end in the right way (II 6 1106b16–22). You are a hothead if little things anger you, but phlegmatic if big things do not (IV 5 1125b26–1126a8). I infer this: we have no good reason to say that Jones is just if we acknowledge that he has no emotional reaction to any act of injustice on his own part or anyone else's.

Life would be simpler if we could confidently act on straightforward principles such as "always run from danger" or "never run from danger." But both of those principles and many others like them are just wrong. Courage requires us to take arms against danger in some contexts but not in others, and we have the difficult task of figuring out when it is appropriate to do which. So it is with most virtues and vices.[10] The reaction of those first learning about the doctrine of the mean is often that it is too vague to guide our action with any precision. Perhaps that is just Aristotle's point: if a principle guides action precisely and absolutely, it is probably a bad principle, whether or not it represents an extreme.

From this we see that context matters to virtue, as Koehn (1995, p. 536) argues. So we have reason to call virtues *thick concepts*, in

---

[10] There are a few absolute principles, however: envy and murder, for example are simply wrong (*NE* II 6 1107a10–14).

Geertz's (1983) sense: they are concepts that one can understand only by seeing how they are embedded in a community's practices, which constitute a complex network of concepts, assumptions, and values. It will not always be easy to figure out what is the virtuous thing to do; it differs from case to case. The contexts of war and business, for example, change the ways virtue looks. What a virtuous soldier or executive does on the basis of obligations attaching to the position may not be right for you or me. You and I are not normally entitled to kill or empowered to fire.

If I am employed by an organization, I must play one or more roles in it. These roles create obligations for me, ethical as well as legal: if I am under contract, I ought to perform accordingly unless there is some overriding ethical reason not to. One of the cardinal problems about business ethics is that I might have a role-based obligation to do something that, in the absence of the role, I would find morally repugnant. For example, I might be under pressure to fire my friend Jones, who really needs the job, even if I believe that he does not deserve to be fired. In deciding what to do I must take many factors into consideration – including, for example, whether my friend received due process, whether I can change my boss's mind, whether the firing would be illegal, whether the company as a whole deserves to prosper, and so on. We do know that it is not enough to grasp one of the extremes: it is not enough to do my boss's bidding unhesitatingly and without question, or on the other hand to ignore my boss entirely and always act purely on my own judgment. We also know that we must do the right things for the right purpose in the right way at the right time. All these parameters we must take into account, as in most cases in which our ethical obligations appear to conflict.[11]

Sometimes context enables us not only to evaluate an act but also to identify it. Aristotle says in *Metaphysics* VIII 2 that some things are what they are by virtue of their place (e.g., a threshold rather than a lintel) or their time (e.g., breakfast rather than lunch). So in this sense the context makes something what it is; it is as form to the matter of the thing. Similarly, we can infer that one of two psychologically identical cases of anger may be petulance and the other indignation, depending on whether it is directed at the right things in the right way at the right time in aid of the right purpose.

---

[11] For much more on roles and obligations, see Alzola (2008).

The corporate context of an act may not only alter the moral parameters of an act but also make it the act that it is. I might say "Smith left some ink stains on a piece of paper," when the paper was a contract and the ink stains were her signature and Smith was the chief executive officer (CEO) of the company in whose name she thereby made a deal or committed a crime. My statement would be inadequate and misleading. Much the same is true of other actions performed in the corporate line of duty. "I was only following orders" is not an honest statement, and not an excuse. If you are playing a certain kind of role, what looks like your individual action may in fact be an action of a community or a corporation, but the setting does not absolve you of all personal responsibility.

Principles: the example of generosity

Most virtue ethicists, including Aristotle, do countenance principles. A generous person acts according to principles derived from the nature of generosity; so Hursthouse (1999) argues concerning what she calls v-rules.[12] So Aristotle says (*NE* I 4 1120a25f.) that a generous person happily gives appropriately to the right people in the right amounts. But it is clear that even the most generous of friends cannot find principles that will indicate exactly how needy Jones has to be or how much money one ought to lend him, or any algorithms that show how to prioritize competing principles related to, say, justice.

A virtuous person, a person of good character, will be benevolent and just and will act on principles based on those virtues without believing that the principles offer precise guidance. Virtue ethicists do not ignore considerations of utility or justice, for example; on the contrary, these may be important to the deliberations of a virtuous person. In giving money to a needy person a generous person takes into account that Jones deserves the gift or that it will benefit him.[13]

An ungenerous person is not necessarily ignorant of principles pertinent to generosity. You may know some such principles but be stingy anyway. Mere knowledge of the principles does not make anyone a good person. For that reason alone, having the virtues that constitute

---

[12] As Audi (2012) observes, the prima facie duties named by the great intuitionist and Aristotelian scholar W. D. Ross (1930) seem to be of the sort that are generated by some familiar virtues.

[13] In Chapter 3 I shall argue that Aristotelian virtue ethics not only takes utility seriously but offers a superior analysis of it.

a good character, which is indeed sufficient for ethical action, is not reducible to knowing principles. You must not only know what virtue requires in certain situations but also be inclined to act virtuously. And if you are inclined to act virtuously, you will typically enjoy it when you do. Jones will benefit from your generous act, but that act will be good in itself for you.

Parents tell children not to lie, as employers tell new employees not to be late for work. Beyond that, however, many parents raise children to be honest – that is, to be inclined not to lie, to feel some repugnance when lying even in circumstances that justify it. In that case a principle that proscribes lying will be fairly unresponsive to utilitarian considerations. Employers, similarly, want employees to work well out of genuine loyalty. For virtues involve not only dispositions but also attitudes. Consider gratitude: when you give me a generous gift, I should not only thank you but also be grateful. Ethicists who rely on principles alone will have a hard time saying why one ever has an obligation to be grateful, or to care about one's employer's success. Those who believe that one has an obligation to be grateful must defend the view that one is morally responsible for one's feelings, which do not seem to be voluntary. Aristotle knows that you cannot make yourself feel grateful on a particular occasion, but he believes that over time you can become the sort of person who is grateful on appropriate occasions. (See *NE* I 3 1095a2–13 and II 1–3.)[14] If he is right, it is not absurd to try to help make someone – a student, for example – a certain sort of person.[15]

Even if an ethical person is one who acts according to certain principles, it does not follow that the best way to teach Smith to be ethical is to give her principles to follow. By analogy, even if we can show that she is an excellent employee by stating her sales figures, a training professional will focus on her knowledge, skills, and attitude as a way of improving her sales figures. The analogue in ethics is improving Smith's character as a way of causing her to act according to appropriate moral principles.[16]

---

[14] We shall discuss the cultivation of virtues, including emotions, in Chapter 4.

[15] Bazerman and Tenbrunsel (2011, p. 27f.) take note of the research that shows that studying or even teaching ethics does not make people more ethical. I shall argue, especially in Chapter 6, that teaching virtue ethics may indeed help do so.

[16] Notice that the analogy suggests that mere financial incentives are not the best way to make someone a good salesperson, much less a good person. There is evidence for that claim, as we shall see in Chapter 3.

Aristotle believes that becoming a good person is natural to us, though not easy. On Aristotle's view, acting virtuously is a matter of acting according to human nature. Humans are characteristically rational and sociable, and their excellence or virtue entails being firmly disposed to act accordingly. Acting that way, quite aside from its results, is intrinsically good for the agent. To say what Aristotle means by this and what it implies will be a primary task of the rest of this book, but some introductory points will be helpful.

Sociability, rationality, and emotions: an introductory word

Sociability

According to the standard translation of the Greek word *politikon*, Aristotle says that a human being is a political animal. My translation of *politikon* is *sociable*. In a weak sense of the term, bees in hives are sociable in that they work cooperatively for a common purpose.[17] People in a household are more sociable than bees because, being human, they can choose and pursue their purposes rationally and coordinate their activity to the extent that the purposes require. People also respond rationally to ethical considerations; they can become virtuous, but only in a *polis*, which is their primary ethical teacher and guardian. For humans are not self-sufficient outside a *polis*, and a human life outside the *polis* cannot be a good life (*NE* I 7 1097b8–13, 8 1099a31–b6, VI 9 1142a9f.). So we have not only an innate capacity to participate in political life (*Politica* [hereafter *Pol*] I 2 1253a7–18) but also a desire to do so (29f. and III 6 1278b15–30). It is not surprising that Aristotle holds that political theory is continuous with ethics (*NE* I 2, X 9).

Aristotle says that the *polis* is prior to the individual (*Pol* I 3 1253a18–29). This seems to mean that a person who is not a part of a *polis* is incomplete, as is an amputated foot: neither is capable of its essential function apart from the whole in which it performs that function. Isolated from any community, a person is not fully human. But Aristotle is not espousing any sort of radical collectivism. His *polis* is small enough that any citizen can realistically expect to participate in politics. If you are a citizen, you can see and take responsibility

[17] In this paragraph I am much in debt to Miller (1995, pp. 31–6), though he does not translate *politikon* as I do.

for the consequences of your own actions; you can see how others' decisions affect you; you can see the importance of cooperation and compromise in pursuit of common goals. He does attribute to the *polis* some functions, especially regarding ethics, that exceed what most of us today would be comfortable in assigning to any political entity. At III 9 1280b6–8, for example, he says that a true *polis* must be *epimeles* – attentive to or in charge of – virtue. It is not a mere alliance for mutual protection (8f.). Social institutions, parts of the *polis*, are about friendship. The purpose of the *polis* is living well (33–40) – that is, the good life for each person in the *polis*.

A household supports a weaker sense of sociability than does a *polis*. Parents can prepare a child for the real world outside the family, but one cannot learn virtue without having experience in that real world, and in particular through participation in a *polis* that creates justice for all citizens (*NE* II 1–3, X 9). But one reason why we are sociable both as family members and as citizens is that we are dependent creatures. Children cannot survive without parents; people cannot be fully functioning adults without the *polis*.

We are also sociable in the sense that we are capable of friendship (*NE* VIII and X). Friends may offer us amusement, or they may be useful. But friendship in the strongest sense is a relationship between two people who are virtuous, since they want what is truly good for each other as for themselves. As with virtue generally, this sort of friendship is natural and good in itself because it is a culminating achievement in our lives, though not everyone achieves it.

In one other important way Aristotle takes humans to be sociable. In his discussion of justice in exchange, in *NE* V 5, he speaks of exchange as holding the community together, for people who have no need of each other do not exchange (V 5 1132b31–3, 1133a16–18, b6–8). Because we are dependent creatures we create communities with markets.[18]

Rationality

Rationality is the other definitive human feature. It may be theoretical or practical; we are interested in the latter, in what Aristotle calls

---

[18] But at *Pol* I 10 Aristotle says that trade is exploitative. Perhaps the point is that it can be exploitative but that in the right circumstances it is just. For more on Aristotle's opinions on exchange see Koehn (1992).

practical wisdom. On Aristotle's account, rationality makes me capable not only of drawing inferences about what to do on the basis of my desires but also of desiring the sort of thing that it is right for a human being to desire (*NE* VI 7 1141b12–14). A decision is based on a desire that is in turn based on deliberation concerning some end. The virtuous person aims at what is really good, the bad person at what just seems good (*NE* III 3 1113a9–12 and III 4 1113a22–6). You are morally responsible for what seems good to you: you may fairly be blamed if you get it wrong (III 5 1114a31–b3).

Aristotle does not wholly separate sociability and rationality as essential human characteristics. The highest form of human sociability entails exercising one's innate capacity to be a citizen and a friend in the fullest sense of both terms. That requires a level of rationality that exceeds what suffices to keep a beehive or even a human family going. Natural human rationality permits the agent to choose not only efficient means to ends, but also the best possible ends, which constitute a good life. And that good life is a sociable life as a friend and a citizen. Still, it seems fair to say that Aristotle makes rationality the dominant characteristic of humanity and of virtue. We shall have more to say about rationality in a number of contexts, for it is closely related to almost everything Aristotle says about ethics.

Emotions

Aristotle's claim that certain emotions support virtue is sound. Elster (1998) and Frank (1988) are among those who hold that appropriate emotion is required to support moral behavior. Psychopaths typically know what is right, but their knowledge has no emotional support – so say Cleckley (1988) and Hare (1993). The brain-damaged Phineas Gage, described by Damasio (1994, pp. 3–33), is an excellent and appalling example. Haidt (2001, especially p. 824) discusses these works in an article on emotion and reason. Walton[19] notes similarities between Aristotle's views and Damasio's. Like others similarly damaged, Gage was quite capable of reasoning about ethics, but incapable of any sort of emotion typical of the moral person. Such people sometimes have trouble making decisions, perhaps because the sort of

[19] Walton, C. 1997. "Brain, Feeling, and Society: Damasio and Aristotle on Neurobiology and Moral Psychology." Published and circulated by the author.

emotional capacity that they lack is what makes it possible for normal people to identify salient aspects of a situation on which a decision can be based.[20] We can infer that it is a mistake to believe that emotional people are not rational. Being entirely unemotional amounts to just not caring, and there is nothing rational about that.

Blasi (1999) argues that emotions seem to be based on preexisting concerns, typically moral ones, and therefore are effects rather than causes of moral concerns and actions. And as emotions arise unintentionally, they cannot be causes of intentional actions, which must be the result of conscious moral reasons if they are to be morally acceptable. As we shall see, Aristotle takes a somewhat different view.

Virtues as causes

In saying that virtue ethics is about the sort of person one is rather than about what one does, we should not forget that the two are closely related, for we infer virtues by looking at behavior because virtues cause behavior.[21] As Aristotle says at *NE* I 5 1095b33, an inactive life is not a virtuous one. In thinking about ethics we have some of the reasons for focusing on virtues as well as on action that natural scientists have for focusing on the relations among theoretical entities as well as on observable events. In fact, I shall argue, the virtues have a status similar to that of traits postulated by psychologists to explain behavior. Virtues and other traits may explain desires and emotions as well.[22]

The causal story is a bit murky, however. It is important to Aristotle that virtues and vices are causes of behavior, and not just ways of describing in summary fashion how people behave. But he does not understand causality quite as we do: he does not take it to be a relation based on natural laws that may cover unobservable entities. So he does not worry, as we might, about how believing that *p* relates to believing that *q* when *p* implies *q*. Those are not straightforward relations, for psychological states and events are sometimes described in normative

[20] Klein (1998) finds precisely this point in DeSousa (1987). I shall have more to say about salient aspects in Chapter 2.
[21] Here I avoid behaviorism, which reduces virtues to actual and possible behavior. The relationship is causal, not logical.
[22] This is one reason why virtue is not a simple disposition to behave in a certain way.

or epistemic terms. If *p* implies *q*, does a belief that *p* cause a belief that *q*? It does in some cases, as a rock falling on one's head sometimes causes a concussion. The laws that relate the two events in each case are underlying physiological laws, not expressed in terms of beliefs or rocks. (See, e.g., Davidson, 2001, Essay 1.) The logical relations among epistemic states like belief do not guarantee that there are parallel causal relations: one might believe a proposition but not believe what it implies. The causal relation between the two beliefs mirrors the logical relation only if the person is rational. So a theory in which psychological states like beliefs are variables, the sort of theory that a psychologist or a scholar of organizational behavior might offer cannot have the rigor of a standard scientific theory.

One of Davidson's targets was the view, popular when his essay first appeared in 1963, that the relation between intentions and actions was not causal but logical, since it is a necessary truth that the intention to do A is the kind of thing that is by definition typically followed by the agent's doing A. Anscombe's *Intention* (1957) was an influential argument to that effect. Wrong as this claim probably was, hers was a subtle account, and she and Davidson held some important views in common. Both were much under the influence of Aristotle.

Aristotle believes that the relationship between the agent's belief that action A is the right thing to do and the agent's performance of action A is not invariant. As he explains in his discussion of weakness of will, one might know that action A is the best thing to do but not do it if rationality is lacking. But Aristotle holds that a true virtue does always cause the corresponding behavior (and emotion and so on), because a truly virtuous person is rational.

Business ethics today

Management scholars and virtue

The virtue approach to business ethics is slowly beginning to gain acceptance. One possible reason for the slowness is the influence of scholars in organization theory, who, because they typically try to identify principles of effective management, can see the intended point of ethical principles as well. Many organization theorists want to be scientific. They seek to operationalize their concepts and to observe and measure whatever they can (see Ghoshal, 2005).[23] Business ethicists trained primarily in organization theory often see ethics as a subdiscipline of that field, and tend to assume that its methodology ought to be similar.[24] Although moral philosophers in business ethics do not believe that ethics is scientific, they must converse with organization theorists, who are in what is indeed a closely allied field. In any case, organization theorists outnumber business ethicists and can outvote them in departmental meetings. It is hard to defend the apparent vagueness of virtue ethics, still harder the view that there is no single metric in ethics – in particular, that ethics does not rest on cost-benefit analysis.

Organization theory is influenced by economics and by the view of human motivation that economists offer, as therefore is business ethics. Insofar as economists are hospitable to ethics, they tend to favor utilitarianism and to identify the good with utility. Psychological traits, attitudes, and beliefs are ethically important just insofar as they lead to good or bad results. Scholars of organizational behavior, like psychologists, take these entities seriously, but often seek to operationalize them; so a virtue might be cashed into no more than a disposition to act in a certain way, contrary to what virtue ethicists believe.[25] Organization theorists, like sociologists, rely less on psychological states and events and are sometimes reluctant to countenance them. So business ethicists who take virtues seriously, and in particular regard them as more than mere dispositions to act, may face skeptical colleagues.

Not all of their colleagues will hold that organizations are subjects for hard science, however. Weber, Taylor, and Barnard are no longer fashionable. There is no consensus today that organizations are machines. Tsoukas and Cummings (1997), writing eight years before Ghoshal, see widespread opposition to the old methods, largely

---

[23] MacIntyre (1985) argues on the basis of reasons similar to Ghoshal's that the very notion of social science is misconceived. Ghoshal worries that the "instrumental" conception of human motivation will crowd ethics out (p. 76).

[24] I once heard a distinguished management theorist ask in a conference session, "Why can't you ethicists operationalize your concepts?"

[25] This form of reductionism is not universal, as Hambrick (2005) and Donaldson (2005) note.

because the subject matter is too indeterminate to admit of the scientific approach.[26]

Ethics and effectiveness

Even principle-based ethics poses some problems for organization theory. Insofar as organization theorists assume that people are *homines economici*, not only narrowly rational but ruthlessly opportunistic, they will reject the very possibility of ethics. The standard justification for oversimplifying assumptions is that they permit fairly accurate predictions. Ghoshal (2005) does not accept this justification; he claims that the assumptions prevail not because they predict accurately, since they do not, but because they are easy to model. They are accurate only insofar as they are self-fulfilling. If you believe that your stakeholders are selfish and ruthless, you have reason to be that way too, with unsurprising results. Many business students learn the dubious lesson all too well, according to McCabe and Trevino (1995) and Pfeffer (2005). Frank, Gilovich, and Regan (1993) say much the same about students of economics.

Most business ethicists today have considerable faith in markets, with reason. Consider the quality of life for the average person, or even the well-do-to person, in America 200 years ago as compared to today's relatively widely distributed abundance of goods unimaginable then.[27] While even most economists would not reduce quality of life to gross domestic product (GDP) or any other measure of wealth, there is something to be said for an economic system that has lifted many millions of people out of poverty, which Aristotle considers a barrier to well-being (*NE* X 8 1178b34ff.). A market in which there is strong competition and participants have the information required to maximize their interests will be highly productive. It will enable positive-sum exchanges, as Aristotle would acknowledge. It will be just, too, in the sense that what you get out of the market will depend on what you contribute to it. It will respect negative rights, in that all deals will be voluntary and there will always be some choices.

---

[26] Tsoukas and Cummings discern emerging "Aristotelian themes" in organizational scholarship. Many of its practitioners would agree with MacIntyre (1985) about the pretensions of social science.

[27] For an extended argument to this effect see McCloskey (2006), herself a virtue ethicist.

We cannot define well-being in the way we can define, say, specific gravity. We cannot prove that Aristotelian *eudaimonia*, usually translated *flourishing*, is a superior version of it.[28] But even if it is, material prosperity counts for something; so business can play a role in creating the good life. To make that claim, which few would contest, is not to embrace empty utilitarianism.

One might plausibly infer from all this that ethics in a competitive market is a matter of competing successfully, that the virtue of a firm is effectiveness, and that the virtue of its employees is to do their jobs well. In a well-managed firm the employees will be compensated according to their contributions (Jensen and Meckling, 1976, and many others); so the self-interested employee will act ethically. Milton Friedman (1970) goes so far as to claim that the primary moral responsibility of corporate managers is to compete successfully and make profits for the stockholders.

Not all markets are highly competitive, however, and market imperfections and failures, particularly failures of knowledge, may create ethical problems.[29] But as elsewhere in economics, the model need not be perfectly accurate to be useful in making predictions. Among the outcomes that the free market model predicts accurately, on the whole, is the efficient production of things that people want. That is an impressive outcome, particularly to a utilitarian.

What I am saying here is not news to all economists, and in any case the approximation of reality characteristic of models is not necessarily a problem. Some, for example Cartwright (1983), have said much the same about natural science. Ghoshal's claim that ease of computation rather than predictive power is behind management theory does not necessarily apply to economic theory. All the same, Aristotle would say that a wise economist knows that economics is not mathematics.

Business ethics and utilitarianism

Most business ethicists reject Friedman's view, but they usually take utilitarian considerations seriously even when they are not praising markets. Advocates of corporate social responsibility (Carroll, 1981,

---

[28] We shall discuss it more thoroughly in Chapter 3.
[29] Or they may create benefits. Entrepreneurship involves creating a product or service that has no competitors, at least at first.

for example) believe that corporations often can and should act in ways that benefit society, particularly when the corporation is in a uniquely good position to do so, as was Merck in 1987. Merck has distributed their medication Mectizan to over 200 million Africans suffering from or exposed to river blindness, an often fatal disease. The benefits justify the cost, according to Merck management (2011). Stakeholder theorists (e.g., Freeman, Harrison, and Wicks, 2007) argue that the interests of certain stakeholders other than stockholders create obligations for corporations, which ought to seek win-win situations with them. Their examples suggest that the winning that they have in mind is largely financial, though that was not true in the Mectizan case. Few business ethicists object to every instance of cost-benefit analysis that imputes a dollar value to human life.[30]

Nearly all business ethicists believe that business can be an ethical enterprise, and they favor organizations that are effective, hence productive, hence necessarily profitable. To the question "Why should I be moral?" the standard utilitarian answer is that I should be moral because the business system can be productive if and only if people like me act honestly, work responsibly, and otherwise contribute to productivity. Everyone fares better if everyone acts ethically than if everyone acts unethically, though I may do very well if everyone but me acts ethically and I convincingly pretend to do so.

Business ethicists and organization theorists are often called upon to say whether good ethics is good business. An affirmative response typically takes the form of evidence that something like a code of ethics correlates with higher than average profits.[31] One can also claim that a reputation for trustworthiness is a business asset. Occasionally business ethicists dismiss the question by arguing that ethical obligation is not contingent on corporate effectiveness, as indeed it is not. In a provocative article, Stark (1993) reports with apparent astonishment that business ethicists believe that a business ought to cease to exist if it cannot succeed without being unethical. Most business ethicists would probably find that belief tautologous. What most of them do not believe is that businesspeople must weigh ethical considerations against effectiveness. They believe that effectiveness is not

---

[30] This is sometimes hard to avoid, as when one must decide how much more or less to spend on a car's safety equipment to save more or fewer lives of drivers and passengers.

[31] See Burke (1985, pp. 451–6).

fundamentally unethical – on the contrary, it is good from an ethical point of view, all else equal – and that business ethicists have something important and palatable to say to businesspeople and business students.

In addition to the utilitarian focus in business ethics there has been some attention to issues like meaningful work and sexual harassment, but scholars of organizational ethics usually respect the point that one may quit an unsatisfactory job and that employers have economic reasons for not treating their employees badly. Scholarship on ethics in international business often justifies multinational enterprise as an engine of prosperity. Even critical analyses of sweatshops usually acknowledge as a point in their favor that they provide relatively good economic opportunities to people in the developing world and can be a first step towards a stronger and more just economy. But few if any business ethicists would deny that some sweatshops are cruel and exploitative and highly profitable.

Ethics as a strategy

It is important to avoid the implication that ethics matters only insofar as it leads to economic success. Business ethicists like to point to the evidence (e.g., that collected by Collins and Porras, 2002) that the most profitable companies are those whose strategies and policies are driven by a prosocial corporate mission. So Johnson and Johnson and Whole Foods Market, for example, aim to satisfy their customers first, then their employees, then the communities in which they operate, and their stockholders only fourth. Corporate management believes that the stockholders are best served if the other three stakeholder groups are given priority. So, happily for all concerned, profit and ethics coincide (Johnson and Johnson, 1943).[32]

This is good news, but the fact remains that some companies succeed by being unethical – by selling bad products, by competing unfairly or eliminating competition, by seeking rents, by exploiting vulnerable workers, by taking irresponsible risks, sometimes under pressure from investors. In any case, to say that one should operate ethically just

---

[32] In recent years Johnson and Johnson has had some ethical lapses, but as I write the stock price is still more than respectable.

because that is the best route to competitive success is to make ethics a strategy, not a free-standing obligation.

Effectiveness is a good thing from a utilitarian point of view, but utilitarianism is not the only basis for ethics. There are also considerations of justice and rights. Many forms of utilitarianism also make some questionable assumptions about the good life, or ignore the difficulties in defining it, as I shall argue in Chapter 3.

Even if we add considerations of justice and rights to those of utility, however, there is a problem: principles sound good in theory, but they are often hard to put into practice. In the difficult cases they offer us little guidance. A story will illustrate the point. It is a business story, but its lessons go beyond business.

Choosing a consultant: a true story

Arnold joined the strategy unit of Bell Associates[33] in the fall of 1977 after completing an MBA. In November of that year, one of the senior members of the unit, a man named Greg, told Arnold to prepare to be sent to London to teach some of Bell's consultants and their clients how to do business-related research. He was to be there for two weeks.

Arnold considered himself qualified to do the project, but the assignment surprised him. There was in his unit a young woman named Deborah, who had spent some years managing Bell's strategy research arm before becoming a consultant. This seemed a perfect job for her. So Arnold asked Greg why Bell was sending him rather than Deborah. "Because," Greg replied, "the Brits won't work with a woman."

For more than twenty years I asked the students in my business ethics classes whether Bell should have sent Deborah or Arnold to London. In the early years Deborah got very few votes, sometimes none; in later years she steadily gained support. Students did fairly well in stating the reasons against and for sending Deborah. There is a risk of failure if she goes; that would be bad for Deborah as well as for Bell. Sending Arnold is a matter of picking a consultant who will establish rapport with the client, the most important stakeholder in the case. It is quite common to assign consultants partly on the basis of probable personal compatibility. You cannot abolish prejudice by pretending that it has

[33] I have altered the corporate and personal names.

no effect. Some students, on the other hand, argued that Bell Associates should consider taking a stand, even a risky one, for gender equity. Rarely did a student ask whether anyone had actually discussed the matter with the British. It was not clear that anyone had, or that the British really were especially prejudiced against women.

Eventually I would tell the students how the story ended. Shortly before Arnold was to leave for London, a general partner called Hank Saporsky learned of the assignment and asked whether, as he expected, Deborah was going to do it. No, said Greg; the Brits won't work with a woman. To which Hank replied, "Nuts to the Brits!" – or words to that effect – "We're sending Deborah." So Deborah went off to London and performed brilliantly. At the beginning of her second week she was asked to stay on "for another fortnight," and in the end spent many fortnights in London and worked with many delighted clients.

From time to time a student would protest that Deborah's success proved no more than any other anecdote. She might have bombed; no one could confidently predict the outcome. This is a good point, though a utilitarian one. The story does not show that standing up to sexism always leads to a good result, or even that is always the right thing to do. The students readily agreed on the injustice of discriminating against someone on the basis of gender, but equally readily they agreed that that principle might not be straightforwardly applicable to this case. If the Brits will not work with a woman no matter what she has to offer, they are being unjust, but what is Bell's obligation in the face of the Brits' alleged intransigence? And how do we factor in the fiduciary duty to the Bell partners?

Greg worked the problem out by focusing on risk and return. He understood that from a technical point of view sending Arnold would entail a cost, in the sense that Arnold would perform less well than Deborah, though probably adequately. But Greg reasoned that the expected value of sending Deborah, taking into account the probability and the cost of her failing, made Arnold the right choice.

Hank took a broader context into account. He believed that even accommodating gender prejudice was incompatible with the values of the firm. In his view as a general partner, there were some things that Bell Associates – and he personally – just did not and would not do. Hank's position made it possible for him to act on his own values. He knew who he was and how his being a general partner of a consulting firm fit into the course and defining purposes of his life. So he was confident that he was making the right decision about Deborah.

Hank saw the importance of sending a message of loyalty to Deborah: You are a valued professional and we've got your back, whatever happens. That is a good message for any young professional to hear from a senior partner, but it is especially important to a young woman who cannot be sure that everyone in the firm understands that. It is good for the firm as well, insofar as it helps create a culture of solidarity and trust.

Hank knew no principles that Greg did not know. His decision was that of an experienced and successful manager with a strong sense of professional responsibility and loyalty, though his loyalty never extended to the extreme of supporting those who did not do well, or giving consultants assignments that they probably would not complete successfully. If Hank had not considered Deborah an excellent consultant, he would not have demanded that she be sent. He did not ignore the risks associated with sending Deborah; he just believed that other factors were more important under the circumstances.

Greg's deliberation fell short in at least two respects, apart from his failure to assess the Brits' attitude accurately. First, he failed to consider some of the important contextual factors, no doubt because they did not seem immediate. It did not occur to him that it mattered in this case that the partnership was committed to gender equity and that the decision on sending Deborah to London was more than just that single decision: it was an example and a widely visible sign of that commitment. Second, Greg's view of the matter may appear to have been more coldly rational than that of Hank, but in fact it was less rational. He had too much confidence in his ability to deal with this issue by estimating the expected value of sending Deborah.[34] This was not the sort of situation in which one could make a good decision by trying to maximize anything.

This case raises many issues, nearly as many as there are accurate descriptions of it and of the options available to the agents. Each of these descriptions suggests a principle on which the agents might act. If you want to make a good decision, you must describe the situation and the options to yourself in a way that takes the most important

---

[34] This supports Beabout's (2012, pp. 423f.) claim that one of the great sources of managerial error is the failure to know what one does not know.

considerations into account. Consider these descriptions of the options, each of them arguably accurate: protecting Deborah from the consequences of failure; expressing our confidence in Deborah; faithfully serving the values of the partners, or the interests of the clients, or the former by way of the latter; refusing to accommodate gender prejudice; sending the most competent professional. Some of these descriptions will seem attractive to a utilitarian. Some will appeal to fairness. Most of them deserve consideration. Virtue ethicists can consider all of them, but they know that there is no algorithm for prioritizing them. Some agents make better decisions than others, however. Their experience and intelligence give them a practical kind of wisdom. That practical wisdom will include knowledge of some principles, but not principles that will tell one just what to do in Deborah's case – still less in other cases, which may resemble Deborah's but will inevitably differ from it in some significant ways.

It would be obtuse to describe the decision facing Hank and Greg without reference to their positions in Bell Associates. They had a prima facie obligation to act in the best interests of the partnership. They also had a prima facie obligation to honor the ethics of the consulting profession. These obligations did not make it any easier for them to sort out what they ought to do: they are not trumps, though they deserve serious consideration. Multiple obligations are a fact of life, and not only in business. But it is important not to overstate the conflicting nature of the obligations that Hank and Greg faced, particularly if they had reason to believe that Bell Associates was committed to high professional standards and to gender equity. If that is what they believed, then there was considerable overlap between what they thought best from their own ethical point of view and what their job required.

Ethical decisions and business decisions

Suppose that Greg wanted to make the best possible ethical decision. How would that differ from making the best possible business decision? What sort of consideration or argument would figure in one sort of decision but not another? If Greg is making an ethical decision, he probably will not try to figure out what will maximize happiness, or treat the people involved as ends rather than merely as means, or invoke the difference principle, or respect everyone's rights. He might tell himself to be fair to the organization, to the clients, and to Deborah. He might remind himself to put aside narrowly selfish considerations, to avoid rationalizing, not to internalize ignorant criticism if things do not work out well. All of this self-advice is valuable from a business point of view as well. It overlaps with what a good human resources consultant would advise.

Greg would be wrong to think this way: "There is no ethical issue here. There is only a business issue. The right question is, 'What is best for the firm?'" Some businesspeople with whom I have discussed this case have said that the manager's job is to do the right thing for the client and therefore for the company *rather than what is ethical*. Some of them see Hank as *balancing* ethics (sending Deborah) against effectiveness (sending Arnold) and choosing the former. This assumption that there are ethical considerations and then business considerations and that one or the other ought to be given priority – the latter, usually – is part of what Freeman (1994, and elsewhere) calls the separation thesis. In this case the assumption seems highly questionable. The considerations that led Hank to his decision cannot be divided into business considerations and ethical ones.

The decision to do what is best for the firm, if it is made properly, will take account of the special claims that the firm has on its employees. In making the decision one must understand the obligations of one's role, which introduces potentially decisive considerations. It will be a foolish and irresponsible decision if it does not also take the interests and the capacities of certain stakeholders – in this case the client and Deborah, primarily – into account, though these interests and capacities are not wholly separate from those of the firm. Making the decision carelessly or on the basis of prejudice or because one does not consider a range of factors is ethically deficient and bad for business.

Anyway, what is the force of the "ought" in "business considerations ought to be given priority over ethical ones"? If it is an ethical "ought," the proposition is nonsense. If it is a prudential "ought," it implies that one might be better off letting a prudential "ought" override an ethical "ought." That is a boring point at best.

We might be inclined to say that Smith morally ought to blow the whistle on her boss for some minor misdeed but that she prudentially ought not to, since she would be fired and her career ruined if she did. So apparently the prudential ought outweighs the moral ought in that case. But Aristotle and some other philosophers would point out that she has some moral obligations to herself, and these may override the obligation to blow the whistle. As we shall see, Aristotle assimilates the prudent to the moral to a considerable extent.

I am not claiming that a good business decision is necessarily an ethically good decision. I am opposing the notion that business considerations ought to trump ethical considerations in any meaningful sense of "ought," as well as the notion that business considerations have no ethical component. I also believe that a consulting firm that offers well-informed and objective expertise that its clients need will probably not fail as a result of maintaining high standards of professional ethics.

One thing that Greg had an ethical obligation to do was to focus on some factual issues. Did the Brits actually say they would not deal with a woman? Does Deborah have the personality to get on with professional men? What would the consequences of Deborah's failure be? What would the consequences of not sending her be? Is the partnership truly committed to supporting women? Is she the right person to be sent for the right reason at the right time to work with the right people on the right sort of project?

Whether Greg could make the best possible decision in this case depended a great deal on whether he was an intelligent, experienced, professionally responsible, sensitive, tough-minded manager who valued doing the right thing. Hank was all of that. He made what many will believe was the right decision because he was able to grasp and assess the essential features of the case – facts about Deborah, about the probable risks, about the sort of treatment the company owed Deborah, about the organization's commitment to gender equity and his acceptance of that commitment. He *framed* the situation appropriately, and he trusted his long-honed intuitions enough to act decisively on them.

Hank had to be rational to frame the situation the way he did, but he needed something more, to get past mere rationalization. Upon being told of the tentative decision to send Arnold, Hank had an immediate emotional reaction that pushed him in a certain direction, somewhat like the gut reaction that a seasoned and successful strategist has when contemplating options. That strategist is aware of the data that analysts can gather and knows many techniques for using the numbers in assessing the prospects of strategic business units, but beyond the numbers *sees* that this option is a potential bonanza and that that option is a black hole. This is a practical kind of wisdom.[35]

Practical wisdom[36]

Aristotle says that a virtue is similar to a skill (or craft; the Greek word is *techne*) in some important ways. A skill, like a virtue, is a discipline that requires practice and rational deliberation. Playing the piano well, for example, requires following some rules, but you improve only by long practice. Eventually you get beyond playing the notes and heeding the directions concerning volume and tempo, and develop a feeling for the music and a virtuoso ability to interpret it. Much the same can be said of management. If you are a good manager, you know the standard rules of management, but you know that they do not offer dispositive guidance on all complex cases. You develop a feeling for the cases; and although you cannot demonstrate that this consideration trumps that one, and you may not consciously weigh the considerations, you can respond to requests for reasons for what you did. When new cases come along that raise problems not amenable to straightforward extrapolation from old ones, the good manager can still cope. Superiority in management requires getting beyond the rulebook rather than memorizing it.

We must be careful not to misinterpret Aristotle on this point. It is true that what we might call practical decisions and ethical decisions are similar and may overlap. In particular, neither sort of decision is reducible to rule following; each requires a faculty based on experience. But Aristotle holds that there is an important difference between making and doing; and in his view, business and other productive activities are about making, whereas ethics is about doing.

Praxis and poiesis

At *NE* V 4–5 Aristotle distinguishes between making (*poiesis*) and doing, or action (*praxis*). Skill (*techne*) is concerned with production.

---

[35] This is the topic of Gladwell (2005). We discuss the skilled strategist further in the next chapter.

[36] Much of what I say about the much discussed and controversial topic of practical wisdom here and elsewhere is influenced by Russell (2009), among others. At *NE* II 6 1107a1, VI 1138b18–34, and elsewhere Aristotle identifies practical wisdom with good character for reasons we shall discuss here and in Chapter 3.

Building a house is a productive activity, an exercise in skill. So is improving your health through diet and exercise. Acting in a way that promotes living well, on the other hand, is a *praxis*, a matter not of skill but of practical wisdom. The Greek term for the latter is *phronesis*, sometimes translated prudence. Prudence suggests cautious and self-interested motivation and behavior. The use of the term as a translation of *phronesis* is not quite as misleading as one might suppose. Aristotle argues that it is indeed in one's best interest to be *phronimos*. Caution too is involved, in the sense that *phronesis* requires good deliberation in full view of the probabilities. *Phronesis* is often used outside an ethical context by Greek authors, but in the *Nicomachean Ethics* it is normally an ethical term.

If you are a practically wise (*phronimos*) person, you know how to get what you aim at and you know what to aim at. You know what living well looks like, you know how to do it, and you do it. Pouring a concrete foundation is a means to building a secure house, which is a skill. Actions and desires and emotions characteristic of practical wisdom are good in themselves; they are not really *means to* living well. One should rather say that they *amount to* living well; they are what counts as living well. If I enjoy playing the piano, it would be a bit misleading to say that I play as a means to the end of experiencing enjoyment, as though enjoying playing were a state distinct from playing,[37] though the enjoyment of my audience, a necessary condition of the goodness of my playing, is a distinct state. A further, related difference between skill and practical wisdom is that when you set out to live well, you cannot describe your objective as though it were your dream house. You need to learn, in part through experience, what living well looks like.

Skill and practical wisdom are similar in that the principles that apply to each are more like rules of thumb than precise guides to action. The skill of management requires intuition honed by experience; so does practical wisdom. The intelligent, experienced, professional manager who sees the situation and its opportunities clearly and whole is similar to the practically wise person, like Hank Saporsky, who sees that a certain situation demands that one act on the basis of justice for and loyalty to a deserving professional employee.

---

[37] I need hardly add that this is a long story, which I started to tell in the Introduction. I am not sure that Aristotle has an entirely consistent view of the matter.

Aristotle does not always use the words *praxis* and *poiesis* in a way that strictly distinguishes them, in part because the two notions are in fact not quite distinct. An action may look like a *praxis* or a *poiesis* depending on how it is described. If I act out of courage, my act can be seen as repulsing the foe or as showing courage and thus achieving *eudaimonia*. In fact, most acts done out of virtue are good in themselves but also have some good result.[38] We can say that a virtuous act creates *eudaimonia*, but that is not necessarily separate from the good result. If you generously give Jones some money so that he can buy lunch, we can think of what you are doing as a generous act (*praxis*) or an act that has the good result of Jones getting lunch (*poiesis*) and thereby creating *eudaimonia* for you and him. If my interpretation is right, we are faithful to Aristotle's view if we say that a certain *poiesis* done from *techne* is a *praxis* done from practical wisdom if and only if a good agent intends and enjoys achieving some good result, such as Jones's well-being.[39]

This kind of overlapping of concepts is a familiar move for Aristotle. It is the standard doctrine of his *De Anima* that a bodily event may be inseparable from a psychological event but that the psychological description is primary: the form of the event is a thought, and the matter is its physical basis. As we noted, a psychological event may be petulance or righteous indignation depending on the sort of thing that caused it. A *poiesis* is a *praxis* if it is done in the right way for the right reason in the right context with the right result.

We can now see a way in which Aristotle's virtue ethics overlaps to some degree with utilitarianism. When you do a favor to someone – a real benefit, that is, not just a preference fulfillment – you are helping create *eudaimonia* in that person and in yourself, and a utilitarian will approve. The problem with utilitarianism, from Aristotle's point of view, is that it looks at the action only as a *poiesis:* it focuses only on the effect of an act on people other than the agent. That effect is only part of what justifies us in saying that the act was a *praxis*, done from benevolence or justice or some other virtue.

---

[38] Aristotle says at *NE* I 1 1094a5f. that where the end is separate from the *praxis*, the end is superior. I assume that he is not using *praxis* in its strict sense in that passage.

[39] MacIntyre's claim that in business profit drives out virtue seems insensitive to the notion of *praxis* as characteristically generating both internal and external goods. I elaborate in Chapter 5.

Consider Hank again. The skilled manager is normally paid for making something, creating some valuable product or service. In the case of Hank, the value takes the form of a direct or indirect service to clients, and thereby profit for the firm. At the same time, however, Hank is the sort of person for whom acting professionally and supportively of deserving fellow professionals is in itself a source of satisfaction. In acting professionally, loyally, and courageously Hank was doing something that was intrinsically good for him. He was engaged in a *praxis*.

An example of practical wisdom

Practical wisdom, in business and elsewhere, is not just a matter of following ethical principles. Think of a CEO – call her Smith – who wants to do the right thing by her company and its stakeholders, primarily the stockholders. She thinks long and hard about possible solutions to the problems of corporate governance, and she concludes that it is possible to do better than the prevailing norms mandate. She contemplates bringing democracy to her board of directors. Smith thinks that democracy is a good thing generally, and she thinks that the standard way of electing directors by nominating as many candidates as there are seats up for election resembles the old Soviet Union too much. She believes that principles of rights and justice are important, but so do those who disagree with her about what to do.

Some defenders of the status quo might tell Smith that stockholders can always sell their stock if they do not like the current arrangement. There are two problems with this advice. First, there are few if any publicly traded firms with democratically elected directors, so there is no realistic way to choose something other than the current arrangement. Second, many defenders of the status quo are the very people who praise Friedman's conception of social responsibility in part because it recognizes the ownership rights of the stockholders. These defenders' views raise the question why owners' rights do not include the right to make meaningful choices of directors.

Smith is aware that more democratic governance may lead to a board that is even more incompetent and inattentive to actual and prospective stockholders than are many current boards. She does not know exactly what the best democratic structure is, and no principle will tell her. She has to find a structure that will gain broad acceptance and that will bring success to the firm. She can do some research, but she may well find herself proceeding by trial and error. She may discover that, for example, freer elections give more power to money managers with a short-term orientation.

Suppose that Smith invents a way for stockholders to be more fairly represented by directors and then convinces the other executives and the directors of her company to have genuine elections for the board. With some assistance she designs the process, and the result is a board that differs somewhat but not radically from its predecessor. Suppose that the immediate reaction is negative: the stock price drops. Suppose, however, that in the longer term the firm prospers and the stock price rises, in part because the new directors are actually paying critical attention to what goes on. Elsewhere, despite frantic maneuvering by management and some directors, similar schemes are put in place with generally good results.[40]

From an ethical point of view, Smith achieves success if things work out in the latter way. The new system enhances productivity; it distributes decision-making power more fairly; it better accommodates the ownership rights of stockholders. But Smith has not done all this by merely attending to principles associated with utility, justice, or rights and then applying them to the situation at hand. She has begun with a somewhat vague vision of what her company might look like if she succeeds, but without a map to guide her through the necessary steps. She must also use her knowledge of organization theory and much else.

We can say that her design was guided by considerations of justice, but it might be more perspicuous to say that by thinking pragmatically and navigating cleverly she created a new and attractive example of what justice can be in corporate governance, and she offered a richer conception of the rights that stockholders have. The facts on the ground limit what works, and what works limits what is just and what rights stockholders have, for normally justice is not served and rights are not protected by any action that severely damages the stockholders' interests or otherwise creates a mess. Paradoxically, then, in this and other cases we cannot usefully apply principles until after the fact, when the new arrangement causes us to have a new

---

[40] This may actually happen, for many new corporate forms are being contemplated.

understanding of how they apply and what ethics dictates. We can look at the successful results of Smith's undertaking – the norms that now determine corporate governance – from the point of view of certain widely accepted principles and call them good, at least for the time being. We cannot know with certainty that they are the best possible under the circumstances, still less that they are the best under any circumstances or forever.

On what basis do we call the new arrangement better than the old one? Effectiveness is a prominent criterion. Beyond that, we have familiar reasons for believing that democracy is good and just, though there are some matters that we should not vote on. If the new arrangement does not create serious problems, we can say that there are no good reasons for going back to the way things used to be.

The story suggests that, being a virtuous person, Smith will take considerations of utility, justice, and rights into account, but practical wisdom must enable her to work out what they mean in a complex situation and to act accordingly. She also needs intellectual honesty and courage. But these virtues are among Smith's business skills as well as her virtues, much as an Athenian soldier's courage is part of his being an effective fighter and part of his being a good person. Business and martial skills have certain purposes, but the virtues that they embody are good in themselves. Making and doing cannot always be cleanly separated.

The story has another important lesson. Smith is a kind of entrepreneur, ethical as well as managerial, with nerve to match. Even more than standard management, entrepreneurship is more than a matter of merely following rules. It is about seeing things the right way, and that includes seeing possibilities for action when others do not. Similarly, a virtuous person never just follows the rules. Even in fairly simple and familiar cases principles give imperfect guidance. In new situations, which we know that the future will produce, practical wisdom gets even less help from principles, and must improvise. But none of this means that practical wisdom avoids generalizations or makes no use of them. Aristotle says at *NE* X 9 1180b8–23 that a good doctor is one who can handle individual cases well, and knows that in this or that case generalizations do not apply; but the best doctor also understands a range of illnesses by virtue of his broader scientific knowledge. Knowing when the rules do not apply is quite different from not knowing the rules at all.

Character

A virtuous person is a person of good character. Kupperman (1991) defines character this way: X's character is X's normal pattern of thought and action, especially with respect to concerns and commitments in matters affecting the happiness of others or of X, and most especially in relation to moral choices (p. 17). Kupperman would probably not object if we were to add something about emotion; that would bring his definition close to Aristotle's. Your character is what is distinctive about you. We usually take character to include certain traits, such as a quick wit, that are not obviously either virtues or vices.

Character (*ethos*) includes all our virtues and vices and therefore entails certain values, dispositions, and emotions as well as actions. Aristotle suggests not only that one's character ought to be consistent over time and coherent at all times, but also that character is essential to personal identity. In a person of good character, virtues and values are reinforced by appropriate dispositions and emotions.

According to Aristotle, we have certain enduring desires that can serve as premises of so-called practical syllogisms (discussed mainly in *NE* VII): these are, in effect, reasons to act. These desires flow from our character; they have to do with our well-being and with our most important concerns and commitments, often involving others, since we are sociable creatures. So a person of generous character acts generously, wants to do so, and thinks it good to do so. If you are generous, you are and want to be – that is, you have a second-order desire to be – motivated by thoughts like this: "Jones needs help, so I want to help him." Your immediate thought is not that one ought to be generous under certain conditions but that *Jones needs help*. A friend's need is your motivation – a reason for action, from your point of view. The next-best thing, though short of a generous character, is mere acceptance of your moral obligation: "Jones needs help, so I suppose I have to help him, so all right, where's my checkbook?" To be a person of truly generous character is to have and to want to have a settled disposition to help a friend in need, and emotions to match. It entails wanting to be consistently motivated by a friend's need, wanting to be moved by a minor premise of a practical syllogism like "Jones needs help." Some of our enduring desires, especially those concerning the sort of person we want to be, we call values.

Integrity

Aristotle claims that a substance is more than a pile of stuff; similarly, a human life is more than a series of decisions and experiences. These are linked by memory, intention, commitment, and growth, which are constituents of a character. When things are working as they should, this character causes the agent's actions, which, owing to the importance of habitual action, in turn contribute to the continued development of the character.[41] Maintaining a coherent character is tantamount to continuing your life (*NE* IX 4 1066a13–29). In these passages Aristotle invites you to think of your life as a whole, as a kind of story, and to think always about what will be good for you now and later.

Aristotle's view is echoed by psychologists like Festinger (1957), who argues that people desire coherence in their views. Chaiken, Giner-Sorolla, and Chen (1996, p. 557) argue, similarly, that one wants all of one's attitudes and beliefs to be "congruent with existing self-definitional attitudes and beliefs." We should not overinterpret this point. Aristotle believes that you can develop your character and even change it, though not quickly or easily.

In addition to psychological consistency and continuity, people of character make and uphold commitments to projects, family, friends, and communities, for example, and assume obligations thereby. (See Solomon, 1992, pp. 168, 172–4, and Kupperman, 1991, pp. 135ff.) It is part of your character that there are certain things to which you are committed in a fundamental way: that is, you find their desirability so clear as to be beyond doubt, nearly self-evident; and you assess your other beliefs and actions on the basis of these values. Values motivate action and are revealed in it: you cannot be said to value hard work if you never work hard, or honesty if you regularly act in a sleazy way. Most of us, however, are weak enough that we do not always act according to our values. Valuing honesty, I accept reimbursement for questionable expenses. Valuing courage, I refrain from opposing the boss's ridiculous idea. Our values may be under pressure at work. Jones may act improperly because his boss presses

---

[41] Koehn (1995, 534) and Weaver (2006, p. 347f.) seem to have something like this in mind. MacIntyre (1985, pp. 204, 217) and Annas (2011) would agree as well. We shall elaborate in Chapter 4.

him to do so. Worse, he may over time become accustomed to acting improperly, and comfortable about doing so and urging others to do so.

The unity of the self admits of degrees in at least two ways. At any moment your psychological states can form a more or less coherent whole. You may be in a state of indecision, for example: you may not know which virtue is salient in this situation. Your second-order desires may have no effect on your first-order desires. The other sort of incoherence is diachronic. There may be little psychological connection (by memory or intention, for example) between you at t_1 and you at t_2. Your projects, principles, likes and dislikes, and character-related dispositions may fluctuate over time. We attribute a distinct and strong character to people who are consistent in these respects at a time and over time, though we allow for continuing character development in the progression of life.

Aristotle allows that one can be a beast, wholly outside the realm of ethics (*NE* VII 5). But to be a human being rather than a beast entails having a certain amount of self-consciousness about one's desires. Bad things are pleasant to a bad person, says Aristotle, but the bad person wishes that that were not so, and he dislikes himself for it (*NE* IX 4 1166b7–14).

Tensions among virtues

The virtues seem to conflict in just the way principles conflict. Can I be honest and benevolent at the same time? Can I be loyal and just at the same time? Aristotle says that virtue aims at the mean; so true honesty actually precludes brutal and gratuitous candor, and true loyalty precludes chauvinism. Practical wisdom guides us as we negotiate among these apparently competing and overlapping obligations, such as those faced by managers contractually obligated to play a certain role. There is no algorithm for doing so, no single principle that is both unexceptionable and useful in resolving complex problems. One learns to do this ethical negotiation as one learns to deal with any complex problem, in business or elsewhere, that bristles with unknowns and conflicting opportunities. Thereafter one may have some principles that are a bit sharper and more useful.[42]

---

[42] We shall go further along these lines in discussing dialectic in Chapter 4.

Aristotle believes in the unity of the virtues: that is, to have one virtue is to have them all. To this extent, at least, he is right: the courageous person must be intelligent as well, to distinguish recklessness from courage. The benevolent person must also be just, for lavishing rewards on an unworthy recipient is soft-heartedness, an extreme rather than a virtuous mean. It is not benevolent to give a poor student a good grade. The just person must also be courageous, for one who dispenses justice may make powerful enemies and disappoint friends. Practical wisdom creates a coherent character out of all of the virtues. If any virtue is missing from the whole character, the remaining virtues may be compromised because they will sometimes be perverted in action, as when one wants to act justly but has not the courage to do so.

Antiutilitarian virtues

The story of Deborah shows how difficult it is to find a moral principle that decides a complicated moral issue. There are also stories that show that apparently decisive moral principles mandate an act that just does not seem right. Suppose your brother and an outstanding manager in your organization are both drowning and you can save only one of them. Let us assume that your brother is a person of no great consequence. A virtue ethicist, and most people for that matter, would likely opt for saving the brother, however productive the manager may be.[43]

But why? The answer seems to be based squarely on your character. If you lack the virtue of fraternal loyalty, you are an appallingly unfeeling person. That you decide on the basis of the manager's greater social utility shows how cold-blooded you are. To a lesser extent we might say the same of the decision not to send Deborah to London: to treat a competent, dedicated, respectable professional that way, without even discussing the situation with her and getting her view, is (to overstate slightly) the decision of a crass person and a disloyal colleague.

Loyalty seems to be a virtue, and disloyalty a vice. Good people are loyal, we believe. But why do we believe so? And is it even true? Suppose that you have a choice between saving a Caucasian or an African-American, and you choose the former because you are Caucasian and are loyal to your race. At the very least we would demand

---

[43] Williams (1981, p. 17f.) tells a story like this.

a justification for this show of ethnic solidarity. Most likely we would despise it.

Family loyalty is a virtue, we think, and ethnic loyalty a vice. But both of those propositions require qualification. It would not be virtuous of me to protect my brother from the law if he had committed a heinous crime. If I were a member of an oppressed minority, it would not be vicious of me to devote spare time and resources to assisting others in that minority in escaping or recovering from oppression, so long as I did not object to members of other oppressed minorities showing the same ethnic solidarity.

Considerations like this suggest that virtue ethics lacks the sort of universality that Enlightenment philosophers associate with ethics: it might even seem to be a matter of Us vs. Them. But the decision to rescue your brother is universalizable in the sense that the virtue ethicist could say that all people should rescue the sibling in such a situation. Nor is the virtue approach to this case altogether opposed to the utilitarian one. A particularly subtle utilitarian might claim that it is right to rescue one's brother because a good society requires family relationships that are so strong that they override certain short-term utilitarian considerations. A very strict utilitarian might take note of the importance of family but rescue the manager anyway because doing so benefits society and does not significantly damage the institution of the family. The subtle utilitarian knows, however, that human beings of good character do not think that way. As a matter of psychological fact, acting like a strict utilitarian in that case is evidence that one is pathologically incapable of the sort of emotion that morality requires. Think of Phineas Gage.

To the virtue ethicist it matters what motivates an action; it matters that you rescue your brother because he is your brother. If you are a psychologically normal agent, your motivation does not include the thought that a good society needs family relationships of a certain sort, though that is true. We can say much the same of free-market capitalism, but it does not follow that managers should think primarily about how to help society. The same is true of the nuclear family. A virtuous person is immediately motivated not by the social importance of family ties but by the thought "My brother is drowning."

In any case, the virtue ethicist can point out that, in arguing that there is a utilitarian basis for fraternal loyalty, the utilitarian has things backwards. The utilitarian judges certain institutions (e.g., the family) and their associated virtues (e.g., fraternal loyalty) according to whether they contribute to the quality of the participants' lives. Many family members, however, will judge the quality of their own lives – assess the extent to which they are happy, fulfilled, satisfied – in part according to whether their marriages, friendships, and other associations are strong. It is a mistake, perhaps encouraged if not committed by utilitarians, to suppose that happiness is independent of, and caused by, strong family ties and other things that we value.

It is about you

In some cases virtue ethicists advocate an action that cannot be justified by any of the standard moral principles, utilitarian or otherwise. Consider a person who refuses to perform an evil act even though it will then be done by someone else. What good does it do to refuse? A virtue ethicist will focus on the difference it makes that I am the one who does this act. It is my act; I am responsible; it is an expression of my values; to do the wrong thing would affect me immediately and badly. If what matters most is what sort of person I am, then it matters greatly whether I will do this.

A version of the famous trolley problem raises the same issue. A trolley is hurtling towards two workmen on the track. The brakes do not work. You can save those two people only by pushing a very fat person into the path of the trolley. Most of us, not being strict utilitarians, intuitively believe that that would be wrong. Killing the fat man would indicate something very bad about you. What sort of person would even be capable of pushing someone into the path of an onrushing trolley?

These considerations are related to a crucial point about virtue. It is good for you to be virtuous; to act viciously harms you. In Chapter 3 we shall consider Aristotle's view of the relationship between virtue and well-being.

The next chapter addresses a question that many moral philosophers put to virtue ethics: If virtue ethics is about the sort of person you are rather than what you do, how does it tell you what to do?

2 | Virtues and decisions

How should I decide what to do?

Suppose you are trying to make an ethical decision. What sort of advice would you expect a virtue ethicist to give you? "Be generous," your adviser might say. That sounds as useful as Aristotle's supposed advice on golf: hit the ball well and according to reason and as the professional would hit. Telling you to be generous, or even to act as a generous person would, may seem to give you only the vaguest idea what to do. In any case, you cannot instantly become generous, or even able to hit the ball well.[1] But in fact being told to show generosity and do what a generous person would do – that is, help someone who needs and deserves help just because the help is needed and deserved – can be useful advice. At the very least the adviser, or the one contemplating the action, is identifying a situation as one that calls for generosity.

Suppose the decision is about a fairly new employee in your firm, an intelligent young man not known either for his modesty or for his admiration of you. You learn that he is about to give a presentation to senior management. You realize that he is missing some information that he needs to make his presentation successful. He is not aware that you have that kind of information and can interpret it helpfully, or that he needs it. You are considering whether to approach him and offer what you have.

Your friend Smith might offer this advice: "Look, I agree with you that Jones is a bit of a jerk, but the best thing for you to do is show some generosity. It will help Jones, and the company too, and you won't regret it." Your friend's advice that you show generosity in this situation is not trivial. Courage, for example, should not be to the fore. You might think about justice, but it is a secondary issue here, and it would be easy to misapply it. You might suppose that it would

---

[1] We discuss the first problem in this chapter and the second mostly in Chapter 4.

64

serve this young fellow right if you let him do the presentation without the information, particularly as he did not seek your assistance. But that would not be truly just, particularly in view of your obligation to the company that employs you both. So you would do well to remind yourself, if you are not reminded by someone else, to be generous, to think and act as would a generous person, perhaps some particular person who seems to you a model of generosity.

The advice is useful only if you know what generosity looks like in this situation. That entails making an effort to avoid not only narrow selfishness but also excessive liberality. You should be willing to help this man, but you should not go to the extreme of insisting on helping him if he arrogantly dismisses your offer of help. You may think twice about acting on your generosity if you have good reason to believe he will conceal or even deny your contribution and then hold it against you afterwards. So you should ask whether this is the right occasion for generosity, whether he is the right recipient, and so on.

Understanding should lead to action: you should act from generosity, or, if you are not a generous person, act as though you were generous. It is all too easy to know what to do but just not do it. In some cases your reluctance to act, perhaps aggravated by social pressure, will lead you to interpret the situation in a way that favors what (in your selfishness or your neurotic need for approval) you want to do. You may tell yourself that to help this person is to be exploited and to enable his crass ambition, but it is possible that the real problem is that you just do not like him and would enjoy seeing him get his comeuppance. If so, it would be difficult and painful for you to acknowledge that prejudice consciously, since you think of yourself as a person of appropriate generosity and the kind of team player that the organization needs.

So Smith will be giving you good advice if she helps you focus on the situation in the right way. In saying that generosity is called for, she is causing you to ask yourself how you can do some good for Jones and for the company rather than how you can put this arrogant little twit in his place. The better question will lead to a better answer, though not by itself to an exact one, since neither the question nor anything else gives you exact guidance on what generosity calls for in this case.

And of course even if you think Smith is giving you good advice, you may act against it.

Advantages of virtues over mere principles

The virtue ethicist and the ethicist who tries to apply principles to situations like this give advice that is similar in some respects. The first says that one should activate one's generosity. The second might say that one should apply principles having to do with supporting one's fellow employee. The virtue ethicist, in saying that you ought to do what generosity requires, is recommending that you act according to principles derived from the nature of generosity and by implication reminding you to consider the details of the situation, which would probably include the importance of the presentation, the young man's reaction, the timing, and the way in which it is done.

The virtue-based advice that you receive does not have its own characteristic decision procedure in the way in which utilitarianism, for example, does. But this is not a drawback, since no single decision procedure is appropriate for all cases – perhaps not even for any single case. Jensen (2010) would probably not agree, for he argues that since it is impossible to maximize in multiple dimensions the corporation must accept a single-valued objective function. I take Alzola (2011, p. 22) to be rejecting this view, rightly. Life would be simpler if single-valued objective functions sufficed for corporate or personal ethics, but neither is a matter of maximizing.

So a person of good character, possessed of all the virtues, is ready to act on a wide range of good reasons. A virtue ethicist might say in a particular case that one ought to act with benevolence – that is, to be particularly kind to someone – but avoid the excess of ignoring the dangers in rewarding poor performance. If some public policy is under discussion, it might be appropriate to take a utilitarian approach, but only an extreme utilitarian would ignore all considerations of fairness. In some cases the virtue ethicist might say that one ought to act justly. So the CEO's son-in-law should be fired if he has been caught in an act of gross dishonesty; but then courage will be required if one is to recommend a just punishment. The virtuous person, armed with practical wisdom, knows when to deploy the principles and attitudes associated with benevolence, or those associated with the public good, or those associated with retributive justice, and what to do when they seem to conflict. That hardly makes virtue ethics inferior to any of the standard forms of principle-based ethics.

On the contrary, virtue ethics adds some features to principle-based ethics. As we have discussed, a virtue is more than a settled disposition to act on a principle: it has an emotional component and a component of desire. So if you are a generous person, you want to be and are the sort of person who enjoys being generous and seizes happily on opportunities to do so. If you are a practically wise person, you are able to identify a situation as one that demands generosity – your emotional reaction may help with the identification – and you have a well-developed sense of what generosity requires. You do not have this well-developed conception of generosity before you can begin to apply it, as the somewhat misleading expression "applied ethics" suggests. On the contrary, having a good sense of generosity requires development of one's ethical sensibilities, including a strong feeling for human relations, based on a great deal of experience with situations like the one involving the annoying colleague. It also requires self-consciousness: you must be able to notice and resist when you are inclined to rationalize ungenerous behavior or to give in too readily to unreasonable demands. And it requires an appropriate emotional commitment to generosity: you must be capable of feeling sympathetic.

So while on a particular occasion virtue ethics does provide advice that is at least as good as what principle-based ethics offers, it is characteristically directed to longer-range questions. It generates advice about the sort of person you should be; and once you are committed to being virtuous, you are much better equipped to deal with particular occasions.

To act from generosity or any other virtue is to act according to Aristotle's model of the intentional action of a rational and sociable creature, which human beings are by nature. But although it is natural for humans to be rational, it does not follow, nor is it true, that we are always rational. We like to think of ourselves as having values that drive our preferences and thus our actions, but it is clear to Aristotle – and to social psychologists and others – that it just does not always happen that way.

Practical reasoning and weakness of will

Irrational action is common enough, but the very notion raises a problem. If an intentional action is characteristically done for a reason, how can an action be intentional but at the same time irrational? If I say, "I am fully aware that in all important respects this action that I am considering is a serious mistake, but I am going to do it anyway," you might find my statement not only hard to believe but hard to understand. It is as if I were to say, "I am fully aware that the evidence against proposition p is conclusive, but I believe that p." This sort of thing happens, but we want an explanation when it does.

How can I know what is the right thing to do but not do it? This is the question of weakness of will, which Aristotle answers at considerable length and, in my opinion, plausibly. In so doing he strengthens the case in favor of virtue and virtue ethics and against skeptics who do not think virtues worth postulating. One reason for addressing the issue is that the frequent disconnect between your desires, especially your second-order ones, and your actions has been taken by some philosophers and psychologists to imply that there is no point in postulating virtues or character, for they do not explain anything. I do not agree, but the challenge is worth taking seriously.

Having a virtue entails knowing, though not necessarily being able to state, a principle of the form "It is good for a person to act in a certain way." The not entirely helpful example he gives is this: "Dry food is good for human beings to eat." (This is not to say that Aristotle believes that dry food is appropriate for all human beings in all circumstances, or that in general his first premises are foundational or unexceptionable principles of either nutrition or ethics.) Specifications of principles of that sort typically function as first premises of practical syllogisms. So you may start your deliberation with this thought: "Eating dry food is good (i.e., nourishing) for a human being." Since Aristotle assimilates self-interest and ethics, as I shall argue in Chapter 3, he would also accept as a first premise "Respecting other people's property is good (i.e., just) for a human being." But Aristotle wants to explain how you can claim with apparent sincerity to value something – to acknowledge that it is good – but intentionally act against your value. (*NE* VII 2–4.)

Imagine that a person well informed about nutrition is having breakfast. The choices are granola and a doughnut. The breakfaster knows that granola is better for human beings than are doughnuts, but eats the doughnut because it is delicious. Similarly, you may be able to say if asked that it is good to respect others' property, but you may dump some garbage in a neighbor's field even though you know that that is no way to achieve long-term psychic satisfaction, just as eating doughnuts is no way to achieve long-term health. In both cases you apparently act against your values.

What has gone wrong?[2] According to Aristotle, you can intentionally do what you do not value because there is something to be said for, as well as against, eating doughnuts and getting rid of your garbage easily. You know that you should not eat the doughnut, because it is fattening; but you want to eat it, because it is delicious. You might even say to yourself, "I shouldn't be eating this doughnut." But when you say the words, you are like a drunk reciting poetry: you lack the conviction (a word Audi, 1989, uses) that real knowledge – or real belief, for that matter – entails. You must grow into real knowledge, and that takes time (*NE* VII 3 1147a21f.). At 1147b15–17 Aristotle says that your recognition that, in effect, the doughnut is fattening and therefore bad for you is not proper knowledge but perception. So you, being perhaps a youthful or ethically callow person, act on the wrong description of the act – that is, that you are eating something delicious. If asked, "But isn't it fattening?" you can say, "Yes, I know, but it tastes great." But in an important sense you do not really know, on Aristotle's account, because you perform the act under some other description, which, if you think about it, you will acknowledge is not the salient one. So the knowledge that you lack is not, as Socrates argues, purely discursive.[3] Or, we might say, you perform the act under a different principle, not the right one – not a principle associated with the virtue most applicable in this case.

Consider again the case of the annoying young man. If you decide to let him fail, you are failing to act on the virtue of generosity. You ought to be looking at this case as one in which generosity is called for, but instead you convince yourself that your practical syllogism is about justice, and you wrongly act on vindictiveness.

[2] Precisely how Aristotle analyzes this situation is a matter of long-standing controversy. My interpretation is not radically new; I am indebted to many commentators, especially Audi (1989, pp. 19–24) and Irwin's translation and commentary (Aristotle, 1999, pp. 256–62), but I am not sure that either of them would entirely agree with me.

[3] The knowledge associated with virtues is never purely discursive because it involves emotions, which may distort perception and cause you to see the situation under the wrong description. Psychopaths cannot know what generosity is because they lack the appropriate emotions.

Aristotle distinguishes between the case in which you are tempted to eat the doughnut but resist the temptation because you have continence (*enkrateia*) from the one in which you are not even tempted because you have temperance (*sophrosune*). In the first case your healthy or ethical choice costs you something. In the second case you are so strongly motivated by considerations of health that the choice costs you nothing. There is something admirable about not giving in to one's craving, but it is better ethically and in other ways not even to crave – or, to put it more broadly, not even to want to do the wrong (cowardly, dishonest, unjust, vindictive) thing. Saints are like that; people of pretty good character have such second-order virtues as the ability to withstand temptation.

This form of weakness of will is a matter of acting on the wrong one of different principles that are based on different descriptions of a situation. As we have noted, in ethics multiple considerations push us in conflicting directions, and there is no algorithm for choosing to be led this way or that, or for picking the description of the situation that is the salient one. If you are a loyal employee of a generally good company in which people whom you respect decide to do something that you consider a bit sleazy, you can tell yourself that in cooperating you are acting out of loyalty to your generally good employer. Aristotle suggests that in such cases someone with a good ethical track record – that is, a person of practical wisdom – will react with discomfort at the thought of going along with the sleaze, and that that experience-honed emotion has cognitive weight. But if you are weak in will, you may have a decisive emotional impulse to go along, whether or not you acknowledge that refusing would be the right thing to do.

So Aristotle is clearly aware that we do not always act rationally, that we may choose irrational major premises and irrational minor ones; for example, we may act on deliciousness rather than nutrition if we do not know that nutrition counts for more, and even if we do know it. In so doing we may be reasoning in the wrong direction: instead of drawing conclusions from our good reasons, we start with the conclusions and choose the reasons that support them. Aristotle seems to be aware of this possibility, though he does not explicitly mention the situation in which one ignores the issue of nutrition or takes the coward's easy way out while telling oneself and others that there is some more respectable reason on which one acts. In spite of what he knows about irrationality, however, he is not willing to give up the idea that characteristically human rationality typically has a place in the explanation of behavior, or that ends themselves and not only means to ends can be rational.

Framing

What Aristotle says has immediate implications regarding framing, which is easy to get wrong. You can frame eating a doughnut as a pleasurable experience or a fattening act, as it is both, but a person concerned with health should take the second way of framing rather than the first as salient. In some cases the problem is that the agent acts on a description that is misleading or incomplete: for example, "As a just person, I am seeing to it that this young man gets what he deserves." So it was not difficult for those in financial services to mischaracterize the risk that they were taking for their customers by focusing on the profits to be made so long as things went well.[4] In cases of this sort you are suffering from a stronger form of *akrasia*, for you are not even able to say that you are doing the wrong thing.

Tversky and Kahneman (1981) found extraordinary framing effects even where the descriptions in question were compatible. In one of their experiments, subjects were more favorably disposed towards a state of affairs in which 25% of some population would survive an event than to one in which 75% would die. This indicates serious irrationality. People may make judgments and take actions in large part on how they describe a complex situation to themselves – differently according to which of two descriptions they attend to, even if the descriptions are logically equivalent.

Your environment will influence the way you frame a situation: you will likely do it as others do it, as is the custom in your profession, as the client wishes, etc. Consider the famous Milgram (1974) experiment. Milgram told his subjects that they were assisting him in an experiment on the effects of negative reinforcement on learning. They were to administer electric shocks to "subjects" who failed to answer certain questions correctly. The shocks began at 15 volts, but with each wrong answer the voltage was to be increased by 15, until it reached 450. The "subjects" were actors, who began to cry out in pretended pain as the

---

[4] On framing as an issue in business ethics see Werhane (1999) and Werhane *et al.* (2011).

shocks exceeded 150 volts, then to scream and beg to be released as the shocks escalated further. Eventually they "fainted." In a typical version of the experiment nearly two-thirds of the actual subjects went the whole way: they inflicted what they believed to be excruciating and, according to a label on the console, dangerous shocks on innocent people because they were told to do so.

One way to interpret the experiment is to say most of the participants did not see themselves as causing pain to an innocent subject but instead as following directions and helping Dr. Milgram in his important work. Some, according to Ross and Nisbett (1991), were uncomfortable because they just could not frame the situation clearly. There were no "channel factors" to sustain their impulse to disobey. (I thank Daniel Russell for directing me to this point.) Your self-image will be influential as well: you tend to argue for the moral rightness of actions that favor you. This does look like the form of rationalization in which you begin with a conclusion and then attend to the features of the situation that support it.

Arthur Andersen's auditors might have described their misdeeds in the Enron case as "good client service" or "aggressive accounting" or even "billing a lot of hours." Those characterizations were accurate, but less salient than "misrepresenting the financial position of the firm." It is common enough: Darley (1996) describes the phenomenon of ethical rationalization, which Jones and Ryan (2001) attribute to a desire to be, and be considered, moral. Haidt (2012, p. 54, for example) claims that this happens far more often than we care to admit. Auditors with higher professional standards would act on the ethically salient description of the action. Most auditors could not have offered a coherent argument from their own values that the short-term gain made by giving good client service justified misrepresenting the financial position of the firm. So why did the Arthur Andersen auditors do what they did? On the Aristotelian view, it was because they were ignoring the salient descriptions and focusing on the ethically inessential ones, as one might focus on the delicious taste of the doughnut without giving adequate attention to one's need to lose weight. Aristotle considers this a failure of perception, hence of character.

Perceiving correctly

Aristotle claims that the person of good character, of practical wisdom, perceives any situation rightly – that is, takes proper account of its essence or, we would say, its salient features. As you perceive that a particular figure is a triangle, so you perceive that a particular act is a betrayal, though the latter is harder to do with assurance. This is standard Aristotelian doctrine, propounded throughout *De Anima*: the form or essence of a perceived object is in the soul of the perceiver. He also says in *De Anima* III 2 that events, including psychological events, have essences in an analogical sense; so you can perceive or fail to perceive the essence of an event.

According to Aristotle, this perception involves imagination (the standard translation of the Greek *phantasia*) and noninferential understanding (*nous*). The faculty of imagination is operating when you understand what a perceived object is or when you grasp the moral quality of an act, hence the virtue that should motivate you; in either case you grasp the essence of the item. You are morally responsible for understanding the act correctly. If you get it wrong – that is, fail to apprehend the morally salient features of the situation – then you have a character flaw (*NE* III 5 1114a32–b3 and VII 3 1147a18–35). A person of good character will perceive that a certain act is courageous rather than foolhardy, generous rather than patronizing, honest rather than dishonest, and will act accordingly. A practically wise person will deal properly with an apparent conflict of generosity and justice. Some moral philosophers have used the term *moral imagination* for the faculty that correctly frames morally significant states and events.[5] And the virtuous person will be motivated to act accordingly.

When people argue about morally charged issues, they often make statements of the form, "This is all about X." Then others respond that it is really all about Y. X may be religious liberty, for example, and Y women's health – as though it could not be about both. I have suggested that we sometimes pick a description of a case, hence a principle covering it and a virtue that it calls for, on a self-serving basis. But it is not always easy even for an honest person to get the description right. Many moral problems are difficult precisely because they are about many things. Aristotle says that a person of good character sees what the argument is essentially about, but he (characteristically) does

---

[5] Johnson (1993) has an influential book on the subject. Werhane (1999), Moberg and Seabright (2000), Hartman (2001), and Werhane *et al.* (2011) assess its importance for business ethics. Vidaver-Cohen (1997) considers how organizations can encourage moral imagination. Chen, Sawyers, and Williams (1997), show how organizations can do the opposite.

not offer a rule for giving a simple and correct description of any situation.

Whether or not all events have one correct description, which seems doubtful, some are just wrong, for they invite moral obtuseness or worse. Moberg (2006) claims that framing can lead to blind spots, since it favors one interpretation of a situation and thus ignores possibly significant facts about it. Consider "I was only doing my job," or "He was just trying to be friendly." Or, for that matter, "It is always morally wrong to discriminate on the basis of race."

Recall the case of Deborah. If you look at the situation and do not see gender prejudice playing a role, you are missing something important. If you see Deborah as a red-headed girl with a cute smile and do not see her as a gifted young consultant who deserves the company's support, there is a deficiency in your character, according to the Aristotelian view. You will not frame her situation correctly; in fact there are probably similar situations that you will not frame correctly. The framing effect of the vice of injustice causes you to decide wrongly about whether to send Deborah to London by making you ask "Should we send this nice girl to London to deal with those demanding men?" Asking the question that way almost guarantees a wrong answer.

Emotion is critical, as we noted earlier. Appropriate emotions assist correct framing. Aristotle notes that an irascible person will take offense too readily, whereas a phlegmatic person will not be angry even when anger is appropriate (*NE* IV 5 1125b26–1126a3). You should be grateful for kindnesses, angry if and only if you are seriously wronged, sympathetic towards the wretched, glad to help your fellow citizens. Recall from Chapter 1 that Klein (1998) notes with approval that both the psychologist Damasio (1994) and the philosopher DeSousa (1987) claim that emotion is involved in correct moral perception.

Practically wise people grasp the essence of the situation, says Aristotle. They do not abandon the applicable principles, but they know more than just what the principles say. They have an eye developed in experience, by which they home in on what matters (*NE* VI II 1143b9–15). They are like expert doctors (*NE* X 9 1180b7–23) or businesspeople (*NE* III 3 1112b4–7) or carpenters (*NE* I 7 1098a29–34) or comedians (*NE* IV 8 1028a23–34), who must take seriously the principles of their craft but know when and how to apply them in complex individual cases. Business strategists can tell you what is in the manual but they also have a well-trained sense of what to do in certain difficult situations, which they can see are significantly different from those covered in the manual. We aim at the mean, says Aristotle, but we sometimes have good reason to deviate from it. How far we may deviate is a matter of perception rather than reason (*NE* II 9 1109b19–23), in the sense that there are no rules.

In some complex situations, however, having fairly inflexible principles to apply is a sign of good character.[6] For example, a consultant may be honest and therefore have a personal rule against ever lying to a client. When a situation arises in which failing to lie would damage the consultant's relationship with the client and lead to avoidable bad consequences for the client, the consultant must take "lying to the client" to be a salient description of any action of which it is true, and honesty to be the salient virtue. "Preserving the relationship" or "preventing consequences A, B, and C" cannot be more salient for such a person. This inflexibility is best in the long run for the agent's character, and it is a barrier to rationalization. If, as Koehn (1995, p. 534), Weaver (2006, pp. 347f.), and Annas (2011, *passim*) suggest, an ethical act is one that not only follows from but also develops our character, then that is important. It does not solve all our problems, of course, for it may give such bad results in some cases that we have to abandon it. But it demands at the very least that we have some strong reason for abandoning it.

In some cases we have reason to refine a rule that, when broadly stated, leads to strongly counterintuitive consequences. So we may decide that the rule "Never lie" should be restated as "Never lie except under circumstances a, b, c., etc.," so that lying to a client is not permitted. Luban (2003) would probably not condemn lying to the KGB. When lying is justifiable is a matter of perception, Aristotle would say; there are no airtight rules for the application of the rule against lying. One has to develop a feeling for it, and some people fail at that and succeed at rationalizing.

Moral imagination involves intelligence and rationality. Aristotle distinguishes intellectual virtues from ethical ones, but he understands how closely they are related. He does not give points merely for meaning well. The Aristotelian position gets support from Haidt (2001),

---

[6] For further discussion see Luban (2003, pp. 307f.)

who argues that intelligence is a causal factor in good moral reasoning and behavior but rightly refrains from claiming that it is sufficient for ethics.

Not everyone will be impressed. Aristotle has discovered a problem and then invented the faculty of practical wisdom, which by definition solves it. (He would not be the last philosopher to do so.) There is, however, some sense to the notion that an intelligent and thoughtful person who seriously cares about being a generous friend can, with experience, develop some good intuitions about when to give and when to withhold. If you are such a person and I ask you why you refused Jones's latest request for a loan, you may not be able to give me a response that convinces me, but your response will offer insight into the situation and will reflect genuine concern for Jones. And in any case, one cannot do better by using only principles.

Practically wise people who make the best ethical decisions – at least the ones that gain the most widespread respect and occasion the least regret or resentment among good people afterwards – are not necessarily the ones who can speak most fluently about ethical principles. They are the people who are best attuned to the nuances of the situations with which they must deal, who best understand the meanings and the consequences of the things they contemplate doing, who have the requisite ethical sensibility and moral imagination.[7] So they know what the situation calls for, but in addition they are willing and able to act accordingly.

It is worth repeating that Aristotle calls understanding your situation and your possible actions correctly a test of character. You are responsible for how the situation looks to you, and there is something wrong with your character if you do not have the practical wisdom to see what virtues the situation calls for (*NE* III 5 1114a32–b3 and VII 3 1147a18–35). In Chapter 4 we shall discuss how practical wisdom is acquired gradually over a long period of time through experience and instruction. If Aristotle's view of the long process of socialization is even close to the mark, practical wisdom is a matter of degree, as therefore is virtue. It may be under assault from forces in the community. That matters, because we are communal

---

[7] Here and elsewhere in this section I am indebted to Paine (1991), who in turn acknowledges her debt to some then unpublished work of Kupperman.

creatures. Some people can deal with these forces better than can others.

Sensemaking

Weick and others have made much of what they call *sensemaking*,[8] which somewhat resembles Aristotle's perception and the notion of framing I have introduced here. A large part of sensemaking is fitting a certain event into a narrative. Aristotle wants us to understand an agent's deliberate choices as part of the narrative of a life. He acknowledges the importance of the community to one's character, but character is about an individual's narrative.[9] Sensemaking is communal: one's choices make sense within a collective narrative. Your organization, your profession, your colleagues are among the important factors that can determine what you do and how you interpret what you do. You do not deliberate as Aristotle claims when you make decisions.

The advocates of sensemaking note that in organizations, at any rate, serious decisions are often made when something unexpected requires a quick response and it is not clear exactly what you are supposed to be accomplishing or what your options are. The practical syllogism will not be very helpful, in part because neither the first premise nor the second will be clear. You may be under considerable social pressure to adopt certain premises, frame the situation in certain ways, without having the time or the space to think carefully. Sometimes the best you can do is try to make sense of what happened after the fact.

You may find that other participants in the decision make sense of the situation very differently, and that getting to agreement on how to frame it may be impossible. This is in part because, contrary to what Aristotle would say, no way of sensemaking is right or wrong, according to its theorists. In any case, participants may not even agree on what the decision is about, and therefore what considerations matter.

---

[8] It began with Weick (1969). Weick, Sutcliffe, and Obstfeld (2005) is a useful summary. I have also profited from Parmar. [Parmar, B. 2012. "Where is the Ethics in Ethical Decision Making? From Intrapsychic Moral Awareness to the Role of Social Disruptions, Labeling, and Actions in the Emergence of Moral Issues." Published and circulated by the author.]
[9] Chapter 4 covers this issue in more detail.

Disagreements about how to make sense of a situation are often not seen initially as moral ones, but they may have moral implications or features. For example, a proposed project may have a long-term but not short-term payoff. It may favor some stakeholders over others. The argument over which is better may bring in some moral issues about the obligations of management to current, as opposed to future, stockholders. And technical disagreements often become moral ones when those who disagree begin to suspect each other's motives.

Anyone who has worked in a large consulting organization will recognize this sort of sensemaking. By the nature of the work, unexpected situations pop up constantly, and there is seldom only one way of stating what the situation is about. The consultants compete to identify the issue, as their reputations for strength are on the line. Whoever loses that competition may then have a vested interest in seeing to it that the winner was wrong. There are competing purposes as well. The consultants' best advice may be unwelcome, even fatal. So how important is it to preserve the relationship at the cost of pulling punches? When consultants take a position on issues like this, they do not usually start by contemplating what the company as a whole is committed to achieving and then work out what that means in this case. They offer their views about what should be done and then defend them by reference to principles that reflect a certain take on the case.

Even if Aristotle is too optimistic about rational deliberation, there is no reason to believe that it never happens. We have noted that Aristotle is aware of at least some of the ways in which we fall short of what is after all an ideal. Managers have good reason to encourage an environment in which people are capable of recognizing moral issues, aware of the different ways in which it is possible to frame situations, and sensitive to how others may interpret their behavior and assess their ways of framing.[10]

Aristotle would go further, and argue that managers can improve in their ability to recognize the truly salient aspects of the complex situations with which they must deal. We can grow in practical wisdom.[11]

---

[10] Parmar, B. 2012. "Where is the Ethics in Ethical Decision Making? From Intrapsychic Moral Awareness to the Role of Social Disruptions, Labeling, and Actions in the Emergence of Moral Issues," pp. 268. Published and circulated by the author.

[11] Chapter 4 is about how we can do that.

There are many different ways in which one might make sense of the issue of whether to send Deborah to London, and many ways of interpreting Hal's decision. All the same, many of us would not hesitate to say that Hal got it right.

Virtuous strategy

Having practical wisdom is much like having a nose for strategy. Hundreds of books and journal articles have offered useful analytical techniques for strategists, but there is no substitute for the ability to see possibilities that others cannot see, whether for achieving profitable growth or for resolving some ethical dilemma. In both kinds of case rules are hard to formulate and harder to apply, but experience and intelligence seem to improve one's ability to make good decisions. In real-life corporate strategy, as I learned as a management consultant, there is much to be said for trusting the intuitions of an intelligent and experienced person with a good track record. Beabout (2012, pp. 424f.) cites Gladwell's (2005, pp. 3–8) story about some art experts who, asked to judge whether a statue was a forgery, quickly said that there was something "just wrong" about it, though they had trouble saying exactly what was wrong. Subsequent chemical analysis vindicated them and enhanced their track record.

Skilled strategists are aware of the data that analysts gather; they know many techniques for using the numbers in assessing the prospects of strategic business units. A good strategist can see threats and opportunities behind the numbers. It is a matter of knowing which factors are salient in a particular market – product quality, manufacturing cost, logistics, image, market share, and even quality of management. What is salient will differ from one market/product to another, and the ability to analyze a market involves knowing what is salient. There may be a rule of thumb that market share matters more in the fast food business than elsewhere, but that rule can be overridden by factors like bad management, and it may apply better in East Chicago than in East Vassalboro. It normally takes years of experience – habituation, we might say – to develop a reliable ability to see what is salient. This is similar to the way in which virtuous people see ethically salient features of situations that others do not see, or do not consider reasons for action. An executive might even have strong evidence that a salient feature is a success factor for a business unit but not act accordingly, out of self-serving rationalization. Yet however well strategists understand the available numbers, at a certain point they will have to satisfice and make a partly intuitive decision.[12] Their track record is evidence of their wisdom.

Strategic success and the environment

In fact, however, the track record in itself does not always prove very much. Rosenzweig (2007) has argued that one can easily go wrong – as have Peters and Waterman (1982) and many others – by looking at successful companies and trying to identify the features that account for their success. The standard diagnosis is that a real winner has a supportive culture, focuses on customers, sticks to a widely understood mission, and has other familiar attractive features. But many such companies, having been held up as examples of what the reader can do to succeed, perform much less well after the book in question is published. In any case, the book's readers must understand that other people can read it too, and that in a competitive environment not all readers can succeed. The problem with the diagnosis, says Rosenzweig, is that people in successful companies are likely to say that their culture is supportive, their focus is on customers, and their mission is before everyone's mind: success has a halo effect; all other factors look good. It is no doubt true that having a culture of mediocrity, ignoring customers, and lacking a mission will do a company little good, but the rules that the strategic gurus have identified are often trivial as stated.

The gurus sometimes ignore the effects of the economic and competitive environment, according to Rosenzweig, and thus overestimate what strategy can do. Pfeffer (1982) argues that managers' decisions have far less effect on success or failure than we intuitively believe. If we judge by annual reports, managers seem to agree in part: success is a result of the efforts of our outstanding management team; failure is a result of factors beyond our control. Doris (2002) and other so-called situationists make the parallel argument on the individual

---

[12] Simon (1954) invented the concept of satisficing, which involves accepting a sufficiently good option rather than trying to find the best possible one. Winter (1971) argued that we must satisfice in deciding when to satisfice.

level: our behavior is determined by environmental factors rather than by our character, assuming that it even makes sense to talk about the latter.

Rosenzweig has something like a virtue theory of strategy. His shining examples, Bob Rubin and Andy Grove, know that deciding on a strategy is a matter of dealing with uncertainty. What is needed, in addition to the ability to gauge the probabilities as best you can, is something like courage: you take a leap into the unknown with the appropriate amount and kind of fear; and if things go wrong, you are ready to weigh the odds and do the same thing again next time. You do not worry about looking bad; you do not retreat to the safety of doing nothing or of groupthink. You have the virtues of courage, wisdom, farsightedness, honesty, appropriate fidelity to the stockholders, appropriate respect for the cautionary opinions of other senior managers, and so on. These do not guarantee success, however. Things may go wrong, as Rubin would readily concede: fortune is not always on your side, and you may incur short-term obloquy, which will be unpleasant. But failure does not undermine your satisfaction in having done the best you can do, or your confidence on the next attempt.

We see a virtue theory of strategy as well in Collins's (2001) notion of Level 5 leadership, the capacity that creates great companies from good ones. The only kind of leader who can achieve this transition is self-effacing but steely in resolve. These two traits, which do not often appear together, are not sufficient for achieving greatness: one can be modest and resolute but obtuse or unlucky, for example. But it is striking that a certain sort of character is a necessary condition of achieving greatness from goodness. The strategy itself, according to Collins, is just not enough.

It remains true, however, that we can more easily reach agreement on matters of management than on ethical issues, because we are much more likely to agree on what counts as success in the former case. Even if we could agree on the probable consequences of some act or state, there could easily remain serious arguments – some of them better than others – about its ethical quality. For this reason alone, a judgment on an act or state ought to take into account the intention with which it is done, hence the character of the agent. It matters that a particular act is courageous or selfish or dishonest or kind, and so it matters that the agent is.

Corporate culture, ethical vocabulary, and perception

If you are a person of good character in Aristotle's sense, you know genuine strength and cowardice when you see it. Ethical managers cannot readily change employees' character, but they can help them to become more comfortable and fluent in the language of right and wrong, particularly of virtues and vices, without which their moral imagination will be impoverished, as will their ability to give salient descriptions of morally significant situations. If the language of economics can encourage maximizing, the language of virtue can encourage good character and therefore good decisions.

Vocabulary is one of the prime vehicles of corporate culture, as Schein (1985) and others have argued. An organization in which reckless people are called decisive may create peer pressure that encourages shortsighted disregard of eventual costs. One who acts on impulse will be called strong. One who prefers moderation or consideration of alternatives will be a wimp. An organization in which women are called girls is unlikely to be supportive of women's ambitions. A European at Salomon Brothers who goes home at the end of the afternoon rather than stay and be seen working late is a "Eurofaggot" (Lewis, 1989, p. 71).

The vocabulary of character is not a foreign language to businesspeople. Most businesspeople do regard honor, courage, and respect for fellow workers and competitors as virtues, about which they speak fluently and comfortably.[13] Most would say that it is the legitimate purpose of financial statements to give an honest picture of the financial condition of a firm. But some people in Enron who might have objected on ethical grounds if a secretary had taken some office paper home did not see anything wrong with creating special purpose entities whose special purpose was to hide losses. The organization failed to help develop a mature sense of right and wrong and salient, give it a language, and sharpen it by welcoming critical analysis. If the local moral language is impoverished or insufficiently exercised, employees may latch on to some other, nonsalient description of the situation: "I am supporting my manager, who knows what he's doing," rather than "I am lying to investigators." They may have no emotional

---

[13] For evidence and argument for this view see Whetstone (2003).

reaction in doing so, or have one but ignore it, so that in due course it deteriorates.

Enron provides us with useful negative role models. One way[14] to improve one's decisions is to ask oneself questions like this: Am I falling into a pattern of action like that of Enron's managers? Am I failing, as the Arthur Andersen accountants servicing Enron did, to listen to the counsel of experienced colleagues? What aspect of my actions am I not noticing? Am I adopting an extreme trait and telling myself that I have hit the mean? On the positive side, I may think of Smith, whom I admire, and ask myself what she would do in this situation, or what she would say if I did action A.

Being virtuous and doing the right thing

Consider the manager who refuses to participate in Enron's immoral corporate activity even while knowing that someone else will step in and help get the dirty job done. Such a manager is saying, in effect, that's not the kind of person I am. Whether Jones ought to refuse to participate in activity that seems questionable depends in part on whether Jones is an honest man with the courage to defy management in the service of what he takes to be the best interests of the organization and its legitimate stakeholders, or an egomaniac who habitually tries to show his moral superiority to his colleagues. It is not always easy to tell the difference on a single occasion, but virtue ethics is not primarily about acts performed on single occasions. The ethical value of the act itself depends in part on the character of the agent.

From the point of view of virtue ethics, an employee is obligated to be a good corporate citizen; senior managers are then obligated to maintain a corporation in which a good corporate citizen can succeed. Such a person gives a fair day's work (but does not actually try to maximize the real long-term wealth of the stockholders), takes the accountabilities of the job and the organization's objectives seriously, protects his or her own personal interests adequately, speaks candidly but not disrespectfully to the boss, refuses to follow clearly immoral directives, seeks win-win situations, and opposes or subverts truly evil people. All of this is a result of having an appropriate attitude, which is similar to that of the professional. A good doctor, lawyer, or

---

[14] This paragraph benefits from the influence of Audi (2012).

engineer must not only follow the ethical rules of the profession but also adopt the attitude that the welfare of the client or patient is in itself a reason for action, and that the client or patient is often not in a position to make the crucial decisions about what to do. So it is with good employees in general, and in particular with those who resemble professionals in that they work for bosses who do not have sufficient knowledge to evaluate their work in the short term. A person who is a good employee in that sense will probably not make many major ethical or strategic mistakes, so long as the organization itself is not a bad one.

In any case, management itself, as opposed to supervision, is not just about individual decisions. Whether organizational effectiveness or morality is at issue, good management requires not only setting rules and standards for employees to follow but also socializing them, and thereby managing their attitudes. Similarly, Aristotle says that a good *polis* not only trains citizens in virtuous habits by rewards and punishments but also encourages them to be truly virtuous – to be rationally reflective and to have appropriate emotions. (See *NE* II 1–4 and Chapter 4.) The former way of managing, which is principles-oriented, and the latter, which is virtue-oriented, may be mutually reinforcing rather than incompatible – or may not be – as may be talk about principles and talk about virtue. Which is the more important aspect of management will depend in part on many features of the organization, the people managed, the market, and so on. We shall address these matters further in Chapter 5.

Clearly one's organization, and in general one's community, will have a significant effect on one's character. Recall that Aristotle has reasons for saying that politics is central to ethics. Insofar as it is the fate of many people in industrialized countries today to live in organizations, we have some of the same reasons for saying that management is central to ethics, and that it needs to be hospitable to virtue.

Culture as a threat to virtue

In saying that we are essentially sociable creatures, Aristotle was not thinking about how much organizations exert a powerful socializing and sometimes corrupting influence on employees' character. Sennett (1998) argues that corporate influence is usually inhospitable to good character, but it need not always be. Corporate culture, as well as structures and systems, can be deployed to encourage and accommodate good character.[15] A community goes a long way towards determining its citizens' values – what they count as success, for example – for better or worse. By providing role models and in other ways, the culture of a community may make a citizen want to be a certain kind of person, motivated by certain considerations and not others; that is, it can affect people's second-order desires. This is true in corporate communities as well as in political ones.

There is voluminous evidence that organizations may support or oppose ethical behavior. Fritzsche (1991) argues that organizational forces may drive decisions more than personal values do and (Fritzsche, 2000) that organizational climate can raise or lower the probability of ethical decisions. Jones and Hiltebeitel (1995) find evidence of the effects of organizational expectations on ethical choices. Sims and Keon (1999) argue that the organizational characteristics that most influence employees are situationally determined; so the organization can foster both ethical and unethical decision-making. Trevino, Butterfield, and McCabe (2001) offer a detailed and complex account of the effects of ethical climate. I have argued that corporate culture can affect an employee's second-order as well as first-order desires: people in the grip of a powerful culture adopt the local values and definition of success, and want to be motivated by what motivates their colleagues (see Hartman, 1994, 1996, 1998, 2006, and especially later in Chapter 6).

The status of character

The very existence of character

So great is the influence of environment on behavior that Harman (2003) and Doris (2002) argue that character does not matter.[16] They base their conclusion in part on the arguments of social psychologists

---

[15] See Walton (2001, 2004) and Moore (2002); Koehn (1998) takes a slightly different view. [Walton, C. 2004. "'Good Job', Bad Work: Aristotle and the Culture of the Workplace." Published and circulated by the author.]

[16] My views on this subject owe much to the work of Alzola (2008, 2011, 2012) and to many useful conversations with him. Alzola reviews the work of Doris and other philosophers and social psychologists, and I have made extensive use of his review in this section.

like Ross and Nisbet (1991) and invoke the familiar works of Milgram (1974) and Zimbardo (2007).

Zimbardo created a simulated prison in a Stanford office building and populated it with students who were assigned the roles of prisoner or prison guard and told to act accordingly. Within a short time the guards were viciously tormenting the prisoners, who reacted to the treatment much as actual prisoners would. The roles took over everyone, including at times Zimbardo himself, the prison warden, who became infuriated when one of his departmental colleagues turned up at his office and asked him questions about the experiment just when he had been warned that the prisoners were on the verge of a breakout. So extreme were the emotional reactions of the participants, especially the prisoners, that the experiment was terminated after six days rather than the planned two weeks.

The subjects of these experiments were quite ordinary people, not sadists or psychopaths. In fact, Zimbardo's subjects tested well for emotional stability. Their character seems to have had almost nothing to do with their behavior. Milgram, whose experiment teaches a similar lesson, even found that he could alter his subjects' behavior by changing the situation slightly – for example, by adding a confederate who would sit next to the subject and obey or disobey.

Trevino (1986) expresses a mainstream view in arguing that both organizational and personal attributes affect behavior in organizations. As the former are easier to measure, researchers will likely be drawn more to them than to psychological states, particularly if they believe that only what can be measured exists. Doris (2002) and others go further than that: they raise questions about how it is possible to explain behavior by reference to character.

Questionable reasons

We typically explain another person's intentional action by reference to reasons for that action. In so doing we presuppose that the agent has acted rationally to some degree. If you ask Jones why he did something – that is, what he intended to achieve or what there was to be said for the action – and he responds by saying that he did not intend to achieve anything and that there was no good to be achieved by the action, then we have reason to doubt that his action was intentional at all. As we noted earlier, if Jones states that he is about to do something that he fully realizes is a big mistake from all points of view, we are puzzled: we wonder whether he means what he is saying, and we wonder whether the act really is intentional.

All the same, weakness of will is possible and explainable, as Aristotle shows. But the situation is even worse than what Aristotle describes. Often we do not even know what reasons drive our actions. So Jones might consider himself justified in patronizing and even harassing Smith. If called on it, he might sincerely claim that he is not prejudiced. He might even deny that he is treating Smith disrespectfully, or he might say that Smith happens to deserve this sort of treatment, which has nothing to do with her being a woman.

Why do we so readily think that we are acting rationally and ethically when we are not? To begin with, we have great confidence in our opinions about our reasons for acting because it is characteristic of mental events that their owners can report them. I can know that I am in pain in a way that no other person can, for example, and it is hard to see how I could be wrong in believing that I am in pain. But while my process of deliberation about whether to eat this dry food may seem immediately evident to me, I can be wrong about it. I may be quite clear in my own mind that I am judging Smith fairly on the basis of standard performance criteria while in fact I am prejudiced and judging accordingly, odd as it may seem to me to suppose that I am unaware of some important features of my mental state. So if people ask me why I am doing something, I normally answer them quite confidently, though not always accurately.[17] And of course we like to think well of ourselves.

Jones's character flaw may lead him to think of his decision to fire Smith as a reasonable response to Smith's incompetence, whereas a salient description of it would be that it is an expression of his resentment of women in the workplace. Inclined to fire Smith, Jones may look for principles, especially self-congratulatory ones, to justify it. The real first premise of the practical syllogism is not "It is good to treat people justly" but "It is good to put an arrogant woman in her place." In that case, or in the case of a plate umpire who unconsciously and very slightly favors the home team with his calls, we may begin to doubt that it makes much sense to talk about first premises at all. It is like eating a doughnut because it tastes good, but then claiming to be

---

[17] Often inaccurately, Haidt (2012, p. 60 and elsewhere) would say.

following the principle that one should load up on carbohydrates in case physical exertion turns out to be necessary. Haidt (2012, and in correspondence) and others claim that this is how things usually are, that our principles are largely "for show."

Sincere claims to respect women, to umpire fairly, and to avoid being cruel to innocent people tell us little about the agents' first premises, little about their character. The unreliability of these claims raises the question whether character is an entity worth postulating. What really drives behavior is, the situationists would say, the immediate environment – social pressure, corporate culture, even a pleasant brief encounter. The evidence from social psychology is strong: manipulate apparently insignificant factors in the environment, and we thereby manipulate behavior. Aristotle claims that one's *polis* is a strong formative influence, but he is not referring to more immediate influences that have little to do with reasons to act.

Inconsistencies

This is not only a matter of people being (say) sexist or cruel while claiming not to be. Most people are not very consistent even in traits that they would admit to. And where they are consistent, their traits do not track with virtues and vices. We find people who are conscientious about feeding the dog but not about getting to work on time and people who are courageous on the football field and cowardly in the dentist's chair.

This sort of inconsistency is a problem for virtue ethics, which requires attitudes that differ from one situation to another depending on what is appropriate. It may be a psychological fact that people who are confident in their reasoned beliefs tend to be stubborn across the board, but confidence in one's reasoned beliefs is a virtue and stubbornness a vice. Good character requires the perceptual capacity to assess complex situations correctly. Doris and other philosophers familiar with social psychologists' research find this capacity lacking in most cases; hence, they claim, the notion of character has no explanatory role. The Asch (1955) experiment seems to support Doris. In it the subjects made egregious mistakes in estimating the comparative lengths of lines because confederates in their presence were apparently doing so. But surely Doris would not infer that there is no such thing as perception.

Harman (2003) goes so far as to say that people have no traits, that the environment determines everything for everyone. This appears to imply that there is no such thing as a psychopath, for example. Someone who has served several prison terms for violent crimes is not, has not even become, a vicious criminal. Put the serial killer near a working bakery with pastry smells wafting out and you have a perfectly nice person.

No doubt character has less of a role than we might wish to believe, but it is not clear that it never has any role at all. What are we to say of the subjects of the Milgram experiment who refused to continue? Is there no important difference between those who acted reluctantly and those who did so almost eagerly? What about the people – rare, to be sure – who seem never to rationalize, who are capable of acting against their immediate interests in pursuit of justice, who fear only what ought to be feared? To say that they are people of character is to suggest that character is an explanatory factor in their actions but not in those of all or even most people.

Virtue is a matter of degree; that is important. As we shall discuss in detail in Chapter 4, one's character develops over a long period of time, and there are few people who develop so far and so well that we can count on them to act from virtue in every sort of situation. But this fact does not keep us from having a fairly clear idea of what good character looks like, and we can sometimes act in accordance with the ideal and sometimes realize it when we have not. This is not news to Aristotle, as his discussion of weakness of will shows; he reminds us that men are not gods. That Aristotle holds that the Deity is pure rationality and that human rationality is pleasing to the gods (see *Metaphysics* VII 7–10 and *NE* X 7–8, especially 8 1179a22–4) gives a clue to what he means by that claim.

Aristotle does not believe that virtue is so far out of reach for humans that it cannot be the basis of a realistic ethical theory. He does, however, clearly believe that some people, such as farmers and women, cannot be truly virtuous. This does not make his ethics any more unrealistic than other theories of ethics. Could anyone possibly be a consistent utilitarian or Kantian? Many people are irrational, too, but that gives us no reason to stop talking about the importance of being rational.

By analogy with character, consider intelligence, which typically involves the ability to think rationally in a broad sense of the term.

If I am trying to work out a problem, theoretical or practical, my intelligence is a factor, but just one of the factors. My intelligence may fail: something about the presentation of the problem may make it impossible for me to work out the right answer, which in ordinary circumstances would be obvious. Riddles and tricky logic problems illustrate the point. Tests of intelligence are notoriously unreliable, for you can get two very different scores on two different days. They are of questionable validity as well, since they do not capture all facets of intelligence as we understand it. Still, it seems preposterous to deny that there are degrees of intelligence: some people are smarter than others. Some people are more intelligent about some things than others, as in the case of some virtues. And of course some intelligent people are not very rational in a practical sense, as Kahneman (2011, p. 49) notes.

If I am trying to act ethically or practically, my character is one factor. If I shock the "subject" in the Milgram experiment or abuse the "prisoner" in the Zimbardo experiment, it does not follow that I am a bad person. Human beings do not always act on their virtues; second-order desires are not always effective. If I were a really bad person, I would undertake shocking and abusing without any social pressure and without the evident discomfort that many subjects felt. In Aristotle's terms, I would be base rather than incontinent, though even a base person can experience self-loathing (*NE* IX 4 1166b23–9). Similarly, if I were really stupid, I could not solve a tricky riddle even if it was not presented in a misleading or distracting way.

Questioning rationality and virtue

Many of the arguments against character as an independent variable work equally well against rationality, which Aristotle takes to be a major part of good character. (See Rabin, 1998, and especially Haidt, 2001, pp. 827f.) As Kahneman and Tversky (2000) and others have shown, people are often extraordinarily irrational. It appears that the deniers of character and the deniers of rationality are making something close to the same point. According to them, we neither explain nor justify an action by stating the first premise of an agent's practical syllogism. There is nothing there.

Yet we do routinely invoke rationality in the explanation as well as criticism of human actions, despite the prevalence of irrationality. If all intentional actions must be rational in some way, and if there are some apparently intentional actions that are irrational, we might be tempted to say that there are no intentional actions, that we should stop talking about intentional actions because we are so often irrational.[18] But to give up talk of intentions would be a heavy, perhaps impossible, price to pay. Can we even imagine what it would be like to stop deliberating?

Kahneman argues (2002, pp. 44–6) that there can be intellectual as well as practical *akrasia* – weakness of intellect. You can just fail to reason through a problem, such as an ordinary syllogism, perhaps as a result of the vice of laziness. You can, and Haidt believes that we often do, believe something because you want to. It does not follow that there is no such thing as rational deliberation, practical or intellectual. The claim that it is rational to believe that it is not rational to believe anything is self-defeating. In any case, we have not stopped teaching logic, formal or informal, just because most people are not very logical.

Russell (2009, pp. 125–9) compares the virtues with rationality and invokes the principle of charity as espoused by Davidson (2001). The point, roughly, is this. Suppose that you and I speak different languages. When you make a statement like "*Il pleut*," I cannot understand what you say unless I know what you believe; but the obvious way for me to know what you believe is to hear and understand what you say. Vicious circle. But can I not infer your belief and therefore your meaning from the noticeable fact that it is raining? Only if I (charitably) assume that most of the time when you say that, you have and are expressing a true belief about the current weather. Similarly, we would have a miserably hard time communicating our desires and intentions and explaining our actions to one another unless we could assume that much of the time we can and do act rationally.[19]

Evidence for degrees of strength of character

Baumeister and Tierney (2011) offer evidence that some people have what we can call greater strength of character: they are better than others at postponing gratification, controlling their tempers, sticking with difficult tasks, not being manipulated by their environment, and otherwise avoiding weakness of will. Willpower, as they call it, is

---

[18] This seems to be the inference drawn by Pfeffer (1982).
[19] Russell's argument parallels the one in Chapter 1 about the sense in which virtues are causes.

crucial to a successful life. They cite Mischel's famous experiments (see, e.g., Shoda, Mischel, and Peake, 1990) showing that children who are able to resist eating a marshmallow now to get two later will go on to live better in many ways than those who cannot wait. This ability to consider and compare goods across time, Aristotle suggests, is one of the functions of reason (*De Anima* III 10 433b5–10, III 11 434a5–10, cited by Irwin, 1988, p. 346). Some people just have more of this ability than do others.

As Aristotle focuses so much on weakness of will in discussing character, the findings of Baumeister and Tierney on willpower merit our close attention. Willpower can be cultivated in a number of ways, they say, but on occasion it has much to do with the availability of glucose in one's system. Baumeister and Tierney suggest that willpower is a matter of degree, as we have said rationality and virtue are. But they offer little reason to believe that there are many people who have so much willpower that they are fully virtuous in Aristotle's sense – that is, people who are not even tempted to eat the one marshmallow now, to get out-of-control angry, or to surf the Internet instead of working. Nor does Aristotle claim that there are many such people.

We know that Aristotle takes a teleological approach to nature. At times his statements about rationality and virtue as natural states sound aspirational rather than factual, but he is not a blind optimist. Substances essentially have potency, he says: as a matter of scientific fact, they have ends towards which they characteristically move and which they sometimes achieve. The facts that some trees die as saplings and that some people do not develop a mature character do not change the nature of trees or people. It is not news to Aristotle that it takes far more intervention to get a person to full actuality than it does a tree, and that there are more ways to fall short. We should not find his views altogether alien. It seems plausible to say that only humankind is capable of certain forms of rationality, even though we know that we are often not rational and hardly ever perfectly rational. But we sometimes are, and we ought to be, and Aristotle offers a sense in which we can be.

Practical implications

For managers the question of the status of character is not an abstract or idle one. If Doris and the others are largely right, then managers will probably find that creating a workforce of eager and competent employees is done more effectively by developing a supportive corporate culture than by testing prospective employees for character (honesty, for example) and hiring only virtuous ones. Insofar as the latter is possible, it is worth trying. Insofar as it is difficult, we have no basis for saying that it or anything else that is hard to measure does not exist.

Motivation is not simple, as good managers know. Aristotle suggests that character is a matter of what motivates you, but also that your community is a significant determinant of your character. If there is anything to the situationists' view, we may expect that a strong organizational culture will influence what motivates employees: it may affect the employees' view of organization's mission, for example; it may affect people's notion of personal success. Aristotle and the situationists differ about the degree to which employees are malleable in the short run. That is an empirical issue. The least we can say is that some people are more malleable than others.

We began this chapter by asking how virtue ethics answers the question, "What should I do?" The sort of answer that it offers has value even if the agent cannot manage to take the advice to act virtuously. But virtue ethics gives reason for taking the advice, and in fact for being virtuous, as the next chapter explains.

3 | Virtues, good reasons, and the good life

Ethics and the good life

If we think that people are acquisitive and selfish, mired in original sin, or just plain rotten, we are likely to think of ethics as a constraint: thou shalt not do all sorts of things that thou wouldst like to do, it says. One finds some of this attitude in Christian traditions as well as in the work of Kant and other moralists. No doubt ethics does constrain us sometimes, when we want to do what we should not do. But Aristotle and many other virtue ethicists emphasize that the virtuous life is a good life, one that any human being will have good reason to embrace. And if you are a person of good character, you will enjoy being ethical. You will have temperance rather than mere continence. You will not want to do what you should not do.

Aristotle argues in effect that morality is not primarily about constraint. Boatright (1995; a review of Solomon, 1992) claims that constraint plays a significant role in morality. Aristotle would probably agree. As we are not as perfect as the gods, we sometimes need continence or the restraint of the law against desires that we would prefer not to have, and we have seen that Aristotle clearly understands that we can fail to control ourselves. And of course Aristotle sets great store by laws.

Businesspeople in particular often see ethics as a constraint rather than part of their utility function. Business is competitive, after all, and the Golden Rule is not obviously a sound competitive strategy. If businesspeople accept many economists' assumptions, they will believe that people are selfish in a straightforward way, and they may then make that belief self-fulfilling.

Aristotle's approach is different. In his ethical works he focuses on what is good for the agent, what constitutes a life of *eudaimonia*. The term is usually translated *flourishing* rather than *happiness*, in part because it is arguably possible to achieve happiness but not

94

eudaimonia in the wrong way – for example, through ignorance. We might translate it *well-being*, though *flourishing* implies Aristotle's intended comparison between humans and nonhuman animals as well as plants. For on Aristotle's view, as we have noted, every substance, including the human being, has an essence and an associated end state or purpose. As we are essentially sociable and reasoning creatures, our natural end is to live in communities of a certain kind and to think and act rationally. If you reach your actuality as a person, you are virtuous (or, on the alternative translation, excellent). You are in a state of *eudaimonia*, a particularly broad, deep, long-lasting form of well-being characteristic of good character and psychological health, which is itself a normative notion.[1] Asking what reason I have to be virtuous Aristotle would find as odd as asking what reason I have to be healthy.

Eudaimonia is admirable and enviable. We admire accomplished people with many friends, and if we are friendless losers we probably envy them. We admire courageous people. We neither admire nor envy people whose happiness is based on their ignorance or shallowness. If you disagree, ask yourself whether you would like being thought ignorant or shallow.

From the beginning of the *Nicomachean Ethics* Aristotle describes the good life for the agent and never wholly abandons the agent's point of view. We can describe how Aristotle gets ethics in the other-oriented sense into the picture in this way: the claim that the agent is essentially a rational and sociable being implies that your flourishing will have something to do with living rationally and finding your appropriate place and arguably even your identity in the community, and that will preclude narrow selfishness. It will not preclude special attention to your own immediate interests, which will sometimes be inconsistent with others' interests, but you will accept that others are similarly motivated.

It would be misleading to portray Aristotle as an egoist who notices that it turns out as a matter of fact that the agent's well-being involves

---

[1] The literature on *eudaimonia* and happiness is vast. I have learned much from Prior (2001), McKinnon (2005), and Annas (2011) in particular. Kraut (1989) takes a point of view slightly different from mine. Scholars of management may see similarities between Aristotle's view and Maslow's hierarchy of needs, culminating in self-actualization. Maslow credits Aristotle explicitly (1987, pp. 15–26, 115f.), as Miller (1995, p. 350) notes.

that of others. Talk of "how it turns out as a matter of fact" mis-construes Aristotle, and in particular understates the centrality of humankind's rational and sociable nature. Aristotle does not coun-tenance the analytic-synthetic distinction, and we should take care in using it to reconstruct his positions. He does rely on the essence-accident distinction, and he claims that it is an essential fact about humans that they are rational and sociable. And though it is fair to say that Aristotle starts from the agent's point of view, from the agent's living well, he emphatically does not start from the agent's interests narrowly defined.

Utilitarianism and the good life

We might begin to talk about ethics by saying that its purpose is that all people should have as good a life as possible. Here a utilitarian might say, "As that is the point of morality, each of us should always act in such a way as to promote the good life widely." The Aristotelian can respond, "I have two problems with what you say. First, we have to decide what the good life is; that is part of the job of ethics, as you yourself seem to imply. Second, individuals making each decision with a view to promoting the good life widely will fail to promote the good life widely. Politics is not that simple." More positively, and consistently with those two criticisms, the Aristotelian says, "The good life is the life lived according to the nature of the human being, who is rational and sociable."

A problem for some utilitarians, underlying their assumptions about the possibility of weighing and measuring goodness, is that they have a vague or facile view about the good life. A utilitarian view common today, particularly in economics, is that the good life is about the fulfill-ment of desire or preference. The latter Hausman (2012, p. 34) defines as a subjective motivational comparative attitude: I may desire both A and B, but taking all my desires into account and being unable to have both, I prefer B. This is a mainstream account of economic doctrine. A virtue ethicist will not accept that form of utilitarianism. One of Aris-totle's great achievements is to offer a compelling notion of the good life in support of his virtue ethics.

Whether or not we can agree on an appropriate conception of the good life, our consideration of the issue shows how facile is the usual talk about one's interests and one's pursuit of them, and thereby helps undermine our unreflective assumptions about them. We tend to believe that what is good for us is whatever we prefer, that that does not change, and that the pursuit of what we prefer is self-interested. We therefore also tend to believe that ethics is opposed to self-interest – that if Jones is an ethical person, he characteristically puts others' interests ahead of his own. (But if Smith does the same, how will she and Jones deal with each other?) Given this approach, one can easily assume that success, especially in business, is a matter of satisfying one's greed and that it cannot have much to do with ethics.

Is ethics good for you?

Aristotle does not clearly distinguish ethical values from what we call interests. The two coincide if and only if what is good for the agent is also good for others. If they necessarily differ, then Aristotle's concentration on what is good for the agent has little to do with what we consider ethics. On Aristotle's view they do not differ. Virtue is a good state for you to be in, from your point of view; vice is a bad one. Rather than take the view that ethics is about the well-being of other people and that you should therefore distinguish virtues from vices on the basis of your contribution to their well-being, Aristotle takes the primary question to be about your living well.

But what if I prefer to lie because I believe that lying will help me to live well? Aristotle's response is based on his claim that a virtuous person has the right preferences. I shall begin to examine that claim by discussing Aristotle's notion of rationality, building on the discussion so far, and what it has to do with living well. Then I shall move the discussion of sociability further for the same purpose. But first we need to consider an account of interests and the good life that is more familiar, particularly to economists and organization theorists – an account that is inferior to Aristotle's.

Homo economicus and interests

It sounds plausible to say that you want what is best for yourself and that therefore you are well off to the extent that you get what you want. But you may not welcome risking death for a great cause or even benevolently sharing your goods with others. So you might

agree with Kant that ethics should not be based on anything involving interests, lest the "dear self" pollute your ethical deliberations.[2]
It appears difficult to accommodate the dear self and the demands of
ethics as well. That is especially true if the dear self is what economists
assume it is.

Many economists – rational choice theorists in particular – assume
that human beings are *homines economici*, rational maximizers of their
own interests.[3] The goals themselves are, as on the standard Enlightenment account, neither rational nor irrational. One's interests amount
to the satisfaction of one's preferences. Typically what is preferred
can be bought, and the strength of one's preference is a matter of
what one is willing to pay. So utility is the satisfaction of any old
preference.

We noted earlier that philosophers like Davidson (2001, especially
Essay 1), argue that we must impute a certain level of rationality to
those whose behavior we explain by reference to desire and belief.
The standard economist's theory, not Davidson's, has the air of triv-
iality, since any claim that one has acted against one's interests can be
countered by the argument that (for example) one has an interest in
giving money to the poor. But once the attempted counterexample is
dismissed, the theorist will typically go back to assuming that more
money is universally preferred to less.

An immediate problem with this form of utilitarianism is the difficulty of knowing what an agent prefers. Some economists offer the
notion of *revealed preference:* what you prefer is revealed by what you
do. One supposed advantage of this analysis is that we need not postulate any unobservable psychological entity as an independent variable.
The analysis is a form of behaviorism: to prefer something is to be disposed to act in a certain way. One of the many problems with this theory, beyond its dismissal of the possibility of weakness of will, is that
the analysis of preference by reference to action presupposes that you
have some appropriate beliefs, for example about the probable consequences of your action. But a consistent behaviorist will say that beliefs

---

[2] Arguably this is unfair to Kant's views taken as a whole. He does take virtue
seriously.
[3] Economists will usually say that they make this assumption only for purposes
of prediction, but sometimes one comes around to believing what one began by
assuming for the sake of argument or prediction.

too are just dispositions to act in a certain way. If so, then a dispositional analysis will not work for either preferences or beliefs – unless everyone has perfect information, as economists sometimes assume, in which case the belief that p can be cashed into p. Nor will it work for virtues.

This problem provides some evidence for MacIntyre's (1985, especially chapter 8) claim that social science should not pretend to be scientific. Human behavior is a fit subject for science if we can observe and measure human psychological states. This seems at first look impossible: beliefs and desires, as well as many other psychological states, are surely unobservable and unmeasurable. But if behaviorism were true – that is, if beliefs and desires were dispositions to act – then perhaps we could observe and measure these states. So at the very least, I could infer what you desire from what you voluntarily do. And if the kind of utilitarianism that MacIntyre attacks were true, then we could observe whether something is good for a person, since getting what one wants is good for one. And with a little help from economists, we could look at a large number of people and observe whether some act was morally good. But human thought and action are not open to observation and measurement in that way. There can be no science of reasons and actions.[4] Behaviorism is false.

Even if we could solve that problem, we would still not have shown how ethics and self-interest can be compatible. One famous attempted solution favored by some economists is to say that narrow selfishness is good from the point of view of prosperity, for a productive market requires just the kind of selfishness characteristic of *homo economicus*. As Adam Smith famously observed, the general welfare is typically served when all participants in the market work to benefit themselves.[5] As business is fundamentally a competitive enterprise, I shall be better off if and only if my competitor is worse off. Selfishness seems therefore to be a prerequisite for business success. To try to contribute to everyone's welfare or, for that matter, to act so that justice is done or that rights are protected would be a losing competitive strategy. This sounds like good news: act in your normal self-interested way – do what you want – and it will turn out best for all.

---

[4] Davidson (2001) offers an extended and persuasive argument for this claim. I touched on it in Chapter 1.
[5] But Smith, a virtue ethicist, has views far subtler than this. See Werhane (1991) and, for a detailed comparison, Calkins and Werhane (1998).

But this view, though it is not entirely wrong, has some problems, including a practical one about implementation: the relationship between managers' interests and the organization's success is not
straightforward. Agency theory is meant to address that problem.

Agency theory

Agency theory holds that managers ought to be faithful agents of
the stockholders, and so must further their interests. The obligation
extends thence to all employees. Agency theorists typically presuppose
that all agents act in their own interests, and that the problem is that
their interests may be inconsistent with the obligation to further the
interests of the stockholders. The solution is to arrange matters so that
agents have an interest in acting in ways that turn out to further the
interests of their stockholders. Incentive compensation is a favored way
of doing this. If senior managers are given stock options, for example,
they have an interest in raising the price of the stock, hence in managing well. So goes the argument.

The great crash of 2008 came about in part because executives of big
banks failed to be faithful agents. Many of the banks had been part-
nerships, in which executives had their own money at risk. When the
banks became publicly held corporations, their executives were able
to take risks with other people's money and did so, with catastrophic
results for the stockholders of the banks but not so much for themselves
except insofar as they were stockholders. Evidently it is not so easy to
design and implement effective incentive compensation schemes.

Several of the assumptions of agency theorists are questionable,
and would not impress Aristotle. One typical assumption of agency
analysis is that people are narrowly self-interested in the way many
economists assume. It would follow that incentive compensation is
the most effective motivator. The narrow self-interest assumption is
not necessary for the theory: there will be a problem about agency
if the parties' interests differ, whether or not either party is narrowly
self-interested. But history, including recent history, indicates that the
assumption is widely held. Agency theorists influenced by game theory, as most of them are, usually make the convenient but implausible
assumption that one's preferences are not altered by the preferences
of any other party. Why would a narrowly selfish player care about
anyone else's preferences (Heath, 2009, pp. 499f.)?

As Ghoshal (2005) claims, organization theorists tend to be skeptical about unobservable entities, which do not make theorizing any easier, and therefore look to external states and events to explain behavior. From that point of view as well, incentive compensation will seem a good explanation of employees' behavior. (See Heath, 2009, p. 502; he might have been thinking of Pfeffer, 1982, for example.) Loyalty might explain why Jones works hard, but loyalty is difficult to operationalize. In fact, if Doris and his allies in social psychology are right, there is no such thing as loyalty as we understand it. Better to stick to what is more readily observable; as the old joke has it, the light is better over here.

Even more problematical is the game theorist's assumption of opportunism (Heath, 2009, pp. 502f.). One makes a preference-maximizing agreement; then at the point of deciding whether to keep the agreement, one maximizes again, without reference to the obligation or the intrinsic value of being as good as one's word. If human nature is like this – and some agency theorists claim that it is – then there is no point in talking about loyalty and trustworthiness, or in trying to create them in organizations.

In at least two ways agency theory has ethical implications. First, it suggests that the ethical obligations of management agents to their stockholder principals always override all other ethical obligations. This is at most a suggestion, however: Friedman himself does not make the claim, though he is vague about the exceptions. Heath is more pessimistic, for he argues that the game-theoretical assumption of opportunism implies that an agency relationship is not a fiduciary relationship at all, but instead a set of implicit contracts that assume a certain ineliminable level of self-dealing on the agent's part (2009, pp. 513f.). Second, any principal or agent who believes that human nature is as agency theory describes it would be a fool not to act cynically and opportunistically. In fact, as Bazerman and Tenbrunsel (2011, chapter 6) and others have shown, incentive compensation may actually reduce employee compliance and effort by crowding out loyalty. And in situations of asymmetry of information, surely quite common in many organizations today, that potentially self-fulfilling belief can have heavy costs, not least for stockholders (Heath, 2009, pp. 519f.).

Sandel (2012, pp. 34f. and elsewhere) argues that putting a price on something may "demean and degrade" it. He would probably find incentive compensation a good example of how that happens. Akerlof (1982, p. 543) explains employees' productivity by reference to their "sentiment for each other and also for the firm," which is ignored by incentive compensation schemes. Virtue ethicists will say that there is a lesson here about rules and motivation generally. Jos and Tompkins (2004) provide evidence that compliance-oriented accountability processes undermine the administrative virtues required for responding appropriately to demands for external accountability. MacIntyre (1985, pp. 175f.) tells the parable of a chess-playing child, who is likely to cheat if offered candy as an incentive to win but less likely to do so if he or she enjoys the game for itself and wants to excel at it.

MacIntyre does not believe that managers are like chess-playing children. He argues that the profit motive drives out the virtues characteristic of honest and cooperative toil. He is largely right about organizations in which agency problems are dealt with by buying employees' loyalty through schemes like incentive compensation. There is strong evidence that what is bought is not loyalty and that it does not support either virtues or profits very well. But not all organizations work that way. As I shall argue at further length in Chapter 5, a successful firm requires the cooperative virtues of its managers and employees.

The belief that incentive compensation is the best way to get executives to perform is a piece of the scientific approach to management, according to which people are so simply motivated that it is not necessary to postulate any complex inner states to explain behavior. Thus behaviorist psychology leads to neo-Taylorist management.

Desires

Beyond the difficulties with revealed preferences and agency, the *homo economicus* view errs in assuming that your interests are always served by the fulfillment of your preferences. What you want may not be best for you, for any of a number of reasons. Some desires will lead to disappointment, some to trouble. Short-term desires may conflict with long-term ones; second-order desires may conflict with first-term ones. What you desire will change, sometimes with your mood. Then there are all the factors that social psychologists identify that make our choices irrational: the endowment effect, choice overload, buyer's remorse, rationalization of many kinds, and others.

To understand the relationship among ethics, self-interest, and success in business requires seeing that one's interests are not necessarily simple and that they do not always coincide with one's desires,
which are also not simple, or even with one's preferences. Aristotle claims that character is a matter of what you enjoy: good things
if you are a good person, bad if bad (*NE* II 3 1104b5–9). He dis-
agrees with Hume's claim that reason is the slave of the passions;
desires can be reasonable or unreasonable, good or bad. Achieving a good character entails developing certain desires and emotions
rather than others. As his account of weakness of will shows, Aristotle is aware that you may have certain desires that you would
prefer not to have. Acting on your rationally preferred desires and
turning away from irrational ones by which you as a rational person do not want to be motivated requires at least continence. But
if you are a fully virtuous person, a temperate person of practical
wisdom, your rational higher-order desires determine your first-order
desires.

So there is an answer to the reflective businessperson, or anyone
else for that matter, who asks: Why is it in my interest to be an honest
person rather than rapacious? It may be true that all will be better off if
all are honest, but then why should I not undertake the best strategy for
me, which is to be prepared to act dishonestly no matter what others
do? If character is a matter of what one enjoys, as Aristotle claims,
then these are shallow and wrongheaded questions.

Deciding on one's interests

It is Aristotle's position that character development[6] involves developing one's interests. A person of good character is one whose values,
understood as his or her or most important interests, are the right ones,
and who acts accordingly. The question that this statement raises is
not "How do I create a life that serves my interests?" but rather "How
do I decide what my interests are to be?[7] What do I want to enjoy?"
When I consider what would be a good life for me, I should ask myself

---

[6] We shall discuss Aristotle's conception of it in Chapter 4.

[7] The notion of interest is a tricky one. We might interpret Aristotle as saying that
all people have roughly the same interests, but many of them do not know what
their true interests are. When I speak of interests as being right or wrong, I have
in mind desires of a very high order.

not only what I prefer, but also *what I would choose to prefer* if I could choose thoughtfully and rationally.[8] That question cannot be readily answered by reference to self-interest. (See Hartman, 1996, pp. 80–3 and 134f., and Elster, 1985, pp. 109–40; the latter speaks of adaptive preference formation.)

Your ability to reflect on your desires and to alter your character and therefore your interests on the basis of that reflection is a characteristically human form of rationality. That makes it possible for you to plan your future and construct your life, within limits (*NE* I 10 1100b34–1101a14, VI 7 1141a27–9; *De Anima* III 10 433b5–10, 11 434a5–10).[9] You can do it well; you can also do it badly, as when the process is dominated by a focus on popularity, or when it reflects the diminished opportunities and expectations of an oppressed person. We can see Aristotle's awareness of the importance of preference formation when he takes it as self-evident (*NE* X 3 1174a1–4) that one would not choose to live the life of a child, taking pleasure in childish things, or to enjoy what is shameful. At IX 4 1166b23f. he refers to the vicious person who wishes that he did not enjoy what he enjoys.

Most people, including most principle-based theorists, would agree that the ethical quality of an act provides at least some reason to perform it, but the Aristotelian tradition has more to say than that being ethical can help keep you out of prison, or that it can help forge the bonds of trust that make an organization more effective, or even that it feels good. To be ethical is to live well, and according to one's human nature, as a tree flourishes when it blooms or bears fruit. And the nature of the human being is to be rational and sociable and to think, intend, and act accordingly.

The typical principle-based ethical theory does not undertake to answer questions about creating preferences and interests. Aristotle does, and his answer is that the right choice is to prefer the life of a virtuous person. Much of the *Nicomachean Ethics* is devoted to giving an account of the state of *eudaimonia* and to showing how attaining this state is good for the agent as well as for the agent's family, friends, and community.

---

[8] This is a particularly sophisticated version of Frankfurt's (1981) view that freedom of the will has much to do with higher-order desires.
[9] I have profited from Irwin's (Aristotle, 1999) commentary on these passages and his further analysis of Aristotle's views (1988, pp. 336–8).

Those of us who are not saints cannot choose to enjoy courage and generosity at all times; we find them occasionally burdensome. And while you can get into the habit of enjoying doing some good things, there are limits. No normal person can learn to enjoy root canal surgery, however beneficial it may be. Some virtues can impose short-term costs. Courage would not be courage if the courageous person did not sometimes pay a price for it. Honesty entails opportunity costs. But apart from whether doing the honest thing always pays, if you are a virtuous person you think yourself better off on the whole for being the sort of person who is inclined to do the honest thing.

Rationality and interests

So a fully rational person can decide what sort of life will be most fulfilling in the long run and then be pleased to live such a life (*NE* I 10 1100b33–1101a21). To complete his account of choosing a good character, Aristotle needs to say what it is about a life that is truly desirable, desirable to a rational person, and why.[10]

As we noted in Chapter 1, a substance is not a mere pile of stuff, and a human life, like all substances, has to have some identity and continuity. So we want to have desires that form a coherent whole at any time and through time, rather than desires that contradict each other or violate our values or change often. Without this sort of integrity you will sometimes desire, and may get, what you do not value. That point Aristotle makes in his discussion of weakness of will, which causes us to do what we do not value. You are better off as well as more virtuous if your values and desires are consistent and drive your actions.

In fact Aristotle claims at *NE* X 7 1177b30–8a3 that one is identical with one's *nous*, the soul's rational element, which he says is in some way divine. Not to act according to it would be to choose the life not truly your own. We can infer that he would hold that a life guided by momentary pleasure or avarice or corporate culture is not a life lived well, nor, given what he says about rational choice, freely.

Aristotle does not show that it is impossible to be consistently rapacious, but he does give some reasons for saying that you cannot be a bad person and still lead a happy life. If you are rapacious and you

---

10 Recall that you can desire A and B but prefer B, which may be achieved only if you do not get A. But the Aristotelian ideal is having consistent desires.

sometimes act nicely for strategic reasons, as when people are watching, you will often find yourself doing things that you do not enjoy. You will be acting inconsistently with your values and with some of your desires (*NE* IX 4 1166b7–14). You will have to smile and smile and be a villain, and that is no enviable smile. Unless you are a total degenerate, being vicious will put you at war with yourself: Aristotle claims that the base person wishes that bad things had not become pleasant to him, and he dislikes himself for it (1166b23–9).

A good person may act differently under different circumstances, but that is not a matter of incoherence. It is a matter of having constructed a character strong and confident enough to be flexible and adaptive to time, place, relations, and other features, including new and unfamiliar features, of the particular situation.

Being base also puts you at odds with your community. As we are sociable creatures, that is not good news.

Community

I claimed earlier that you cannot decide on the basis of self-interest what your interests will be. There is evidence, however,[11] that choosing to want to be a good citizen is wiser than choosing to want to be enormously rich. According to positive psychologists,[12] people of moderate but sufficient means are happier than very poor people on the whole, but extremely rich people are not much happier than those who are moderately well off. This echoes Aristotle's view (X 8 1178b33–1179a3) that to have *eudaimonia* one needs to be fairly well off but not necessarily rich. According to the likes of Belk (1985) and Kasser and Ryan (1996), cited in Haidt (2006), for most people strong personal connections are the key to happiness. So they agree with Aristotle that humans are essentially sociable creatures, and that our sociability affects the nature of the good life for us. But we should not readily assume that happiness can easily be measured, or even defined.

Aristotle argues that wealth, because it is only a means to some other end and not an end in itself, cannot be what is finally good in life (*NE* I 5 1096a6–8). He also condemns *pleonexia* (NE V 9 1136b21f. and elsewhere), which is a matter of grabbing more than one's share

---

[11] See Haidt (2001, 2006).
[12] See Gilbert (2006, pp. 217–20) and Haidt (2006, chapters 5, 6, and 11).

of something. He regards leisure as one of the great and necessary goods of life (*Pol* VII 14 1333a35f.). And the more leisure one has, when blessed with adequate material goods, the more necessary are philosophy, self-control, and justice (VII 15 1334a23f.). From all this we can infer, as Skidelsky (2009) does, that Aristotle would not admire businesspeople who work long hours to make far more money than they need and therefore have no time for a life of *eudaimonia*, particularly that of a good citizen (*Pol* VII 9 1328b38–29a2).[13] And if they do succeed in becoming rich, there is a good chance that they will not be very content, because they will always be comparing themselves to those who make more, and therefore working still longer hours.[14] This cannot be a good life.

To explicate the ways in which human beings are sociable would take more space than any one author could spare. For example, one might write many volumes on the ways in which language is necessarily a social activity and how the meanings of expressions are necessarily worked out in the public square. It is worth noticing that rationality is a social matter as well, since rationality requires desiring to live well and living well is a matter of living sociably. We should also recall the point about the person who is bad but must appear good when others are watching. If you do that, you violate rationality by doing things you wish you did not want to do. You also violate your social nature. For whatever else you may be, you are a family member, a friend, and a citizen, and you ought to play those roles well.

Social capital

We see some of Aristotle's views on human sociability reflected in the notion of *social capital*. This is a fairly new concept, and there is no consensus on exactly what it means.[15] I shall take the term to refer to

---

[13] Skidelsky notes that Keynes' prediction that greater wealth would lead to greater leisure has not been borne out. He suggests that the root of the problem is the absence of any conception of the good life other than preference satisfaction.

[14] See, for example, Frank (2004, chapter 8).

[15] The concept has been associated primarily with Putnam (2000). For a review of the early literature on social capital as it relates to business see Adler and Kwon (2002), who find almost as many definitions of the concept as there are scholars who have studied it. Adler and Kwon note that social capital can have negative consequences. What strengthens Us may harm our relations with

certain individual characteristics as well as social and institutional relationships that create assets that generate future benefits, in particular
effective solutions to collective action problems.

The key to solving such problems is trust, which in turn requires
trustworthiness, which is an example of social capital. One obvious
benefit of trust is cooperation. Consider the tradition of barn-raising
among the Amish of Lancaster County. If Jacob Stoltzfus needs a new
barn, the men of the community join him in building it, while the
women make an elaborate lunch. Why does Samuel Zook help Jacob
Stoltzfus build a barn? Because, Samuel might say, it is more efficient
to have a barn built by a lot of people at once rather than to make it a
one-man job.

Samuel also knows that if his barn burns down, Jacob and others will
help him build a new one. That is, Samuel trusts Jacob, as he should,
because Jacob is trustworthy. Trust also comes from the Amish tradition of encouraging an inclination to be trustful enough to cooperate.
The Amish also have a practice of shunning the cynical, who are easily
exposed in a small community in which news about slacking travels
fast, considering the lack of communications technology.

What Samuel might or might not also say, though it is true and
important, is that the members of the community care about one
another: Samuel and others take Jacob's need as a reason for action.
Ostrom and Ahl (2009) claim that what they call second-generation
collective action theories do not assume, as their predecessors do, that
the agents are *homines economici*. On the contrary the players have
"social motivations and endogenous preferences" (p. 21). I believe,
though Ostrom and Ahl do not quite say so, that Samuel's friendly
attitude towards Jacob is crucial.[16] If Samuel is old and knows that
his barn will almost certainly outlast him, he will still help Jacob even
though he will likely never need Jacob's help. It would be fair to say
that that sort of attitude makes both Samuel and Jacob trustworthy,
but that is not all it does.

Ostrom and Ahl also make a claim that we ought to find interesting
in the light of the argument of Doris and others that the immediate
environment determines behavior more than do individual personal

---

Them. For a detailed account of the importance of social capital as it relates to
business ethics, see Sison (2003).

[16] Bowles and Gintis (2011, especially chapter 11) would agree with me.

characteristics: two communities may be similar in nearly all respects but differ in the level of trustworthiness of their citizens. Ostrom and Ahl infer that the trustworthiness of individuals is distinct from and not determined by institutional arrangements (p. 26), though it seems clear that the latter can have some effect on the former.

Consider a village commons in colonial New England. If the carrying capacity of the commons is 110 sheep and there are 100 families in the village with ten sheep each, you might expect Jeremiah Hopkins to be tempted to put more than one sheep on the commons, since he will benefit if he does, whether or not his neighbors do the same. But there is a useful norm in place: one sheep per family. Jeremiah follows the norm because he is trustworthy and trusts the other villagers to do the same, and because he is motivated by the interests of his friends rather than by pure self-interest. If all the villagers do the same, they are all better off than if each acted on pure self-interest. (See Hardin, 1968. I have discussed the commons in Hartman, 1996, especially pp. 74–8.)

Much the same is true of organizations. Employees who can get by with minimal work may decide instead to try to contribute as best they can to corporate success, with the result that all are better off. We have seen good reason to doubt that incentive compensation programs, however well designed, can do the same. In effect they privatize one's work. First generation collective action theorists will approve of this solution, which is consistent with their belief that agents are narrowly selfish. But it is important for employees who are entrusted with responsibilities to be worthy of that trust and to believe that others are as well. Insofar as they care about one another and about the success of the organization, trustworthiness will be encouraged, to the benefit of the commons.

We go perhaps a bit further than Ostrom and Ahn and many analysts of social capital in identifying attitudes that solve collective action problems.[17] In some cases it matters that the participants are friends. Insofar as Samuel cares about Jacob, he cares about the quality of Jacob's barn and the quality of his (Samuel's) contribution to it. But if Samuel is not only trustworthy but also virtuous, he will enjoy being part of the "socially established cooperative...activity" of the barn-raising, as MacIntyre would call it. He will enjoy hammering nails

---

[17] But not further than Fox (1985), who takes a utopian and nearly anarchist view of how to preserve the commons.

not only because he is a good carpenter and therefore hammers nails well and according to reason and as the professional would hammer, but also because he knows that "hammering nails" is an inadequate description of what he is doing,[18] which is helping build a good barn for his friend Jacob. What he is engaged in is a *praxis* and not only a *poiesis*, and that is a good thing. Samuel is like an employee who cares about accomplishing the mission of the organization for the benefit of his fellow employees, the stockholders, and certain other stakeholders.

Aristotle does not have the concept of social capital, but he has just the place for it. He believes that the people of the *polis* should be bound together by relationships and attitudes that we recognize as creating social capital. As we noted in Chapter 1, the citizens participate in politics not to win benefits for themselves or their factions but to see to it that justice is done and that the people live well. Emotional ties too bind citizens, according to Aristotle. A successful community requires at the very least that citizens take the interests of the community and its citizens as strong reasons for action. There is no reason to believe – and Aristotle does not believe – that a democracy in which individuals pursue their own interests rather than what is best for the community as a whole will be a good community. A *polis* is not a collection of individual citizens making deals to get the best outcome for themselves that they can manage; it is a community of citizens sharing certain values and pursuing them. (See, for example, *Pol* IV 11 129b23–5 and *NE* IX 6 1167b5–9.) From the point of view of a liberal like Rawls (1971), this is a bit too much unity.

Intrinsic and instrumental goods

In the discussion of *praxis* and *poiesis* in Chapter 1 I interpreted Aristotle as saying that nearly all virtues create some benefit, or they would not be virtues. But a virtue is a state of the soul, a good thing in itself. It is intrinsically, not merely instrumentally, good for you to be honest, courageous, and just. At the same time, those virtues stand you in good stead in the community, and so are instrumentally good as well. Intrinsic goods and instrumental goods converge because human beings are sociable creatures, who cannot flourish with character traits

---

[18] Recall from Chapter 2 the ethical importance of understanding actions under adequate descriptions.

that are incompatible with a self-created life in a community. So while it is true that virtues are primarily internal states, their typical external effects are a necessary condition of their being virtues.

A virtue is in some ways like the faculty of vision. When I see something, I am in a certain internal psychological state, but that internal state constitutes seeing if and only if I am related to some seen object in the right way. It is not surprising that Aristotle believes that we get intrinsic satisfaction from using our senses. (See *Metaphysics* I 1 980a21ff., the second sentence of the work.)

To say that it is in my best interests to be a good friend and a good citizen because I am by nature the sort of creature whose end (fulfillment; purpose; actuality) is to enjoy being sociable looks like rigging the game: Aristotle seems to be just stipulating that we are essentially creatures who flourish in achieving our end, which is to be good citizens and so on. We may not be so confident that it is in our nature to be moral people and that being moral people makes us happy. But there is much to be said for deciding to become the kind of person who enjoys being a good friend and a good citizen and gets the most out of friendship and citizenship. For whether or not we accept Aristotle's views about our essential nature, we can agree that much of what people enjoy and nearly all that they accomplish require the cooperation of others. This is true nowhere more than in business. It follows that trust is important, as therefore is trustworthiness, as is honesty. In the absence of enforcement mechanisms we can sometimes rely on virtue. If I am your true friend, I am no more likely to cheat you than I am to cheat myself. If I am a good citizen, I will not be motivated to be a free rider – for example, to work hard to get the government to reduce spending overall but to increase it for programs that benefit me. If I am a good employee, I am even less likely to be a free rider, since we expect employees to share the organization's values more than a citizen must share those of the state. (On this last point we probably differ from Aristotle.)

Ostrom and Ahl show that communities similar in nearly all respects may differ with respect to social capital. That suggests that the virtue of the populace may not be sufficient to preserve the commons. Nor is any system proof against vice. It is not the case, as Friedman seems to believe, that firms that focus entirely on profit are more successful, other things being equal, from a moral point of view. Nor is it the case, as designers of incentive compensation schemes assume, that self-interest can be easily harnessed so that it serves corporate interests.

Naturalism and the good life

In Aristotle's view the essential facts about humankind go a considerable way towards determining what is ethical. Many moral philosophers of the past century have not accepted Aristotle's position or his way of getting to it. This is in part because they believe that it is characteristic of ethics that you and I can agree on the empirically determinable facts of the case but disagree about the ethics of the case; so they reject his inference from propositions about human nature to propositions about ethics. For example, you and I might agree that 1 percent of the populace of some country has 20 percent of the wealth, but you might think that that is unjust while I do not. Most philosophers would deny Aristotle's view that the purpose or natural end of some substance is anything like a straightforward, empirically available fact about it. This is not to deny that on moral issues one of us may be right and the other wrong; it is rather that the empirically determinable facts on which we agree do not imply ethical facts, on which we may disagree.

So-called naturalists, closer to Aristotle, will claim that, for example, from "Jones enjoys inflicting pain" we can infer "Jones is evil." Opponents of naturalism argue that the inference requires another premise, such as "Anyone who enjoys inflicting pain is evil," which is a normative statement; we cannot infer the "ought" just from the "is." So there is a gulf between science and ethics, hence between psychology and ethics. To operationalize ethical terms is to take an ethical stand. So, for example, if we define the good as utility and then define utility in the way economists do, we have stipulated a kind of utilitarianism that even most economists would not embrace. The case of Deborah seems to be a situation in which people can agree on all the facts but disagree on the ethics of the matter. It would remain so even if we knew precisely how much happiness would be generated for precisely which stakeholders by sending Deborah to London as opposed to sending Arnold.

But while we can and do argue about what counts as good or harmful, there are limits to our disagreements. Someone who claims that ethics is essentially about inflicting pain or putting things on top of other things or obeying Kim Jong Un is just mistaken about the nature of ethics. Anyone who says, "Jones is a really good man who just happens to enjoy vandalizing others' property and torturing children" is in much the same situation as one who says, "Jones is a very intelligent fellow who just happens to be unable to think rationally, understand complex issues, solve problems of any kind, or retain information." It is a necessary truth that ethics has to do with human well-being.[19]

Though we may disagree about many issues, such as whether and when Smith may coerce Jones for Jones's own good, there are nevertheless some areas of firm agreement about ethics; that much is indicated by our use of words like *cruel*, whose denotation cannot be cleanly separated from its connotation because its connotation determines what sort of person or behavior it denotes.[20] We might disagree about whether, say, hanging is cruel but still agree that stoning to death is cruel. Our language permits us to agree to the extent of understanding what we are talking about but at the same time to disagree and to argue rationally about it.

Some, but by no means all, who argue for a clear division between is and ought go on to say that ought-statements are neither true nor false. But the sophomore skeptic mentioned in Chapter 2 will probably not say anything like this: I grant you that Jones did stand up to his bullying boss, but that is no reason to say that he acted courageously. Or like this: Yes, Smith always keeps confidences, tells the truth, pulls her weight, and does what she undertakes to do, but who's to say that she is trustworthy?[21] It is of course possible that Jones was not acting courageously, that instead he was showing off to win the admiration of Smith. But to say even that is to concede that virtues can be invoked to explain and justify some actions, and that the invocation may be true or false.

Loyalty and trustworthiness can explain behavior in organizations. So can dishonesty and fair-mindedness. If Jones, an employee, works

---

[19] Saying what ethics is about is itself an ethical claim, though not a very specific one. In Chapter 7 we shall discuss a conception of ethics that seems to bring this claim into question.

[20] See Putnam (2002) on cruelty and much more. Among other things, he argues that many who advocate the fact–value dichotomy have a narrow notion of fact, which they have inherited from the positivists.

[21] Recall the claim, made in Chapter 2 and supported by Whetstone (2003), that managers are comfortable with virtue talk.

hard, it may be because he will get paid more for doing so. But in the absence of incentive compensation, Jones may work hard because he sees other employees working hard and feels that he owes it to them and to the company to work no less hard than they do, because it is unfair to be a free or even inexpensive rider. External events and states do not explain everything, money is not the only motivator, and some of the motivating states must be named in normative language.

Limits on the good life

The controversy over what counts as a good life is an old and hardy one; I cannot summarize it, much less resolve it, here. But I can urge that we not underestimate the extent to which certain facts about human beings determine the limits not only on what could conceivably be considered ethical but also on what we can call the good life and what constitutes well-being.

One might argue that well-being is about feeling good: it is subjective, and it matters not why you feel it. It is true that there would be something odd about saying, "Jones feels good all the time, but he is unhappy." On the other hand, we might argue over whether Jones is really happy if his good feelings are the result of ignorance of some sobering facts, or of pleasant things happening to him rather than anything that he has accomplished, or if he is satisfied with the life of a couch potato or an elevator operator whose great thrill is to take the elevator to the roof (Hartman, 1996, p. 36).

Think of physical health as an analogue to virtue and its *eudaimonia*. There is something just naturally good about being healthy, but that does not automatically make it attractive. Particularly if you are out of shape and overweight, exercise is painful and eating and drinking moderately is frustrating. You may think that robust health is not worth the trouble, especially if you have been a contented couch potato enjoying watching sports with your friends and drinking a lot of beer. But if you do change your ways, over time you not only see progress but also begin to feel good about jogging and pumping iron and about cutting back on beer and potato chips. Having achieved a certain level of fitness, you may wonder why you ever thought it would be painful. Of course some fat chain-smoker might outlive you, but the odds are on your side. More to the present point, health is its own reward. It is an acquired taste, as are some virtues, but you have good reason to decide to acquire a taste for health and for a desire to enjoy working out.

It is at least possible that an overweight television watcher experiences as much subjective pleasure as a person who enjoys health and fitness, but it is not probable, for only the healthy person can experience the subjective pleasure of having achieved health through rational self-discipline. And so with good character: as a virtuous person you have the positive subjective experience of having become able to act in ways that contribute to your good character.[22] That is a form of pleasure unique to human beings, and to only some of them. Having achieved your character, you would not be pleased to change places with the dullard who gains little from life.

Philosophers who follow Bentham in holding that well-being is a matter of one's mental state are in the minority, but there is a subjective aspect to the happiness of the physically or mentally healthy person. Aristotle is no Benthamite.[23] In his view there is something deficient in your life if you have not designed it yourself; there is something lacking in your life if you are not a citizen participating in the life of your community, or if you have no good friends, even if you feel just fine.

Well-being and sociability

To call humans sociable is not to say only that their individual interests typically require the help of others for their achievement. There will indeed be much that Jones cannot do in the absence of the cooperation of others: building a barn may be one such thing. But it would be a mistake to focus only on the good results of sociability for human beings. Aristotle holds that it is natural to you to live in a good *polis*, and that therefore you ought to be a politically active citizen. He believes that you should have true friendships, which are natural to you and good in themselves: they are not just about strengthening a network of useful contacts. Friendships and family relationships at their best are among the greatest pleasures of life. If you are missing these, your life is sadly lacking. As the positive psychologists say, the happiest people have a close family and many good friends. In

---

[22] For more along these lines see McKinnon (2005).
[23] See Hausman (2012, pp. 78–80) and Annas (2011, pp. 128–44).

saying this they suggest that family life and friendship constitute rather than cause happiness. If so, happiness is not (as Aristotle believes that *eudaimonia* is not) a mental state over and above the blessings of our lives.

MacIntyre accepts this view in claiming (1985, p. 187) that excellence in a practice – a "coherent and complex form of socially established cooperative human activity" – is a form of virtue and creates its own intrinsic goods. For example, cooperative work on a practice requires, and so cultivates, not only technical skill but also trustworthiness, honesty, sensitivity, pride in one's work, loyalty to the group, unselfishness, and other virtues. The practice may generate external rewards like money and prestige, but the internal goods are more important, and we should not reduce their motivating force by introducing observable independent variables like incentive compensation schemes. If we are people of the right sort, we enjoy using our skills in cooperative activity. MacIntyre doubts that this is possible in a firm, but I shall argue in Chapter 5 that he is wrong. People can enjoy being team players where the activity calls on their rationality and sociability.

There are some cases in which team play is not much fun. A military unit in battle is probably not exactly enjoying the camaraderie that unites the soldiers, but there is a kind of satisfaction in it all the same, and the satisfaction has something to do with the notion that it is right and good for us happy few to fight together upon St. Crispin's Day, quite apart from whether we care about Harry's political ambitions.

Varieties of the good life

Thus far the claim that what is ethically good is somehow grounded in human nature seems at least plausible. Insofar as human beings act according to their rational and social nature and support others in doing the same, they are enjoying the good life and being ethical. The obvious objection is that some people appear to be perfectly happy with a life that is minimally rational and only social enough to enable them to get by. Surely, a liberal in the Rawlsian mode would say, we want ethics to accommodate a range of lives that a range of people might find appealing. The claim that a simple life consisting primarily of the satisfaction of modest desires is a failed life seems to be a piece of elitism. Different people will find fulfillment in different places, and we need to be careful about claiming that one style of life is by definition better than another. So let me try to be careful. Without committing myself to any detailed account of what the good life is, I say that a reasonable view, a mean, lies between the proposition that there is a detailed and unarguable account of what is good and the proposition that the good is whatever someone happens to like. Rawls himself falls between these extreme views when he claims that there are some "primary goods" that any rational person will desire (1971, p. 92). With the notion that what is good is just what someone likes we associate the Enlightenment view as presented by MacIntyre. But the extreme views are both false.

The claim that our nature determines what is good for us and that what is good for us is to find a place in a good community may remind us of the determinism of sociobiology or social psychology. Either our genetic makeup or our immediate environment largely determines what we do. Not so, from an Aristotelian point of view. For if we are rational, we can reflect on and create our lives, even to the point of choosing our interests. We know that Aristotle is a careful student of the ways in which most of us fall short, but we do not fall short because it is in our nature to do so.

I have argued that Aristotle sees rationality and sociability as working together. It does not seem to worry Aristotle that they may work against each other. The Milgram experiment shows how social pressure can undermine rational deliberation, but at the other end of the spectrum we should not always reject the effect of the community. What is required here is a mean between a form of individualism bereft of community and a form of sociability that forfeits all independent deliberation.

Aristotle thinks that rational beings are partly responsible for the creation of their own character (*NE* III 5 1114b23). This statement, in the context of his views about sociability, suggests that you have an obligation to make yourself the sort of person who has enough autonomy to permit a wise choice of a life that is coherent and sustainable in a *polis*. It does not follow that any particular set of values is right for all agents, but some values are good and some wrong for anyone.[24]

---

[24] Giovanola (2009, p. 436f.) suggests that the "capabilities approach" (most thoroughly described in Sen, 2009), which emphasizes the freedom and the opportunity to function appropriately, is close to the Aristotelian view. The capabilities are universal, but you have your own particular way of using them (p. 437).

So you might decide to become a professional soldier or a professional singer, but you ought to be courageous in either case, whether in facing a fierce enemy or in singing a demanding aria before a large and discerning audience.

Freedom to choose and the good life

In a liberal democracy we assume that citizens will have a variety of what Rawls (1993) calls "comprehensive conceptions" of what is most to be valued. So long as your comprehensive conception does not cause you to interfere with others, you are entitled to it. This sort of political freedom Aristotle does not advocate. As we noted, he holds that in good communities there is a high level of unanimity. People should have interests of the right sort, which are shaped by the good *polis*, to which virtuous people want to contribute. That is one reason for saying that ethics is continuous with politics. But even among those with good interests there can be disagreements; so there is a place for discussion and deliberation among the citizens as they consider what justice demands. Still, Aristotle's good *polis* does not resemble the kind of liberal democracy that we find in the late Rawls. He does not seem to have a strong sense that even the best possible government is likely to be too ignorant and clumsy to micromanage people's lives very well. But Aristotle's typical *polis* is a small community in which people know one another, and in which the government is in the hands of wise and virtuous men who care about the common good. We do not know what he would say of a modern nation state, or even a big city.

Choosing characteristically has certain results: one often gets what one chooses. Deliberation whose result fails to contribute to the development and maintenance of a life that includes the enjoyment of family, friends, and fellow citizens is self-undermining and therefore irrational. Deliberating without rationality is all but an oxymoron. The rationality of one's desires is a crucial part of ethics, and of *eudaimonia*. What could be good about having desires that make one a bad friend or a bad citizen? What could be good about a constant desire for instant gratification, or for incompatible outcomes? These dysfunctions are not the result of the sort of rational choice that is essential to human beings.

It would be a mistake, however, to focus only on the results of deliberation. Aristotle believes that the act of free choice in itself is valuable. Choosing – wishing, deliberating, evaluating, deciding – is a crucial part of the life of a rational human being, as opposed to that of a non-human animal. In the realm of human activities, deliberative choice is important if anything is, and it must be done rationally. Surely you would not be living a good life if your deliberation led to unexpected or undesirable actions.[25] To be rational is to be a creature that deliberates and chooses in a way that only humans can. Deliberation and choice are essential activities for any human life, and therefore for a good life. They are good in themselves, but you can deliberate and choose badly, even about your life as a whole.

This is not to say that deliberation and making a decision is always fun. Sometimes it is difficult, even agonizing.[26] Responsibility can weigh heavily, especially if the decision is a hard one and its best possible outcome will entail a cost. It may be easier to let someone else decide, even when your interests are at stake. But most of us want to be the sort of person who can make autonomous decisions. We do not admire or envy those who cannot or will not. And in any case, *eudaimonia* is not the same thing as fun.

Considering the importance of autonomy in deliberation is bound to lead to considering the limits of the good life. Aristotle does not seem to countenance very broad limits: though he would no doubt agree that we need soldiers and tradespeople and that they can be more virtuous or less, he does not regard them as living a life of true *eudaimonia*. MacIntyre opposes modern liberalism, which he thinks is unanchored in any defensible account of living well, of which no account can be given that omits the essential relationship between the individual and the community. Liberals want no such anchor. Kupperman (1991) seeks an intermediate position in criticizing the greatest of all the recent liberal philosophers.

---

[25] There are, however, slaves, whose enslavement Aristotle thinks is appropriate if they are incapable of characteristically human deliberation and choice. (See *Pol* I, pp. 4–7, 13.) On this basis we can fairly accuse Aristotle of a deficient notion of rights.

[26] Baumeister and Tierney (2011, chapter 4) argue that the act of deciding can itself weaken one's willpower.

Liberalism

One of the great differences between Aristotle's view of the purpose of government and that of the modern liberal is that Aristotle believes that the role of the *polis* is to support virtue in the populace, whereas the liberal holds that the *polis* should support the liberty of the individual.[27] Aristotle and Aristotelians like MacIntyre do not believe that it is a good thing that people are at liberty to choose a childish or slavish life. That kind of liberty MacIntyre takes to be an essential weakness of modern liberalism.

Kupperman, a virtue ethicist, opposes Rawls's (1971) view that a good government is not committed to any determinate idea of the good.[28] He accuses Rawls of not taking "intellectual and aesthetic achievements and the development of character" into account in assessing a society, and of not seeing how questions of resource allocation relate to questions about "what the important goods of a society are" (Kupperman, 1991, p. 96), as though culture had no effect on how resources get distributed. Rawls must be prepared to accept a coarsely hedonistic "Tepid New World" – like Brave New World except egalitarian and democratic – rather than an intellectually and aesthetically superior society in which the worst off are "materially" worse off (p. 97). The Founders, prevented by the Veil of Ignorance from knowing their conception of the good, will have no basis for criticizing Tepid New World (p. 98) or for preferring anything else. Followers of Aristotle and opponents of Enlightenment and particularly social contract liberalism can also criticize Rawls for believing that one can conceive of a human being apart from any community, as Aristotle cannot.

Most individuals in the Rawlsian Utopia will know their conceptions of the good and be able to act accordingly, within broad constraints. The government imposes no conception on its fellow citizens, but instead permits various conceptions to coexist and possibly compete within the community. Kupperman believes that a good government will encourage richer views of the good life, for example by stocking

[27] Here we are talking about liberals with libertarian tendencies, in the tradition of Mill, rather than advocates of "nanny government."

[28] It was two years after Kupperman's book came out that Rawls's *Political Liberalism* argued that a state should not enforce a "comprehensive conception" of the good. But much of the argument of that book appeared in 1985 or earlier.

libraries with classics like *Huckleberry Finn*, which help develop moral imagination and practical wisdom (1991, p. 99). Rawls declines to grant the arts state support (1971, p. 100), perhaps because he is aware that many citizens do not want their tax dollars to pay for *Huckleberry Finn* and other classics.

Kupperman (2005, p. 208) believes that it is appropriate for a government to contemplate "quality of life issues." Surely there are some affirmative moral values that a good community shares. And if there are not, morality can hardly exert even the social control that liberals advocate. But the extent to which the government should encourage these values, especially if there is no consensus about them, is not obvious to most of us today, though Aristotle had considerable confidence that the elites governing a good *polis* should go quite far in encouraging them.

Like other virtue and character ethicists, Kupperman sees in the likes of Rawls the repugnant notion that whatever satisfies people can define the good life, and worries that liberalism is morally adrift. But Rawls envisages a community in which people "have a highest-order interest in regulating all their other desires, even their fundamental ones, by reason..." (1993, p. 280). Rawls does not argue that one could ever definitively describe the best possible kind of life, but neither does he give evidence of believing that any kind of life that is satisfactory to the individual is as good as any other.

In a Rawlsian world there is no reason to expect that under the appropriate conditions disinterested people will create a community that discourages creativity and encourages tepidity. It may turn out that in a Rawlsian community some people will want to read Sophocles or listen to Bach while others will prefer Danielle Steele and country western. That is not necessarily a good thing, but justice in government does not require pressuring people to change their reading and listening practices. In any case, justice need not be the only virtue in play, and the state is not the only influence on culture. The liberal view is not that tepidity is good, but that we should let a thousand flowers bloom and then see which ones survive reflection and experience and who is best equipped to water them.

Yet virtue ethicists in the Aristotelian tradition are surely right in claiming that values can be widely accepted without actually being worth valuing. So what, we might ask, is worth valuing? To begin with, no matter what may be valuable, it is necessary to value whatever is required by our ability to ask ourselves what is worth valuing – that is, what the good life is. That requires a measure of rational reflection, as therefore does the good life. (Rawls makes much the same point in the passage cited just above.) And it is an unalterable fact that persons live with other persons; we might promote that fact to a necessary truth by showing that human beings would be profoundly and unrecognizably different if they did not live together in communities. This is to make the now familiar point that the human being is a rational animal and a sociable animal.

What is inadequate about Brave New World and Tepid New World is that their citizens fall short of their potential as human beings. They are not capable even of asking themselves what a good life might be. But Rawls does not seem to doubt that people in his Utopia will be capable of that; and if they are, they will not be satisfied with tepidity. In that respect Rawls is not neutral about tepidity, or about equal respect and equal opportunity. Nor, despite the egalitarian element in his conception of justice, is he neutral about the right of each person to choose among a wide range of possible commitments.

Aristotle, Kupperman (1991, p. 155, for example), and Rawls too (p. 280, quoted above) would regard commitment to self-interest as empty. I believe all three would agree that in making one's most important commitments one decides what one's interests will be. Aristotle and Kupperman would consider a strong character a necessary condition of a good life, and I have no reason to doubt that Rawls would agree.

Kupperman and Rawls do not differ seriously about what the good life looks like. If they differ at all, it is over the role of the government, as opposed to families or voluntary associations or other social entities, in defining and promoting the good life. In the *Politics* Aristotle gives the *polis* a stronger role in moral guidance than does either Kupperman or Rawls, but he has in mind a *polis* that, unlike a federal or even state government of our time, has a more homogeneous population and a select and elite group of full citizens.

In spite of their differences concerning the appropriate role of government in sponsoring virtue, none of the three would claim that there is any form of governance, actual or theoretical, that guarantees that its citizens will live well. A good community requires virtuous citizens, but they do not arise inevitably from some good form of governance.

The need for character in any case

Berkowitz (1999) is among those philosophers who believe that a liberal regime will succeed only if citizens learn virtue in strong families and in rich associations. He notes (p. 26, for example) that Rawls does not adequately consider what a liberal regime ought to do to encourage these and other virtue-producing institutions. Aristotle would no doubt agree. Those who doubt that *homo economicus* becomes *homo honestus* in perfect markets or well-designed compensation schemes will agree as well. Berkowitz himself offers no theory on what a government ought to do to promote virtue that sustains liberal democracy. He sees instead an "unstable equilibrium" between liberalism and the demand for a minimum of good character. That means that, to use familiar terminology, there is a mean between these, but no algorithm for hitting it. A certain amount of experience, including trial and error, is required. There is some reason to say that education is the way to achieve the necessary practical wisdom, but education itself is a politically contested area. In any case, the goal is to have a government that supports but does not control stable and loving families, neighborhoods full of good neighbors, civic associations, and other institutions that are crucial to the success of any polity. To the extent that there is no such government, virtue is at risk. But if people are not virtuous, there will be no such government. Aristotle allows that it is conceivable for a *polis* to be good collectively while the people are bad individually, but it is preferable to have good people, since the goodness of all follows from the goodness of each (*Pol* VII 1332a36–8).

I have argued and shall continue to argue that in the right circumstances not only government but also business, including both organizations and markets, can support good character. As we know, however, the circumstances are not always right. Some skeptics will go further and say that the culture of capitalism is toxic from the point of view of virtue.

Sandel (2012) is such a skeptic.[29] A critic of Rawlsian liberalism, he argues that to a great degree Americans have reduced value to price: the notion that you get what you pay for has been extended into areas in which goods have traditionally not been priced. We pay children for

---

[29] Sandel is carrying on a long tradition of skepticism about what ought to be for sale. See Claasen (2012).

good grades; we pay people to wait in line for us; rich people spend millions on political advertising and watch professional sports from expensive skyboxes. In so doing we invite corruption, we undermine important intrinsic goods, and we miss the point of public events that rich and poor have heretofore enjoyed equally and together. Sandel is no more swayed than Aristotle would be by the claim that these sales involve willing sellers and willing buyers.[30] Some of the things that we do willingly are bad.

Sandel agrees with Aristotle's view that money should be considered a means to what is good, and not a good in itself. Both of them hold that some things should be valued and that others should not be, even if they are. Sandel infers the corollary that there are certain goods to which money should not be a means. These goods, many of which have to do with virtue and equality, ought to be valued for themselves and not according to supply and demand. To commodify them is not only to privatize what ought to be public goods but also to devalue them. It is unlikely that our views about the value of parenthood, for example, would survive if parents could sell their children to the highest bidder. Sandel would not be surprised to learn that incentive compensation schemes can work out badly because they undermine managers' loyalty to the company, which is often a stronger motivating factor than the bonus that commodifies one's work.

There are serious questions about what human beings ought to value. Not all that we want is desirable, as Aristotle says. We might be inclined to believe that Rawlsian liberalism leads to the crude form of utilitarianism that neither Aristotle nor we would accept, or that capitalism leads to the sort of commodification that Sandel criticizes. But there is danger in the other extreme, the idea that a good government should permit only what it thinks is virtuous, whether in the political sphere or the economic one.

Clearly the government can make things better or worse: for example, it can establish public spaces and provide educational opportunity for all, or it can privatize everything that most people want and sell it all to the highest bidders. Either can happen in democratic capitalism. But the fault is not in our system but in ourselves. Whether our politics

---

[30] In fact Aristotle claims that to sell a shoe rather than to wear it is to fail to use it for its proper and characteristic purpose (*Pol* I 9 1257a6–13). He does not go so far as to say that one should never sell shoes.

and economics support the good life is largely determined by whether we who vote and buy are virtuous. So we must believe if we believe that there is such a thing as virtue. Of course if Doris and others are right about virtue, there is little hope.

Large questions

Sandel raises questions of special concern to business ethicists. Does business itself sometimes have a corrosive effect on communities and the character of their citizens? Or are organizations sometimes hospitable to virtue much as a *polis* is? The answer to both questions is a cautious affirmative.

While some of what Aristotle says about the *polis* applies to companies in interesting ways, the two are not the same. Depending on one's point of view, the purpose of the *polis* or of any good state is to improve its citizens' lives or to give them the opportunity to improve their own lives. The purpose of a company is less clear. Neither Aristotle nor we would say that the primary purpose of a company is to make its employees virtuous. Usually a company has a mission; always it must make a profit. Normally it can support virtue in its ranks without compromising its primary purpose, perhaps even as a way of supporting that purpose, which need not be its only purpose. It may also undertake to serve some internal and external stakeholders, particularly employees and customers. But beyond the purposes that a company sets for itself, the community safeguards markets and otherwise supports business as a whole because business does or should perform a crucial public service.

In spite of this good news, we simply cannot say that most companies make their employees virtuous, or that failure to support virtue will always undermine a company's profitability. We can say that it is in several respects a good thing for a company to be supportive of its employees' virtue, and that taking the interests of employees and certain other stakeholders as reasons for action is also a good thing and can help a company succeed. We shall discuss that issue further in Chapter 5.

Business can be a positive ethical force. It does not follow that it usually is. In particular, it will not be if businesspeople are unethical. But in the course of this book, especially in Chapters 5 and 7, I shall argue that there are some features of capitalism that support the virtues and that we can learn lessons from Aristotle about how that can happen.

Our next step is to consider what Aristotle says about the development of character, in which the *polis* is a crucial factor. I have claimed that the ability to construct one's character is a defining characteristic of human beings. Chapter 4 describes how Aristotle thinks we do it.

4 | *Developing character*

How we begin to acquire character

We have seen that Aristotle claims that a person of good character has and acts on certain virtues, hence dispositions and emotions and even interests that are consistent with the essential human characteristics of rationality and sociability. But how does one acquire these virtues and other items? I cannot simply decide one morning that I am going to be an honest or courageous or patient person. I must cultivate the virtues, and I cannot do it on my own: I must be socialized.

Aristotle gives his account of character development in the early chapters of *NE* II and in some passages in *NE* III. A typical human being is born with the capacity to be courageous or cowardly or otherwise virtuous or vicious, but does not possess any virtue or vice at birth. You acquire (say) bravery by first acting as a brave person acts until it becomes a habit, much as you become a harpist by playing the harp. In that way your decisions create your character (*NE* III 2 1112a2f.). You cannot become a good person by studying ethics as a purely philosophical subject: that would be like trying to achieve health by listening to what a physician has to say about health and not acting accordingly (II 4 1105b13–19; cf. II 2 1103b28–30). Aristotle does not choose the analogy lightly. As I suggested in the previous chapter, health and virtue have much in common. Truly healthy living requires actually undertaking a certain mix of diet and exercise rather than just reading about it.

But you can practice badly over a period of time and thus become a bad harpist, so you need a good teacher. Similarly, you can set out to practice acting courageously but fall into the habit of acting in a foolhardy way. To avoid this, you need moral guidance, which typically comes from your *polis* or from your parents, though Aristotle puts greater emphasis on the *polis* as teacher. This is not surprising, given what he says about the function of the *polis* as upholder of virtues and communities: noted in Chapter 1. You should start doing the right things early in life, and thus develop good habits and in due course become a good person. It is a long process.[1]

Rules can play a part in your early development. Telling a child not to lie, for example, and enforcing the rule against lying will help the child get into the habit of telling the truth. We come to have correct desires through the mechanisms of pleasure and pain – reward and punishment, as we might say if we follow Skinner (1972). In fact the development of character is a matter of learning to enjoy right actions and find wrong ones painful (*NE* II 3, especially 1104b5–13). So by guided habit one is learning the right emotions and desires.

But adult education is more than habituation: for those who have moved beyond reaction to reflection, virtue is about reasoning (*NE* X 9 1180a7–12). So, for example, later in life we learn why truthfulness is important. Then, knowing its purpose, we may learn that one can tell the truth in a way that defeats its purpose by misleading listeners. We learn that there may be times and places and ways and circumstances in which lying is appropriate, as when the secret police ask you where your dissident friend is. But even then we may tell a necessary lie with some feelings of repugnance, owing to our habit of truth-telling, with which we have become comfortable.

We have noted that Aristotle takes emotion to be an important aspect of virtue. It is a person of good character who, needing to act rightly in the face of danger, willingly braves the danger and acts without undue fear. But Aristotle demands more: the truly courageous person does not have to push aside any serious temptation to cut and run. One faces the foe or takes the risk with alacrity. But as we know, Aristotle says in his discussion of weakness of will in *NE* VII that you may want to be courageous and believe that a courageous person will join in this attack, but still run the other way. Or you may join the attack by overcoming an almost paralyzing fear and running towards the enemy while wishing it were not necessary to do so and whimpering the whole time. Or you may foolishly believe that there is nothing to fear. In these cases you fall short of true courage. Preparation in the form of repeated drilling is the usual way to help soldiers face the enemy bravely, but Aristotle would doubt that mere drilling imparts

---

[1] With approval Moberg (1999) cites Costa and MacCrae (1994), who provide evidence that character is not well fixed until about age 30.

true courage, which requires knowing how, when, why, and under what circumstances to stand fast.

In a workplace a strong corporate culture may support good or bad values, as we have noted, in part by habituating people to certain ways of acting. Beyond rewards and punishments, role modeling can encourage good habits. Talking openly about corporate values and about a corporate mission with which employees can identify is often effective as well. Rules too, including ethics codes, may enforce good habits, particularly if people understand their rationale. But as Bazerman and Tenbrunsel (2011, chapter 6) point out, rewards and punishments by themselves do not always have the intended effect. Aristotle agrees.

Habituation

Consider how little Philip learns to speak. At first he repeats words in just the contexts in which his parents say them; then he says the words in similar contexts. But in some cases the context is similar in the wrong way. So he says "daddy" when his father is present, but then also when some other man is present. In correcting him, the parents are educating him in the use of the word "man," which he will then use more reliably thereafter, as he gradually acquires the concept man. In due course he develops more difficult concepts, such as those relating to states, events physical and psychological, and even to right or wrong.

Philip extrapolates from the cases in which his initial words have been confirmed: he reacts to cases that are similar to or different from the original ones in important respects. So a dummy is not a man because it is lifeless, and breakfast and lunch are not the same meal because they are eaten at different times. In due course Philip may progress from habitually making correct statements about persons and lunch to learning some rules that allow him to extrapolate from familiar cases: for example, that breakfast is eaten first thing in the morning and lunch around midday.

Philip begins to learn courage by doing as his parents say in taking or avoiding risks, and by following the examples of others. If he follows bad examples, his parents and others correct him, we hope. In this way Philip gets into the habit of performing brave acts, on the whole, but even then he is not fully courageous. For one thing, he makes telling mistakes. He cannot quite distinguish between courage and machismo, for example; so he sometimes takes inappropriate risks because his peers are doing so, or because Andrea is watching. He is fairly good at doing and avoiding the sort of thing his parents have taught him to do and avoid, but he does not extrapolate very well from the paradigm cases. He might act courageously on the football field as a result of hours of practice and playing in games but be terrified of going to the dentist. Even when Philip gets it right and takes the right amount of risk, he does so without having thought about why what he has done is courageous, or about why he should or should not do it.

Philip learns any concept by extrapolation to new situations and actions. When a new case presents itself, we look for important similarities to the old ones that form a basis for framing the new case one way or another. Sometimes the decision is arbitrary. Sometimes there is a solid scientific basis for the decision. Sometimes we extrapolate on a pragmatic basis. If we take the analytic–synthetic distinction seriously, we think that some features attach to things by definition. Aristotle thinks that some similarities are more important than others because they reflect essential rather than accidental differences. So a good act is one that is performed by a good person, and there is nothing arbitrary about the essence of a good person.

Consider the development of one's concept of a human being. Even young children can usually identify and reidentify a person correctly, and can distinguish a person from a robot. But true mastery of the concept requires knowing a great deal about what a person is – the essence, as Aristotle would say. And arguments about what a person is are moral arguments in part.

If I blow the whistle on my boss, is that an act of treachery or of justice? The case is difficult in part because it resembles both cases of treachery and cases of justice. We might be able to state principles giving necessary and sufficient conditions for treachery and others for justice, but they will be of little help in cases that seem to meet the criteria for both. Aristotle's view is that cases like this require practical wisdom for correct framing, and practical wisdom has an emotional component. We might prefer to say instead that in some cases no one way of framing is salient, that instead one needs to be aware of the variety of ways in which each case can be described.

Aristotle is aware that the process of induction does not automatically lead to a coherent concept of the item in question. We use words in ways that differ from their original meanings, or have analogical meanings, or relate differently to some focal concept.[2] All the same, he believes there is such a thing as getting the concept right, that is, understanding the essence of whatever is before us. Aristotle does not believe that this is easy: in some cases there are simple principles for projection; in others, particularly ethical cases, there are no evident and airtight ones. In a disputed case it may be necessary to test our intuitions against a tentative principle for applying the word to decide whether some event or act is a virtuous one.

Crary and Aristotle

Alice Crary (2007), undertaking to show how moral thinking is broader than moral judgment-making, deals with two features that some philosophers find it difficult to attribute to moral language at the same time. We want to say, as moral realists do, that some moral statements are objective; but we also want to say that they are action-guiding.[3] Crary argues that a concept is objective in the broad sense that it determines the same content in different circumstances even if the sameness of content is not determined by reference to some standard external to our discourse. It may be objective from the point of view of the people who use the concept and have a sense of how to use it right and extend it to new circumstances. For while these people may argue about how to use it right, they nevertheless typically believe that there is a fact of the matter about which they are arguing. This analysis includes moral concepts, she claims.

How to deal with new cases is an issue for Crary as for Aristotle. She holds we have "a sensitivity to the importance of similarities and differences," but "there is no question of rigidly specifying the content of the envisioned sensitivity" (p. 41). And moral development is in part a matter of improving that sensitivity, which Aristotle would recognize as part of practical wisdom.

Aristotle deals with the problem of objectivity and action guidance by drawing on his teleological science. He takes it as a fact that a human life has certain ends that are good because they are natural; so to call a trait a virtue is to relate it to a good end and thus both

---

[2] In an important and controversial essay, Owen (1960) discusses how Aristotle deals with this matter.

[3] I am not convinced that there is a problem here. A sign that reads "Wet Paint" is factual but guides one not to sit on the bench. But this is a very long story.

state a fact about it and indicate a reason for having and acting on that trait. Aristotle does not worry about objectivity very much. On the other hand, ethics is not an exact science: for while there are right and wrong answers to ethical questions, we cannot always be sure what they are, and we cannot find them by applying some detailed and reliable formula.

Crary argues that the sensibilities – which, as in Aristotle's case, include emotional reactions – that we bring to bear in speaking and acting on the basis of what we consider important constitute much of what morality is about. She holds that talking about importance in this way, even when the concepts in question are not ones that we normally consider ethical, opens the door to cases in which one is engaged in moral thought (p. 44). We cannot readily separate our assumptions and sensibilities about what is important into the moral and the non-moral. Some of them may seem nonmoral but still be a part of moral thinking in the broader sense on which Crary focuses.

By way of illustration Crary cites Gilbert Ryle's critical views of Jane Austen's *Pride and Prejudice*, among others of her novels (pp. 138–49). Ryle assesses the sort and degree of pride that each of the main characters in *Pride and Prejudice* exhibits and makes it clear that, while not all of their forms are obviously moral – the donnish and passive pride of Mr. Bennet and the "vacuous complacency" of Mr. Collins (p. 141) are not what we would present as standard examples of virtues or vices – they are nevertheless central to who each of the characters is, and linked with the traits that we do readily call virtues or vices.

Aristotle similarly appears not to distinguish our acquisition of the concept man from that of the concept just. In both cases a child gets into the habit of saying the word under the right circumstances – a complicated matter, according to Aristotle, and it takes time to learn how to do it – but then eventually needs to reflect on how it ought to be done, especially in difficult cases and unfamiliar ones. He assimilates moral cases to nonmoral ones at least as much as Crary does. On the Aristotelian view, to identify anything is to identify it as a substance, or a property of a substance, or an event involving substances; in any such case there is some reference, perhaps indirect, to a substance and therefore to a purpose or good end. To be able to identify something as a human being or reidentify it as the same human being requires knowing what a human being is. That necessity, in turn, as we can infer from arguments about abortion, requires dealing with some moral issues. No concept, no human feature worth talking about, is without moral content. For by definition a human being has certain purposes and tends toward certain good end-states, which form the basis of ethics.

Aristotle has a point. Even today we define many psychological features functionally: pathologies are teleological concepts. Aristotle holds that every feature of a human being is essentially related to the whole of the person's life, hence to the purpose of the person's life, hence to the good life, hence to virtue. Consider intelligence, for example. Aristotle distinguishes ethical from intellectual virtues, but all virtues require practical wisdom, which no unintelligent person has. Of practical wisdom we can also say that it knits the traits of a virtuous person together. Aristotle believes, quite reasonably, that flourishing involves more than just what we would consider moral virtues. It includes a sense of humor, for example, and other fairly self-regarding traits. Aristotle would probably accept Ryle's characterization of Mr. Collins's personality traits and would regard them as not contributing to his flourishing. They are part of his character, but they give Elizabeth and us reason to ridicule him, not to hate or fear him.

Skills and habits

The ability to act truly courageously is like a skill, of the sort that a carpenter or a musician might have after years of experience and, in due course, reflection. Perhaps you remember learning to play the piano. When you start learning and your mother makes you practice an hour a day, you are not good at it and you do not enjoy it very much. You do it to avoid bad consequences from your mother. As time goes by, though, your playing improves and you begin to enjoy it. You also become conscious of technique. You learn that playing well is not just a matter of hitting the right notes: expression counts. Eventually you play superbly and get extraordinary pleasure from it. Having learned some of the technical aspects of playing, you can say why Glenn Gould is better than John Tesh.[4] As Newton (1992, p. 359)

---

[4] Yogi Berra once said to a sportswriter who was also an amateur pianist, "We just bought a piano. Can you come over some time and show us how it works?" Berra evidently espoused the principle-based theory of piano playing.

says, employees may develop that way in their jobs: first they follow instructions; then after a time they act by habit; finally, at least in some kinds of job, they understand the purpose of what they are doing and creatively find new ways to do it. It is fair to add that they also come to enjoy it more.

Recall that Aristotle distinguishes between doing (*praxis*) and making (*poiesis*). The former activity can be enjoyed just for itself; the latter is valued for its consequences. When you start learning to play the piano, your activity is a *poiesis*, because its purpose is to please your mother, or at least keep her off your back. Eventually it becomes a *praxis*. We might push Newton's point a bit further and say that, in some jobs at any rate, the purpose becomes not just getting a paycheck but doing the work in a virtuoso way.

An organization might use habituation to discourage sexual harassment by rewarding and punishing good and bad behavior. It is of course possible to make rules that will be useful insofar as they are based on a clear understanding of what sexual harassment is and what is wrong with it. The problem is, notoriously, that it is difficult to say exactly what constitutes harassment; and in the absence of a clear definition, the law may seem to be demanding that people, especially men, walk on eggs. So it often is with rules and principles. But if it were possible to get all male employees to speak and act with respect for women, in due course they might accept them as fellow employees and feel comfortable in treating them accordingly and deplore treating them otherwise. Many men cannot immediately change their attitude about this; but they can act respectfully or courageously or justly for a time, perhaps trying to imitate a role model, until they get into the habit of doing so. They will still make the occasional gaffe, or bend over too far backwards, but they are making progress towards acquiring the virtue. "Assume a virtue if you have it not," Hamlet urges Gertrude. He suggests that she refrain from having sex with Claudius that night, and the next, and over time it will become easier to abstain. "For use can almost change the stamp of nature."[5]

If all goes well with Gertrude, she will not only get into the habit of not having sex with Claudius but also become comfortable with her

---

[5] I follow Audi (2012) in using this passage to make a point about habituation. Aristotle would emphasize that one cannot literally change the stamp of nature, however; hence the "almost."

abstention, and she will be moved not only by her son's importunate emotions but also by considering what is wrong with having sex with Claudius: it is incest, technically, and he is a bad man. In the case of sexual harassment, it is a good thing for a man to get out of the habit of calling women "sweetie" in the workplace and interrupting them all the time in meetings, but true virtue is a matter of acting better because one genuinely and with good reason respects women.

Free will

People of strong character can resist environmental pressures to act against the considered first premises of their practical syllogisms, so they have more autonomy than those who succumb against their better judgment, or just do not recognize the pressures that influence them. Autonomy in this sense – the ability to form and act on intentions that are based on one's well-considered values – is virtually equivalent to practical wisdom, which is a necessary and sufficient condition of good character. But we do not withhold blame from the weak-willed: their incontinence is a fault in them. Character development aims at something better. We are ethically obligated to acquire the right traits and desires and the ability to act on them.

All this tracks with Aristotle, but there is a possible problem in his account. He holds that one's family and *polis* strongly influence character development. If you are fortunate, your parents and fellow citizens will offer you good role models, rewards and punishments, and ethical education. But what if you are not so fortunate? Is it your fault if your family and your *polis* are bad and raise you accordingly? Aristotle claims that you are jointly responsible for your character (*NE* III 5 1114b23), but it is hard to see how you can be responsible for your character at all if you cannot choose to avoid being brought up in a degenerate family or *polis*. In any case, acting on the basis of habit does not seem to be acting autonomously.

Aristotle is well aware of factors that make actions voluntary or involuntary, and thus beyond the reach of praise or blame; that is the topic of *NE* III, especially chapters 1 and 5. Acting under physical compulsion is an example of an involuntary action. But if you do something wrong out of ignorance because you are drunk, it is your fault, because you voluntarily drank to excess (III 5 1113b30–3). Ignorance of a certain kind may also excuse you: you may know that trespassing is wrong while not knowing that you have strayed onto my property. In this case you know the universal but not the particular. (Whether your ignorance is a legal excuse is another matter.) But if you know that selfishness is wrong but fail to see that what you are doing is selfish, you are responsible. Nor does any other sort of weakness of will excuse you. Aristotle says that your choices form your character (III 5 1114a6). If you are responsible for your character in that way, you are also responsible for what appears to you to be good, because your character determines what appears to you to be good (III 5 1114b1). If demanding more than your share seems to you simply a case of standing up for yourself, or if you are insensitive to some ethically salient aspect of a situation, there is a problem about your character.

The issue of causal determinism

Aristotle does not contemplate the determinist objection, familiar in recent centuries, that the decisions we make, even as we develop a character, are themselves the products of unknown preexisting causal conditions beyond our control and knowledge. One likely reason for Aristotle's apparent failure to face this problem is that he does not embrace causal determinism generally, or understand causality as we do.

Yet Aristotle's position on free will is not far off the mark. It makes sense to think of free will as the ability to form and act rationally on intentions that are in turn based on rational values and desires. Weakness of will is a good example of the absence of free will, since your will is weak rather than free and effective. In a state of weakness of will you are caused by inappropriate factors in your environment or by your own psychological pathologies not to act rationally, and the reasons you offer for your actions are rationalizations at best. On this account, free will is a matter of degree. So, arguably, is the appropriateness of praise and blame, because one may be more or less susceptible to them. (But the appropriateness of praise and blame does not track precisely with its effectiveness, or with freedom of the will.) Paradoxical as it may seem, you may not be able to decide whether to have freedom of the will; you may find it difficult to get into the habit of acting rationally and therefore virtuously. Your ability to act freely can be a matter of luck in upbringing or in some other respect.

Aristotle does not believe that you are always a passive victim of your desires, however: weakness of will is not universal. As we have noted, he does believe that base people are victims of desires that they wish that they did not have, because bad things have become pleasant for them (*NE* IX 4 1166b23–9). Their first-order desires are not under the control of their second-order desires. That we must avoid in our moral development. Elster (1985) advocates "self-management" to keep inappropriate desires and emotions from diverting us from our most rational intentions. This may involve staying away from situations in which we are vulnerable, as well as what Elster calls strategic preference formation, noted in Chapter 3: we cultivate certain desires that support us in acting according to our values. This cultivation presumably includes getting into the habit of acting as if one had certain preferences and certain reasons for action and thereby eventually coming to have them. So we develop habits of desire and of reasons for action, and not just habits of action. (See Werhane *et al.*, 2011, for further advice along these lines.) Notice that managing yourself in this way requires having a fairly clear notion of the way you want your life to go. As Aristotle says, you need to aspire to a life defined by desires better than those of a child (*NE* X 3 1174a1–4) or a base person.

Rational choice is characteristic of human beings, and a good thing in itself. You are responsible for your choices to a significant degree. But Aristotle links human nature, rationality, virtue, and *eudaimonia* so closely that he leaves little or no room for free choices that are bad. These are the result of the process of choice going wrong, as in the case of weakness of will, which undermines your autonomy. Whether or not we entirely agree with Aristotle, most of us would say that people in the grip of some pathology, including severe weakness of will, have autonomy that is so sharply limited as to be unworthy of the name.

One might be tempted to object that this account simply ignores causal determinism. For how can I be free to act when all of my actions are the results of prior causal conditions? But it is far from clear that a caused action is an unfree action. If my action is caused by my knowledge and my sound and careful deliberation based on values that take appropriate ethical and other practical considerations into account, it is as free as an action can be. A certain action that I take – say, applying my car's brakes – might be caused in part by my seeing a toddler walking out onto the street and in part by my aversion to killing innocent children. There is no reason to believe that the presence of these causal conditions, my vision and my values, undermines my freedom.[6] Now if I had hit the child because I had poor vision or was in the grip of an ungovernable compulsion to kill innocent people, I would have been performing an unfree action. Whether my good vision and rationality in one case or my bad vision and irrationality in the other are results of my upbringing is irrelevant to the question of freedom. Kant calls this sort of approach a subterfuge, but it matters that you have the ability to make a rational decision even if it is caused by some previous conditions of your eyes and brain. Does it matter that something causes your 20–20 vision, which in turn causes your rescuing the toddler? Could it be otherwise?

Rationality has a central place in this account of free will. If virtue is nothing but good habits, without reflection, then even the virtuous do not control their own lives. But becoming virtuous is a matter of rationality as well as habit.

Rational reflection

Getting beyond habit

Aristotle says that we proceed from habit to reflection on the way to virtue (X 9 1180a7–12), but his account of weakness of will shows that our progress does not take a straight line. It is possible for me to come to a reasonable conclusion about how to deal courageously with the boss but still be too weak of will to do it, possibly because I am in the habit of keeping safely quiet. Duhigg (2012, pp. 129–32) argues that sometimes you increase your willpower by developing new habits to drive the old ones out. Like Gertrude, you may assume a virtue, take a deep breath, and with trepidation say to the boss, "Margaret, there may be some problems with what you're suggesting." You keep doing this, and over time it will become easier to act courageously as you know you should. Still, knowing when and how to challenge Margaret is not only a matter of habit.

It is worth noting that Duhigg (pp. 138f.) finds evidence that one can strengthen one's willpower across the board. So, contrary to what Doris and others may lead us to expect, it is at least possible to gain

---

[6] Recall that these factors are real causes. See Davidson (2001, Essay 1).

courage in the office, in the dentist's chair, and elsewhere – and develop other virtuous habits at the same time.

So long as virtue is just a habit, Philip is likely to be courageous in some situations but not others. He will cheerfully accept hard contact in a football game, since he has played a lot of football, but he resists the dentist's drill and shrinks from asking Andrea to the prom.[7] Aristotle would say that Philip is not truly courageous if he is cowardly or reckless off the football field. To be fully courageous requires Philip to have a clear idea of what his values are and to be concerned about them – to be concerned, that is, about the kind of person he is. Knowing what courage is and why it is important to act courageously enables Philip to be confident in his belief about what is the courageous thing to do in a particular situation. Clearly all this demands a high level of rationality. This point seems to suggest that what looks like courage in a bad cause is not true courage, for it is based on false beliefs or untenable values. That is what Aristotle says about "courage" shown for bad reasons or in a bad cause. It might be more courageous to refuse to fight in an unjust war than to fight in it.

Socrates was wrong in thinking that knowing what is the courageous thing to do is a sufficient condition of doing it. He was probably also wrong in thinking that it is possible to give a neat, unitary definition of courage or anything else. But being able to give some sort of true account of what courage is, perhaps by stating certain v-rules, surely contributes to one's ability to act courageously. If Philip is genuinely courageous, he knows that courage requires him to speak candidly when the boss asks his opinion even if she will probably not enjoy hearing it. That is worth knowing, but it is not enough. He must know what courage looks like in practice. If the boss proposes to do something that Philip thinks is a mistake, Philip should state his reasons for disagreeing with the proposal, but he should not call the boss an idiot. In some cases Philip will state his objections but then get with the program if the boss does not budge. In other cases Philip will dig in his heels, or perhaps resign, or perhaps blow the whistle. True courage sometimes requires Philip to be very practical and extremely wise, and to have supportive emotions as well. His courage entails acting at the

---

[7] Doris and others think that this is the way things usually are, because people are not rational enough to regiment their beliefs and desires according to reason. Aristotle himself would concede that that is true of many people.

right time, in the right way, with respect to the right person, and so on.

Suppose that Philip has good reason to believe that in the long run the boss will get over her initial irritation and respect him for challenging her, but his will is weak, and he decides not to challenge her because the thought of it makes him very nervous. In this and many other ways we are all sometimes irrational. Our values and some of our desires are inconsistent: we want what we wish we did not want, sometimes because emotion plays an inappropriate role; and we act on desires that are inconsistent with our values rather than on those we know should be guiding our actions. As we have discussed, a variety of factors can undermine our virtues, as we weaken or rationalize. That is one reason why it is important to have the right emotions.

Aristotle seems to believe that our emotions are creatures of habit. To become accustomed to something helps us lose our fear of it, our disgust at it, our indignation about it. Emotions of this sort cannot easily be reasoned away. On the contrary, we are more likely to cast about for a rationalization of emotion-based prejudices. But Jones may stop feeling unmanned and resentful as he gets accustomed to reporting to Smith and to thinking of her not as a woman but as a good manager, assuming that she is.

What rationality adds

If you are a virtuous person, you have a rational basis for what you do. In particular, you understand not only the importance of (say) honesty, but also something of its purpose, of how it contributes to our lives together. But to say that virtue entails rationality is not to say, nor is it true, that the genuinely virtuous person has achieved the sort of knowledge of courage or benevolence that a mathematician has of the triangle. On the contrary, ethical maturity is a matter of getting beyond attentively following rules. At a certain point you are on your own, in the sense that you make decisions without having a principle to tell you exactly what to do. Hank Saporsky had no manual to consult before deciding to insist that Deborah be sent to London. If he had been asked why Deborah ought to go, he could have given an insightful answer, no doubt having something to do with the importance of a corporate commitment to her and others like her. But his answer would not have proved that he was doing the right thing. It was not like deciding to fire a consultant who had been systematically cheating on time and expense reports. It was a new situation, one that did not match any previous situation feature for feature. It did not require new virtues, but it did require Hank to think anew and independently. One reason for praising Hank's character is that he is open to continuing development of his virtues as new situations arise. He can deal with these situations because his decisions are grounded in his character, which can adapt without wavering.

You want to avoid the situation in which, like the base person, you find pleasant what you despise: in that case your lowest-order desires are out of control. In the opposite case, you have reached the pinnacle of adult education when you are able to address the highest-order question, "What sort of person do I want to be?" I argued in Chapter 3 that the sort of person you are determines what your interests are; so the Aristotelian question is in effect asking, What do you want your interests to be? I noted that according to Aristotle you will not want to have childish or shameful interests; you want interests that are consistent with your fully developed humanity. This question would not be out of place if you are taking a business ethics course. Do you want to be the sort of person who can enjoy only overwhelming financial success? Or the sort of person who enjoys a life in which work plays an important but not dominant role and in which that work offers challenge, variety, growth, association with interesting people, and compensation that lets you live comfortably? The question is not which one you prefer. It is a higher-order question about which one you would choose to prefer if you could make that choice. It is not a straightforward question about self-interest, though in Chapter 3 we saw some evidence from positive psychologists that the latter sort of life is happier.

It is characteristic of the human being and of no other creature to be able to construct a character. A good character is an achievement of reason. You are responsible for understanding that it is not good for you to pursue the pleasures of a child or of a base person, and for becoming the sort of person who wants to act accordingly. You are responsible for seeing your life as a whole, not a mere succession of experiences, and seeing to it that it is appropriate for a creature that is a rational and sociable citizen in a community of rational and sociable citizens. As in the case of physical health, you start with exercise, which gradually you come to enjoy doing well.

What is natural is not easy

Becoming the right kind of person and acting accordingly is natural, in the sense that one is born with the capacity for it, but it is also difficult. Habituation is necessary but will not suffice; the process requires rationality in working out what one ought to do. Aristotle's model of rationality is the practical syllogism, which begins with a statement of what one wants and ends with an action. This seems straightforward: I figure out what is good for me and act accordingly. But as we have seen, Aristotle himself acknowledges in his discussion of weakness of the will that it just does not always work that way. As a host of social psychologists have argued, most people are not very good at working out what is good for them or, even if they succeed in that, at acting accordingly.

Consider Smith, who gets on well with people of other ethnic groups as well as her own. When she was a child, her parents told her that all races are equal, and they policed her language as well as her actions. They saw to it that she became accustomed to hanging out in diverse company, and she now enjoys doing so. When she says that she judges people by the content of their character, she means it and acts on it. She is in a better position morally than a person who has acquired no such habits, and who reacts to human differences in a way that reflects our hard-wired tendency to favor our in-group. (On this issue see Messick, 1998.) But there are some racial issues that are not amenable to habit-formed intuitions: think of affirmative action and racial profiling, for example. She must be able to reason about these issues and to reflect on her own perceptions and emotions. And if she is a just person, she will abjure not only racial prejudice but also prejudice against evangelical Christians and wealthy Republicans.[8]

Not all instances of a virtue are psychologically similar. That is why mere habituation will not create virtues that carry over from one sort of situation to another. Military training, even with live ammunition, will not make soldiers truly courageous. The willingness to take risks can be learned as a habit more easily than can the willingness to take the calculated, justified risks that courage requires and of which recklessness is incapable. Feeding the dog every day is a habit, and

---

[8] Respectful and open-minded disagreement, which we shall discuss in Chapter 7, is not the same as prejudice.

not necessarily a sign of the virtue of conscientiousness. Understanding one's obligations – to one's dog, to one's employer, and to others – and faithfully meeting them is a sign of true conscientiousness, developed with reflective intelligence (Elster, 1985, pp. 15–26). It is the ability to reflect that brings together an assortment of learned dispositions and creates a virtue. That ability may also create virtues by separating states that are psychologically similar. For example, reflection may teach you that there is a difference between standing up for what you believe and being intolerant of dissent.

To the extent that Philip is able to reason about what he ought to fear rather than just relying on habit, he will understand why he should not fear the dentist any more than he fears large tacklers when he is carrying the ball. Of course just knowing that the pain of the drill will be less than the pain of being tackled is not enough to reduce his fear; we know how weakness of will can operate. It may turn out that the role of reason in this case will be to make him go to the dentist in spite of his fear, so that he eventually gets accustomed to the drill and thus less fearful of it. If so, reason requires the assistance of habit.

It is important for people with some good habits to consider why these habits are virtuous – that is, for example, what is involved in being just and how it contributes to a good life. From this consideration will emerge some broad principles concerning the nature and application of justice. Simply knowing these principles will not make the agent just, according to Aristotle, though it will help. As we have discussed, one must come to see people and situations anew, in situations that do not easily fit the principles as we have understood them.

This is not as easy as it looks, according to Bazerman and Tenbrunsel (2011, chapter 4) and many other social psychologists. We convince ourselves that we are fair-minded people and that our judgments on women and others are made on the basis of pertinent evidence, however prejudiced they may actually be. But one can avoid even the most obvious inferences from one's espoused principles. Think of our enlightened Founding Fathers, who in the Declaration of Independence declared it self-evident that all men are created equal but later in that document charged King George with having encouraged slaves in America to revolt.

Here we return to a point broached in Chapter 1. Is it so hard to be virtuous – to have virtues that cover a diverse range of cases and to avoid self-serving rationalization – that it is an unrealistic ideal?

Aristotle does suggest that few succeed in being wholly virtuous. One might infer from this that Aristotelian virtue ethics is disqualified as a viable approach because it fails the test of attainability. I do not draw that inference. There are a few people who really are virtuous, and they can serve as role models for the rest of us, who sometimes act virtuously because we have some sense of what virtue is and are capable of partly satisfying our desire to be people of good character. We try to become more like the heroes of virtue, including the great religious prophets; we fail, but we make some progress in that direction.

What managers can do

If free will essentially involves the capacity to deliberate and act rationally, then the problem of free will is at least in part an empirical matter, on which certain social psychologists have something to say. For managers and management theorists those findings will have practical implications. If one is to influence the behavior of employees and others, it is useful to know to what extent they do act on their values, as opposed to mere habit or social pressure of some kind. Changing behavior by appealing to rational self-interest and encouraging willpower does not work well in every kind of situation. Baumeister and Tierney (2011, chapter 10) give willpower its due, but they acknowledge that, for example, losing weight successfully is largely a matter of manipulating one's physical and social environment and oneself, as a technique of what Elster calls self-management. This is consistent with Duhigg's view that you sometimes increase your willpower by developing new habits to drive the old ones out. (None of this will be news to Weight Watchers or to Alcoholics Anonymous, or to Doris and others, for that matter.)

To get employees into good habits may be a step in the direction of making them more virtuous. Keeping them from temptation and offering no incentives for bad behavior will help. But there are ethical issues here.[9] To motivate employees in ways that ignore or undermine their values – managing by fear, for example, or lies – is a form of manipulation that undermines the character of agent and victim alike. There is

---

[9] It should be clear by now that in saying this I am not claiming that in discussions of psychology and ethics we can readily distinguish the empirical from the normative.

a moral dilemma, however. We believe that people ought to be treated with the presumption that they are rational, but there is evidence that many are not. We may say that good managers will encourage and reward rationality, but that may be difficult, particularly if managers themselves are not rational.

But Aristotle is not satisfied with finding the most effective management tools. He wants to show how to achieve the kind of rationality that supports virtue. This requires adult education in what he calls dialectic, to which we now turn. As we do so, I must acknowledge that there is controversy about exactly what Aristotle means by dialectic and whether he consistently uses it in *NE* is controversial. (See Salmieri, 2009, for example.) I use the word to refer to the method that Aristotle explicitly uses in *NE* I 4 and at least occasionally elsewhere.

Dialectic

Fully developed character involves, among other things, making good judgments in part on the basis of good principles. Aristotle holds that one arrives at acceptable judgments and principles by the process of dialectic. The process starts with common opinions (*koina*), or at least the opinions of those widely regarded as wise people.[10] The objective is to have as premises of practical syllogisms consistent principles that justify correct opinions. (See *NE* VII 1 1145b4–8, for example.) This is not to say, however, that we can readily use these principles to guide our actions in complex or novel situations.

We have noted that Aristotle's view, laid out in *NE* II 3 and 4, is that a good upbringing that inculcates good habits prepares one to consider definitions of the virtues. A person who is well brought up and therefore has good habits and appropriate emotions is capable of making correct judgments about some individual cases of virtue and vice, and capable of making somewhat more general judgments as well. But Aristotle undertakes to show how we can justify these judgments by coming to understand justificatory principles (*archai*; the singular is *arche*), which typically take the form of definitions of virtues, which are or generate v-rules. We collect common opinions, giving preference to those of wise people, and then look for principles that show why they are true and thus justify them – or at any rate many of them, since

---

[10] The most influential treatment of this topic is Owen (1986).

some will be shown to be false. When Aristotle uses the word *arche*, which may be translated as *principle* or *beginning*, he sometimes has in mind what we would consider moral principles, while at other times he is thinking of particular moral judgments. The ambiguity is confusing, but he explicitly claims that a starting point of an argument that leads to a principle is called a beginning (*arche*) while the principle itself is a beginning in a different sense: it is the starting point of the justification of a particular judgment. (See *NE* I 7 1098b2–8, for example.) He sometimes distinguishes the two kinds of beginning by saying that particular judgments are known to us, whereas the broader principles are known by nature. So the broader principles justify some of our particular judgments but rule others out.[11] If a principle generates a particular judgment that is strongly at odds with our intuitions, or perceptions, as Aristotle sometimes calls them, we have good reason to abandon either the principle or the intuitions. He does not use any term that we can translate as "intuition," but I shall use it to refer to individual perceptual or ethical beliefs in a way that I think is consistent with Aristotle's analysis as well as with modern usage. "This woman is incompetent" and "Consultants should always tell the truth" are examples of intuitions in my sense. I have no special perceptual faculty in mind.

Here we may think of Rawls's (1971, pp. 48–51) reflective equilibrium: you compare your principles with your judgments about particular cases and adjust one or both in an effort to make them consistent. Neither the principles nor the judgments are prior; each is subject to adjustment by reference to the other. If your principles are nothing more than the result of rationalizing the intuitions on which you act – a common occurrence, according to the likes of Haidt – they do no justificatory work. On the other hand, if you embrace principles that have no connection to any plausible intuitions, they will have little credibility.

Aristotle thinks of common beliefs as being widely held among intelligent people in a fairly homogeneous community. He is aware that there are barbarians, including cannibals, who do not share these beliefs, but he gives no sign of thinking that they might possibly

---

[11] Aristotle does not say in the *Nicomachean Ethics* that the particular opinions that are *archai* may turn out to need correcting, but he does say elsewhere that what is "known to us" may be false (see *Metaphysics* VII 3 1029b8–10 and Irwin's translation of Aristotle (1999, p. 176).

be right and wise Greeks wrong. It is indeed hard to argue with those with whom we disagree about everything. You and I can reach agreement on many important points only if we can start our conversation with something that we hold in common. Aristotle does believe that there is much on which we can agree because there is much that seems intuitively obvious to all of those with whom we converse. But our initial intuitions may require some elaboration or even alteration.

An example of dialectic

It is not unusual for a discussion in an ethics class to proceed dialectically. The instructor asks students what they think the purpose of ethics is. Some student says that the purpose of ethics is to make people in general happy. The instructor asks whether the purpose of ethics implies any principles. A student then offers the ethical principle that one ought always to act so as to maximize the world's happiness. The instructor then tells a story about a deputy sheriff who is investigating a killing that appears to have been done by a homeless man, the scourge of his village with his begging, public drunkenness, and other petty offenses. There is evidence enough to convict him. But before the deputy can make the arrest, he finds further evidence that incontrovertibly shows that the victim was killed by the town's leading citizen and greatest benefactor, a woman who accidentally took a combination of medications that caused her to lose her mind for a short time, during which she did the killing. The homeless man and the civic-minded woman have forgotten everything. The deputy can easily suppress the damning evidence. The instructor asks: If the deputy is a utilitarian, which of the two will he arrest?

Most students will say that utilitarianism requires the arrest of the homeless man, but they also believe that to do so would be wrong because it would be unfair. This intuition is strong enough to undermine the utilitarian principle as it is stated. Some students try to save a version of the utilitarian principle by pointing out that there is always a risk of the woman's guilt being discovered later, with results that no utilitarian could welcome. Better to make a policy of punishing only the guilty. But the intuition that will not go away is that the woman rather than the man should be punished because she is guilty and he is innocent, that, quite aside from the possible consequences, it is just unfair to punish the innocent rather than the guilty.

Some students may also argue that the deputy is sworn to uphold the law and therefore has a moral obligation to do so, and that the villagers have a right to expect him to do so. This obligation and this right also trump utilitarian considerations.

By now it is clear that the utilitarian principle needs some modification. The intuitions are too strong for it. But the instructor might encourage the students to scrutinize some of the intuitions. Must a government servant such as a police officer or a soldier uphold the law in every case? Our strong intuition is that Deputy Menendez of the Pinal County Sheriff's Department has that obligation, and we may support a principle to just that effect. But what about a deputy sheriff in the American South before the civil rights movement? Should he always follow orders, including instructions to treat black suspects much more harshly than white ones? Some will say yes, others no. So it is not immediately clear how to reach consensus – whether to adjust the principle or the intuition.

We can imagine a dialectical conversation outside the classroom as well. Suppose your friend Jones is in the habit of being conscientious about feeding the dog every day but not about showing up for work on time every day. Then you might ask Jones why he is conscientious about feeding the dog; then, once he has given you his reasons for being conscientious about that task, you can point out to him that the same reason applies in the case of getting to work. That may not be the end of the matter, but it will help him understand why his conscientiousness ought to apply more broadly.

Introducing facts

Daniels (1979) argues that in dialectic – or, as he calls his version of it, wide reflective equilibrium – we must take certain facts into account. Some who argue that the deputy sheriff is justified in beating an African American demonstrator because all deputies are under orders to do so are motivated in part by their belief that African Americans are congenitally inferior to whites in a way that justifies treating the races differently – that is, treating African Americans more harshly. The principle that they say justifies the beating is "Deputies should always obey orders." The principle that actually supports their view of the case is "Blacks should be brought to heel." Clearly there are some facts in play, but they are in dispute.

Racists' intuitions, too, differ from those of nonracists in a way that would interest Aristotle. The former would describe the beating as "subduing a troublemaker in obedience to orders"; the nonracists would describe it as "beating an innocent man." Neither description is inaccurate, but there is something incomplete and even obtuse about the first one. It seems not to be the result of what Aristotle calls correct perception, which is a function of good character.

The example suggests that one's *archai* of both kinds, intuitions and principles, can affect each other. They surely can, and in a way that shows that dialectic is far from straightforward. I may feel strongly that my intuition is right even when it is not. I may believe in a racist principle that appears in my intuition: when I see this situation, it matters to me that the victim is black, and I describe it accordingly. And my racist principle is the result of induction from many cases in which my intuition has been that some black person is behaving badly, and that intuition may have been supported by the norms of my racist community. In the process of dialectic I must compare my racist principles with others having to do with equality and deserving, and I must examine my intuitions and see how well they fit with the facts of the case. Of course my intuitions will affect my acceptance or rejection of the facts of the case. So I may claim not to be a racist and say that this particular person, who happens to be African American, was obviously asking for trouble. This is the kind of false perception that Aristotle says indicates a flaw in my character.

The limits of dialectic

Even if we reach consensus on principles, it does not follow that we shall agree on how to apply them. Recall that Aristotle does not believe that our knowledge of ethical principles is unassailable, or their application always straightforward. He takes them as seriously as a doctor (*NE* X 9 1180b7–23) or a businessperson (*NE* III 3 1112b4–7) or a comedian (*NE* IV 8 1028a23–34) must take seriously the principles of money-making or medicine or comedy, but also knows how to treat different situations differently. Ethics is more like carpentry than geometry (*NE* I 7 1098a29–34). The distinction is important: we know just how to apply the principles of geometry to a geometry problem, even a problem in actual space and time.[12]

If I know a little about plane geometry, I can easily work out the area of a parcel of land if it is rectangular and I can measure the sides. If I know a little about medicine, I may not be able to offer a diagnosis on the basis of my knowledge of a patient's symptoms. A good diagnosis requires skill, which requires experience and intelligence. Physicians often encounter conditions that are not the same as conditions that they have seen before, and that therefore cannot be assessed by straightforward application of any diagnostic rules. True skill is the ability to deal with these new conditions.

Successful dialectic leads to good principles and good intuitions. But the latter, though they must be consistent with one's principles, must also be based on correct perception. For example, one must know whether a southern deputy's thrashing of an African American suspect was a case of obeying the law or being cruel, whether a particular act was a matter of betraying one's company or refusing to participate in unacceptable practices. If you believe that a southern deputy sheriff acted lawfully and therefore correctly, your belief may be influenced by an emotional reaction that you would not have had if the victim had been white. That emotional reaction is largely a result of habit: you have grown up being instructed that blacks are inferior and therefore not entitled to the same treatment as whites, and you have grown accustomed to believing, feeling, and acting accordingly. Dialectical argument will put pressure on your intuitions about race, but possibly not enough to change them. As intuitions depend in part on emotions and emotions are in part creatures of habit, your intuitive reaction to Jackson – your seeing him as a good manager rather than a black man – will require getting into the habit of treating him that way and in due course thinking of him that way.

Werhane *et al.* (2011, p. 113) refer to this sort of understanding when they discuss moral imagination, which "entails perceiving norms, social roles, and relationships entwined in any situation." Described this way, moral imagination is similar to what Aristotle calls correct perception in an ethical context, which we might call moral perception:

---

[12] Many present-day virtue ethicists agree. Nussbaum (1990), Hursthouse (1999), Foot (1997), and others argue that we can apply principles but must be wise about it.

one sees the salient features of the situation, and those features will often include norms, roles, and relationships. So, for example, Hank sees Deborah as a promising employee and himself as a senior partner of a firm that values professional standards.

Sometimes, however, familiar relationships and principles do not tell one what to do in a new and complex situation (see Annas (2011, pp. 18f., 74) in interpreting Aristotle; and Werhane (1999, p. 93)). Suppose you are considering whether to send Deborah to work with people who have a demonstrable prejudice against women and will lose confidence in Bell Associates if she fails. Your intuition in this situation is incompatible with the familiar principle that consultants should be assigned on the basis of probable success with a client. So either the intuition or that principle must yield. If Hank decides to send Deborah to this client, his intuition has some credibility in that he is a person of practical wisdom. But you seldom get to the point at which you can say with perfect confidence that your intuition is a clear application of an unexceptionable principle, and the principle that you do have will have somewhat indefinite conditions. Then eventually you will probably face a situation that introduces new conditions. For that you will require practical wisdom, which operates beyond the straightforward application of available principles.

Organizing dialectic

Dialectic typically involves other people, though you can think dialectically on your own. It is a familiar truth that there is much to be said for having your ideas challenged and for hearing those of others. Another important advantage of having another party to the conversation is that it reduces the probability of rationalization, that great enemy of rationality in ethics. According to Lerner and Tetlock (2003, p. 433; quoted in Haidt, 2012, p. 76), "exploratory thought," a reasoned consideration of available options, is possible only when the thinker or decision-maker faces a well-informed, truth-seeking audience whose views are unknown. Otherwise the purpose of the conversation is likely to be not the truth but persuading the other party and perhaps oneself as well, or just winning. Aristotle probably had such ideal conversations in the Academy and the Lyceum; that would help account for his faith in dialectic. Philosophers sometimes come close to these conditions by undertaking conversations with intelligent people who may disagree with them.

There is controversy about whether groups are better than individuals at ethical reasoning. (See, e.g., Abdolmohammadi and Reeves, 2003.) It would be hard to show that they do, since the conclusion would have to rest on a morally contestable notion of what counts as improvement. If we could reach a consensus on that issue, we would have to examine a number of kinds of reasoning, including dialectic, that groups might undertake.

Rare, however, is the organization in which conversations of this sort regularly take place. If you are a good manager, you will get better advice from your subordinates if they know that you care greatly about the issue under discussion, that you know the pertinent facts, and that you have not made up your mind. But if there are multiple advisers in one conversation, there will usually be some whose overriding goal will be to defeat the others. It takes a good manager to control and learn from that sort of situation.

Successful dialectic improves one's principles and one's intuitions. Some people seem to have reliable intuitions,[13] but the notion that there is any such thing as expert intuition is a contested one.

Expert intuition: Deborah again

Kahneman (2011) distinguishes between what he calls System 1 and System 2 thinking. The former is fast, automatic, intuitive, and more influential than we think, and therefore the source of much irrationality. System 2 thinking is slower, more deliberative, usually more rational, "lazy" in not readily involving itself in one's intentional activity, and much less influential in guiding our thought than we think, or hope. In Aristotelian terms, System 1 thinking is about *archai* in the sense of individual opinions. A minor premise of a practical syllogism might be a product of System 1 thinking. On the whole, System 2 thinking is about *archai* in the sense of principles, such as those that can be major premises of practical syllogisms, though one can think carefully and rationally about individual judgments as well.

Aristotle's treatment of weakness of will shows that he understands the strength of one's immediate and irrational reaction to what is

---

[13] This is what Gladwell (2005) writes about.

delicious or otherwise tempting but not consistent with our considered values. The practical syllogism is a model of rational thought, but it does not describe how we always deliberate. Those who do deliberate and act rationally have not only rational values (e.g., they understand that dry food is good for humans or, we might say, that a virtuous person is honest) but also correct perceptions (e.g., that this is dry food, or that some action one is contemplating is dishonest). This ability to see an action for the sort of action it is – that is, to see the ethically best description of it, which typically identifies a principle under which it falls – is part of moral imagination, a desired outcome of dialectic, by which we not only find the best possible principles but sharpen our intuitions.

Kahneman too, for all he says about System 1 thinking, seems to agree with Aristotle in countenancing rationality at the level of intuition. He and Klein (Kahneman, 2011, chapter 22) agree that there is such a thing as expert intuition, though they argue that it is less widespread than the would-be experts themselves believe. Expert chess players have it: they can look at a board and just see threats and opportunities that mediocre players cannot see. Clinical psychologists surprisingly often do not have it: their predictions are usually less good than statistical predictions based on few parameters, as Meehl (Kahneman, chapter 21) showed. Kahneman and Klein argue that true expertise requires an environment regular enough to be predictable and prolonged practice that enables the expert to learn the regularities, particularly through feedback.

What does this tell us about what Aristotle calls perception and Werhane calls moral imagination in the context of ethically significant and complex situations? To begin with, we should guard against overconfidence. We can say that a practically wise person, a participant in dialectic, is one who is good at applying principles to complex situations by virtue of an ability to see similarities between one act or situation and another. The practically wise person sees that certain norms or certain obligations associated with roles or relationships apply in new situations as they applied in significantly similar cases earlier (recall what Aristotle says about Pericles and doctors), though there is no authoritative guidance on which similarities really count.

This is no common ability, and you will have reason to be skeptical if I express great confidence in my own judgment in hard cases. But consider Hank Saporsky again. He appears to have identified a feature of Deborah's situation whose importance had escaped the notice of Greg. He realized that Deborah was a young and somewhat inexperienced consultant with great potential for growth and contribution to Bell Associates, and that she therefore needed and deserved the strong support of the organization. He had been in this sort of situation before, and on the basis of his experience had come to believe that visible support makes a great difference to a consultant's long-term success. He had no prejudices that would prevent him from taking this fact seriously. And he was ready to take responsibility for his decision and its consequences.

Whether Hank drew an inference from prolonged practice in a sufficiently regular environment is plausible, though not certain. If asked to defend his decision, he might have said something like this: "Over the years I've come to believe that our confidence in our excellent young people is self-fulfilling, and that we don't determine excellence on the basis of gender. I've also noticed that clients and others who are prejudiced are able to set aside their prejudices for individuals who impress them in the way Deborah has shown she can impress a client. And anyway, what's the downside here? We're not exactly betting the firm."

That explanation does not fully reveal Hank's flexibility. In a somewhat different situation he would probably have acted somewhat differently. Deborah might have been less skilled, or Arnold more so. The clients might have been Saudi rather than British. The firm might not have been committed to its female consultants. In those cases he might have acted differently. He acted with an eye on the time, the place, the clients, and other details that had to be right for him to make the decision that he made. His decision was intuitive, but he was confident of his intuitions as expressing his values under the circumstances. As a PhD psychologist, he could see patterns in cases of unfair discrimination, but he was also alive to these crucial details, which differed from case to case. That is what a person of practical wisdom can do; it is what is involved in hitting the mean. If Kahneman is right, that kind of practical wisdom is rare indeed.

Facts and dialectic in Aristotle

In the case of what Daniels (1979) calls wide reflective equilibrium we bring in pertinent science and other facts as background. Irwin

(1988, especially chapters 1–3) finds in Aristotle what he calls strong dialectic, which resembles wide reflective equilibrium in that it too incorporates pertinent facts but also Aristotle's analysis of them. Aristotle's metaphysical works supply him with a conception of substance (it is the individual essence) that derives from common opinion but is superior to it because it makes clearer sense of it. The notion that a substance is identifiable through change by virtue of the persistence of its essence and that a human being is a substance with an essence underlies Aristotle's arguments in *De Anima*, his primary work on psychology. So when Aristotle undertakes dialectical inquiry in the *Nicomachean Ethics*, he is dealing not only from common opinion but also from his own views about human nature and the good life. Not least important of them is that humans have natural ends, which help determine the nature of the excellent life. These views do not radically undermine commonly held opinions, but usually sharpen them.

Recall, for example, that Aristotle dismisses the preference fulfillment conception of human good by saying (*NE* X 3 1174a2–4) that no one would choose to live a life with the intellect of a child and a child's idea of fun. Why not? Can Aristotle be sure that any reader would concur? But Aristotle has already argued, with his metaphysical views in the background, that the excellent life is about actualizing one's human capacities. We may be inclined to agree with him; if so, our assent will probably have something to do with our own consideration of what makes a life worth living, based in part on our own views of the nature of humankind. We do not envy the happy idiot.

Similarly, when we consider business ethics dialectically, we have as background some notions of the purposes of business and of what is likely to achieve those purposes. Most business ethicists accept the increasingly widespread view that capitalism is a source of prosperity but that it must be restrained in some areas. Most of us believe that work and autonomy can be mutually reinforcing but often are not and sometimes cannot be. Most of us oppose discrimination on the basis of irrelevant personal attributes. Most of us can identify instances of bad behavior in organizations and in markets. It is important to have some guidelines for thinking more thoroughly about those issues; so, as I shall argue in Chapters 6 and 7, there is a place for dialectic in a business ethics class and beyond.

Ethical progress

We make ethical progress as our moral perception improves. For example, many men, but not all, can now look at a woman in the workplace and see a manager rather a girl who has been given a management position. Many white people, but not all, can now see Barack Obama as President of the United States rather than as an African American. This is in part a matter of learning new facts, but also a matter of giving certain facts new prominence. When we think of Deborah, we think of her first as a well-qualified fellow professional; from our point of view, that is an essential fact about her, and her being a female is secondary. We might not have done so in 1977.

Our emotional reaction, a crucial part of moral perception, is part of how we see Deborah. If we resent her success, or experience a feeling of sexual attraction that makes it hard to follow her presentations, or are put off by the color of her lipstick, we will have a hard time taking her seriously as a colleague. In fact our attitudes may influence how we judge her work. It is often hard to change people's perceptions overnight: they tend to be impervious to new information, which can usually be reinterpreted or filtered or ignored, and they cling to information that confirms their biases. When Jones raises his voice, one thinks, he is being tough; when Smith does so, she is being hysterical.

Suppose I believe that women should not be management consultants, that they and society are better off if they become teachers or nurses until they marry. You might try to use dialectic to change my mind. You could start by getting me to admit that justice requires that jobs be distributed according to qualifications. Then you could try to get me to admit that there are at least some women who have the necessary qualifications for management positions, and that therefore women should be judged on their own merits. But I might respond that the nuclear household is the basis of a good society and that it requires full-time wives and mothers to keep it flourishing; so women should not become managers and undermine the flourishing of the nuclear family, hence of society. This claim is not easily refuted, in part because it is the sort of claim that people believe because they want to. So we might be inclined to say that dialectic works best among those (few) who are able to clear their minds of prejudice, typically by a process that involves emotional change. Habituation is the obvious way to change one's emotions, but they are more easily changed if one understands that they are irrational.

We can at least try to clear our minds of prejudice. And libertarian conservatives who take Milton Friedman seriously ought to be downright eager to acknowledge that Bell Associates should hire and promote on the basis of what is best for the firm, not for society as a whole. If so, then a libertarian conservative should be opposed to using "Deborah is a woman" as a premise in any practical syllogism invoked in this case. What will count is the value of Deborah's performance; that is a salient fact. But Aristotle gives no sign of believing that identifying or even accepting a salient fact is always easy. We know that performance assessment is notoriously vulnerable to prejudice, and trying to do it by invoking quantifiable indices has all of the disadvantages of ethical rules and not many of its advantages. Bringing a variety of points of view into the dialectical conversation will improve it: where we cannot be certain which description of a situation is the essential one, we can at least try out a variety of them. But even that does not guarantee anything.

Dialectic as a joint enterprise does help develop moral perception, however. New viewpoints and facts of possible salience will encourage you to look at your values and compare them to your more specific principles and judgments, including the minor premises of your practical syllogisms. If you think that Deborah's being a woman is a salient minor premise, it may be useful to ask you to defend its salience, for example by offering good reasons to believe that women tend to be poor consultants. Being required to mount that defense may not immediately cause you to change your views, but it may facilitate reconsideration in due course, and alter some of your intuitions.

Endless education

Aristotle is a naturalist, an essentialist, and something of a traditionalist. He does not contemplate the sort of technological, economic, and social change to which we are accustomed. But dialectic, which we should understand will not get us to the final truth on every issue, will continue to be a useful device even as things change, since it takes account of facts much as wide reflective equilibrium does. As a naturalist, Aristotle can absorb new facts and assess their significance, for he thinks of his ethics as fact-based. Given the importance of emotions and the absence of algorithms, he might have some difficulty accepting our views about women, slaves, foreigners, and others. But he has the equipment to do so, as do we, along with prejudices and blind spots some of which we no doubt retain. There is good reason to believe that dialectic will continue to be useful for the foreseeable future, which will offer new problems and new intuitions. Aristotle does not foresee a time in which, for example, physical differences between men and women become far less relevant to their place in society. He does not foresee any possible controversies about intellectual property or the threat of telecommunications technology to privacy. Aristotle may not have considered dialectic a way to make ethical progress in a time of radical change, but we can think of it that way, and still learn from him. In Chapter 7 we shall explore that point further.

There is no reason to believe that we shall ever need a whole new set of virtues. But the ways in which courage, benevolence, justice, and the rest work in practice may well change, and we cannot predict how. No doubt human beings will continue to be rational and sociable creatures, but our notions of what is rational and of what social arrangements make the most sense will change. Aristotle knows that we are not entirely rational, but all the same we can see that he is something of an optimist about our rationality. We know, too, that we are sociable creatures – sometimes to too great a degree: social influences can interfere with our rationality. But they can support it as well, as habituation can supplement rational consideration. If you get accustomed to working with women or members of some ethnic minority, you will probably become more comfortable with them, better able to distinguish them as individuals, more inclined to see them as colleagues, as part of Us rather than of Them.[14] This process may precede avowing that women are men's equals, or it may follow the avowal and make it sincere.

So there is no end in sight to our moral education. We form new habits, acquire new facts, face new situations, and try to make coherent sense of them all amid the clamor of emotion, social pressure, and other generators of blind spots as well as of insight. But we do not discover any algorithms that guide one's choice of a salient description of an

---

[14] Messick (1998) claims that we have difficulty making distinctions among members of an unfamiliar social or ethnic group. They all look the same to us.

action or a state of affairs, and we cannot always make our emotions support what rationality we do have.

The fact is that dialectic is a difficult process and not a straightforward one. We do not normally abandon our intuitions and associated emotional reactions the moment they seem to be in tension with our principles. Instead we sometimes tweak our principles to make them fit our intuitions, or we even change them. Consider the individual mandate that is part of the Affordable Care and Patient Protection Act, or Obamacare. For years many prominent Republicans, including Senators Hatch and Bennett of Utah and Governor Romney of Massachusetts, had followed the lead of the Heritage Foundation and other conservatives and supported a mandate,[15] without which emergency rooms must offer uninsured patients expensive care that will ultimately be paid for not by its beneficiaries but by the insured. But when a Democratic president offered a scheme with a mandate, these Republicans and virtually all other conservatives not only opposed the mandate but also argued that it was unconstitutional. It is difficult to believe that their change of heart was the result of a dialectical examination of their intuitions and principles.

Haidt (2012) argues that that is just how most people think most of the time. Of the odious Claggart, villain of *Billy Budd*, Melville (2001) writes, "His conscience was lawyer to his will." Haidt would say that Claggart is not unusual. Principles offered in defense of our singular judgments and actions are just public relations. They do not motivate us, any more than a concern for constitutionality suddenly began to motivate those prominent Republicans.[16] To put Haidt's view in Aristotelian terms, weakness of will is nearly universal. In terms used by Doris and his allies, Haidt is in effect denying that character is a major factor in our thought and action.

Haidt considers himself an intuitionist, in the sense that we make nearly all our moral judgments on the basis of intuition, unless we are philosophers (2001, p. 829). But Pizarro and Bloom (2003, p. 194) offer what amounts to a remarkable challenge to Haidt: they argue that

---

[15] Romney supported the Bennett–Wyden bill, which included a federal mandate. Obama himself opposed the mandate during his primary campaign.

[16] Haidt may consider himself an exception. He gives thoughtful reasons why he has abandoned his long-time liberalism in favor of a view closer to conservatism in some important respects.

intuitions may "serve as a starting point for deliberative reasoning," almost as though they were describing dialectic. They point out that we can influence our intuitive reactions in at least two ways. We can remind ourselves to take a certain perspective on events: for example, we can remember to put ourselves in the place of someone whom we might be inclined to judge harshly. We can also control our emotional reactions by controlling our environment in a way that encourages good reactions and good second-order desires (that is the term they use; p. 195). They cite Aristotle, though not any specific passage, and they are right to do so. A necessary condition of reasoning properly is having good intuitions, and we get these through habituation guided by good teaching. And as we develop principles to guide us, we can reflect back on our intuitions and see which ones need to be changed. But putting these principles into practice and aligning our intuitions with them requires us to develop practical wisdom. This involves cultivating the desires of a mature person rather than those of a base person or a child. Habit plays a role in the process of cultivation.

I shall argue in Chapter 6 that education in virtue can be a positive force in getting people, including businesspeople, to be more rational in the sense we are discussing. As Haidt himself says, training in philosophy can help one think more rationally.

5 | Virtues in and among organizations

MacIntyre

Alasdair MacIntyre (1985) is an Aristotelian, a virtue ethicist, and a critic of liberalism in general and of the Enlightenment in particular. He notes that ethics before the Enlightenment was based on a strong form of naturalism, a teleological and often religious view of human nature. He supports Aristotle's view that rationality is a matter not only of being able to draw valid inferences from certain premises but also of having correct premises about what sort of life is appropriate for a human being. There is nothing rational about an abiding motivation to paint everything blue or to torture small animals or, Aristotle and MacIntyre would say, to strive to earn a billion dollars. We fail to understand both our sociability and our rationality if we believe that self-interest is mere preference satisfaction and that benevolence always entails costs.

According to MacIntyre, philosophers of the Enlightenment not only abandoned the teleological conception of the human being but also supposed that the individual could be fully human even in the absence of certain essential relationships. The idea that a person may or may not be part of the fabric of a society makes no sense from his or Aristotle's standpoint: it would be like saying that a foot or a hand may or may not be part of a body (*Pol* I 2 1253a19–22). In part for this reason, MacIntyre holds that the notion that ethics is determined by a contract between the individual and society is a great mistake.

Hume, whom MacIntyre's considers part of the problem, is well known for saying that it is not contrary to reason to prefer the destruction of the world to the scratching of my finger. Thereby he suggests that rationality is about means to ends, and that no end is naturally superior to any other. If that is true, there can be no rational account of the good life and no basis for morality apart from whatever we happen to desire. And in the absence of reason in determining what is to be desired, we are relying on emotion alone, says MacIntyre. So he calls his target *emotivism*.

What MacIntyre calls emotivism and I call empty utilitarianism is a theory of human behavior as well as a moral theory. Those who think that it works as a psychological theory are inclined to find it satisfactory as a moral theory. The separation thesis would not permit this sort of inference: it holds that a theory cannot be both a psychological theory and a moral theory. MacIntyre rejects the separation thesis and rejects emotivism as wrong empirically and morally. But even if, as Doris and others claim, it is a weak psychological theory, it can still be a good moral theory.

All this relates to MacIntyre's other great claim, which is that social science should not pretend to be scientific. I extrapolate a bit, but in a way that has support in MacIntyre's text. Human behavior is a fit subject for science if we can observe and measure human psychological states. This seems at first look impossible: beliefs and desires, as well as many other psychological states, are surely unobservable and unmeasurable. But if behaviorism is true – that is, if beliefs and desires are dispositions to act – then perhaps we can observe and measure these states somewhat as we can observe and measure typical dispositional entities. So at the very least, I can infer what you desire from what you voluntarily do. And if the kind of utilitarianism that MacIntyre attacks is true, then we can observe whether something is good for a person, for getting what one wants is good for one. Then, with a little help from economists, we can look at a large number of people and observe whether some act is morally good. But as I argued in Chapter 3, human thought and action are not open to observation and measurement in that way. There can be no science of reasons and actions. Behaviorism is false. Radical individualism, unreflective economics, empty utilitarianism, the notion of utility as preference satisfaction, and a common sort of organization theory are wrong.

It does not follow that anything like a scientific approach to certain organizational questions is impossible.[1] For example, though we cannot clearly observe beliefs or precisely measure the strength of desires, we can conduct surveys that give us a useful idea of what employees want and what they think. If three-quarters of all the employees in an organization state in a confidential survey that they believe that all

---

[1] I think Donaldson (2005) agrees with me on this point.

their senior managers are dishonest and cruel and that therefore more transparency is called for, the organization undeniably has a problem. It would be foolish of the senior managers to dismiss the results because they are not really scientific, though there are some who would do just that. Aristotle claims that it is a mark of erudition to refrain from demanding more precision than the subject matter admits of. We might add as a corollary that one should not demand more precision than is required for practical purposes. Sometimes it is safe to assume that people see what is going on and know what they want. But sometimes that assumption is not safe at all.

We are inclined to believe that we typically act to achieve some result that satisfies us. In fact, MacIntyre says, sometimes we enjoy intrinsic goods: some actions are good in themselves. I stand to gain from acting in a friendly, cooperative way: the organization will probably benefit from it, and will probably reward me for it. But human beings, sociable creatures as we are, naturally enjoy friendliness and cooperation and other active virtues for themselves as well as for their good results. As we know, that is Aristotle's view.

Practices and institutions

Central to MacIntyre's critique of business is the notion of a *practice*, which is meant to translate the Greek *praxis*. As we noted in Chapter 1, *praxis* (doing) contrasts with *poiesis* (making), and suggests an activity that is good in itself. A practice is a "coherent and complex form of socially established cooperative human activity" (1985, p. 187). These activities are performed according to "standards of excellence." Virtue – that is, excellence – in practices creates goods internal to the practice. For example, cooperative work on a practice requires and so cultivates not only technical skill but also trustworthiness, honesty, sensitivity, pride in one's work, loyalty to the group, unselfishness, and so on. The practice may generate external rewards like money and prestige, but the internal goods are more important. The practices are schools of virtue; this is where, if anywhere, ethics may be found in an organization.

MacIntyre accuses managers of ignoring values, which they consider none of their business (see pp. 24–6 on Weber, for example), and aim at effectiveness, which turns out to mean profit, which Aristotle would consider a means to some end and not a worthy end in itself. Any external goods that they create, like money and prestige, are typically owned by individuals rather than being shared, and are "subjects of competition in which there must be losers as well as winners" (pp. 189–91). That is, markets are zero-sum games, whereas internal goods are shared, and create win-win situations. We can infer that if a company does have a prosocial mission, MacIntyre has reason to attribute some virtue to it, though he does not say so.

Practices require institutions to support and protect them, to hire and pay the practitioners, marshal them, and give them an organizational home. Corporate institutions must aim at profits and market share, hence at high productivity and low costs; so managers focus on the external goods thrown off by practices. But institutional imperatives are typically at odds with the practices. Aiming at maximizing profits undermines the intrinsic enjoyment of the internal goods that one might find in cooperative activity in an organization. If, as Bertland (2009, p. 25) says, "... the role of an institution is to provide opportunities for individuals to develop capabilities to function at a level worthy of human dignity," business organizations fail badly, according to MacIntyre.

Leisure

Aristotle seems to take a more radically antibusiness approach by claiming that virtue requires leisure.[2] We might take him to mean that only people of independent means can be virtuous, because they do not need to work or do anything else that they do not want to do. This would be a slightly misleading interpretation. Aristotle suggests that any activity that is good in itself is a form of leisure (*Pol* VIII 3 1338a1–6, *NE* X 71177b16–26). That would include not only the sort of thing one enjoys doing in one's free time, but also work that is intrinsically good.

According to Aristotle, some forms of work do not qualify as leisure even in that broad sense (*Pol* VIII 2 1337b10–15). He takes it as evident that the work of farmers and merchants is entirely aimed at some extrinsic good, such as a wage for the worker and in some cases return on investment for the owner as well. Most such people do not do

---

[2] On this issue I am indebted to Ciulla (2000, pp. 192f.) and Miller (1995, 226–8).

this sort of work to help a friend or enjoy intrinsic satisfaction; so they are not living well, not developing the virtues.[3] They are therefore not qualified for full participation in the governance of a *polis* (*Pol* VII 9 1328b38–29a2), which is supposed to promote justice in support of the virtuous lives of its citizens.

MacIntyre takes a similar view in noting that for employees the purpose of work is normally corporate profit, and the benefit for them is a wage. From this MacIntyre infers that the work is not good in itself and does not promote virtue. This is true of much of the work created by the industrial revolution, which largely eliminated relatively autonomous craft work and made employees parts of the machinery.[4] Frederick Winslow Taylor thought he was creating a win-win situation by closely controlling employees' movements to increase their efficiency and then sharing the increased profits with them; so one works just to get paid. It is the model of the utilitarian justification of work, and MacIntyre despises it. But he does not show that Taylorism or anything remotely like it is found in most profit-making organizations today.[5]

Some objections and amendments

MacIntyre makes two main points against business. First, the pursuit of profit crowds out the virtues in organizations. What might have been intrinsically valuable cooperative activity is spoiled because it aims at profit. So the work of a businessperson is not intrinsically good. It is pure *poiesis*: it is not an enjoyable cooperative activity, so it is not a *praxis*. Second, firms do not aim at any good end. MacIntyre (1985) criticizes Weber (pp. 24–6) for simply dismissing questions about the values of the ends at which managers aim. The problem is not just that businesses are supposed to make money: it is that money is a means rather than an end, and businesses countenance no further purpose, and thus evade any ethical questions about what they are creating. MacIntyre's two criticisms of business are related. To refute them

---

[3] The suggestion that work can be fulfilling or servile depending in part on the purpose seems lost on MacIntyre.
[4] See Ciulla (2000, pp. 88f., 92–96). In Marxian terminology there is a problem about alienation. It should not surprise us that MacIntyre has been influenced by Marx.
[5] Heugens, Kaptein, and van Oosterhout (2006) argue that it simply is not.

is a matter of showing that in a good organization people do enjoy cooperative activity done in support of a prosocial corporate mission.

MacIntyre does not consider managing a practice, but it is like a practice in that it can be done excellently, and it can create internal goods of its own (Moore, 2002, 2005a, 2005b, 2008, 2009). Managers can protect the practices while ensuring that they provide the organization with the external goods necessary for it to compete successfully. MacIntyre's claim that the profit mandate must undermine internal goods in an organization is not obviously true, nor does he provide much evidence for it.[6]

External objectives in general do not always undermine internal virtue. Aristotle allows that a soldier in a national army not only develops military virtues but also benefits his nation by fighting for its defense. Aristotle argues (*NE* X 7 1177b2–4, 16–20) that virtuous actions, as in war and politics, are good in themselves but also aim at some good result. In this respect they differ from the kind of godlike philosophical contemplation that has no further aim. He would not claim that the goal of national defense undermines the development and exercise of courage, duty, and honor. But then how does the overriding purpose of winning the war differ from the firm's (supposed) overriding purpose of making a profit?

Internal goods are necessarily connected with external ones in the sense that, although virtues are internally good states of the soul, virtuous people characteristically and essentially generate external goods. Consider courage, for example. It would not be a virtue if courageous soldiers and politicians did not benefit the state. There is some relationship between a practice and the quality of its product. If I take pleasure and pride in making a violin, with or without the participation of others, I am pleased with and proud of the quality of the music that the violin produces. If we could maintain a strict separation between *praxis* and *poiesis*, we would probably say that making a violin is a *poiesis*; but like many virtuous activities, it can be valued for its intrinsic rewards as well as for its results. There would be no good craftsmanship or any sort of virtue in enjoying making an ugly sounding violin. A group of investment bankers who enjoy working

---

[6] See Jackson (2012, chapter 3), who argues that one will take that view only on the assumption that profit is the single purpose of the firm – a view that MacIntyre does seem to take. Profit may be a result of virtuosity, Jackson claims.

in an atmosphere of trust and cooperation to create a financial instrument that is far riskier than it appears to potential customers cannot be acting virtuously, whatever internal goods characterize their practice. Similarly, what may pass for honesty, cooperation, accountability, and so on will fall short of excellence in an organization dedicated to bad purposes, such as manufacturing tobacco.

Koehn (1998) offers the example of the Nazi architect Albert Speer. Sundman (2000, p. 251) argues that a manager in an evil enterprise may still be a good manager, as opposed to a good person. I am not so sure. We might hesitate to say that a teacher who follows the curriculum of a school that supports terrorism is a good teacher.

It is not clear that the primary purpose of the company in hiring Jones to make violins is to make a profit: the profit itself might be considered a necessary condition of achieving the mission of the organization. But in any case, Aristotle suggests that one can make and sell things virtuously. In particular, as he says in *NE* V 5, justice in exchange is a matter of people trading away what they do not need and getting what they do need. His account is sketchy, and it does not begin to deal with most of the ethical issues that markets raise. For example, he does not discuss monopolies or purchases of things that will not turn out to benefit the buyer. But the point remains that Aristotle does believe that buying and selling can be done justly and that justice in this case is based on reciprocal and positive-sum benefits.

MacIntyre not only fails to show that concern for profit crowds out virtue: he does not give an adequate account of the circumstances under which work may be intrinsically good. Beadle and Knight (2012) address the similar issue of meaningful work, but they do not find that meaningfulness has much to do with whether the work is a *praxis*. They argue that meaning can be created by many sorts of factor, including characteristics of the individual (pp. 441f.) and the opportunity to negotiate the terms of the work (p. 439), but not characteristics of the job (p. 441), surprisingly. They note that there is serious empirical work to be done here – and of course conceptual work is appropriate as well if meaningfulness is at issue – but that one point is already clear: a virtue perspective is a necessary condition of talking about intrinsically meaningful work as an ethical issue (p. 436). Evidently it is not sufficient.

Good employees and good organizations

Contrary to what MacIntyre seems to believe, internal virtue in his sense can be a success factor for an organization, and it is no less virtuous for that. Employees' excellence in what he calls "socially established cooperative ... activity" characteristically generates social capital and so helps preserve the commons in organizations. It does so particularly where employees take the mission of the organization to be of value.

Consider a CEO of a large company that manufactures excellent products, sells them at competitive prices to well-satisfied customers, and makes profits that sustain growth. The board might decide that the CEO ought to be given stock options as an incentive to perform well; or the board might instead decide just to give CEO a good salary. We know that some economists and organization theorists say that the CEO will perform better if given the incentive of stock options. We also know that that is not always true; often incentive compensation changes the manager's view of the job and its purpose. And the theory that that is how managers must be motivated is, MacIntyre would probably say, exactly what you get when you begin to think of social science as a natural science: you greatly oversimplify your view of human nature so that you can quantify it and in other ways make it fit for scientists.

It is odd that MacIntyre focuses so much on practices in organizations and so little on other areas in which virtue matters. He should approve of the CEO who performs well without incentive compensation owing to something like loyalty to the organization and a professional attitude towards the position of chief executive. The excellence of the organization is itself an incentive for the good CEO, and running the company in the right way with the right results is a source of pride and satisfaction. And as no CEO can be a manager or a leader all alone, the good CEO will enjoy the associative virtues and the social capital that they create, in part by treating employees respectfully and honestly and thereby encouraging them to take the success of the organization as a source of pride and satisfaction.

Moore: characteristics of a good organization

Moore (2012), a sympathetic but firm critic of MacIntyre, collects evidence to support the claim, also made by Ghoshal (2005), Bazerman and Tenbrunsel (2011), and others, that individual financial incentives are the enemy of virtue. They attract "self-centered narcissist[s]" to the executive ranks. They undermine the sort of social capital that corporations should be encouraging among their employees: the motive to reciprocate, the desire for social approval, and the desire to work on intrinsically rewarding tasks – the bases of practices, in MacIntyre's sense. Drawing from his own research and that of others, Moore offers eight "parameters" for developing an organization that is both virtuous and successful. The parameters go well beyond what MacIntyre values, or even notices, in organizations. Many of them have to do with social capital.[7]

First, focus on the purpose – by which Moore seems to mean the mission – of the organization. It is important to persuade employees that the mission of the organization has its own importance and that it confers value on their jobs. Being proud of the quality of the products or services they create may motivate employees, contrary to the *homo economicus* assumption. Wanting the organization to do well, the employees will be less likely to act on what they take to be their narrow interests and become slacking free riders. In such cases the belief of most employees that other employees are pulling their weight will be true because it is self-fulfilling. Thus a good external mission strengthens internal social capital.

There is a mutually supportive relationship between the success of the organization in fulfilling its mission and the cooperative work of trustworthy, unselfish, loyal employees. As we noted in Chapter 1, Collins and Porras (2002) find evidence that long-term financial success is a result of a clear and compelling mission. Johnson and Johnson, Whole Foods, and some other successful companies have taken this to be fundamental. Firms like this offer counterexamples to MacIntyre's claim, rejected by Moore, that profit must undermine virtue.

MacIntyre agrees with Friedman that the purpose of the firm is to generate external goods, for stockholders first of all. I see no good reason to think of a firm as having only one purpose or serving only one group of stakeholders, though some stakeholders deserve priority. Moore may have changed his view slightly. In 2006 he and Beadle inferred from the 1919 *Dodge vs. Ford Motor Co.* case that

---

[7] Pastoriza, Arino, and Ricart (2007) put the primary responsibility for developing social capital on the chief executive, who is in charge of shaping employees' motivation.

"Anglo-American capitalism" takes the purpose of a corporation to be profit for the stockholders. But *Dodge* is not the last word on the subject, in law or in practice. Allen (2006, p. 42) notes that courts in Indiana, Pennsylvania, and Connecticut have ruled in the opposite way, and that we have not reached a consensus on this issue. One way to deal with the ethical gulf between MacIntyre and Friedman is to use the old philosophical device of denying a premise that they hold in common: that the purpose of the firm is only to enrich the stockholders.

Second, Moore advises, hire and nurture prosocial employees – cooperative, honest, conscientious people. This is not bad advice, but it is difficult to say in advance who will be a cooperator and who will try to be a free rider. That much should be clear from the work of Doris and others on the questionable status of character – or, as I would prefer to say, its fragility. Moore clearly does not accept the Doris view of character; in fact, he finds evidence in the literature that conditional cooperators comprise about half of the population and free riders about a third (p. 307). Showing the conditional cooperators that the conditions are right for cooperation is crucial, and it is helped by cracking down on the free riders.[8] This does not require knowing ahead of time exactly who the free riders are. It may be that the most one can do in the absence of adequately subtle psychological testing. Moore is assuming that the right kind of organizational structure and its systems are necessary but not sufficient for the organization to be a good one, and it should be obvious by now that I agree.

Third, design jobs so that they offer an opportunity to be virtuous. This seems to mean not only that the employee has reason to be honest, but also that the job demands skill, conscientiousness, autonomy, cooperation with others – that is, the virtues characteristic of a practice. It is not easy to do this for menial jobs,[9] but many if not all employees can be made to see that they are respected. This and most of the parameters are about creating a certain sort of corporate culture.

[8] Maitland argues that solving the assurance problem in this case will require management to be prepared to punish free riders. [Maitland, I. 2009. "Economic Imperialism and its Enemies: The Case for Governance." Published and circulated by the author.]

[9] But it has been done for coal miners. See Trist and Bamforth (1951). Even a job that does not require great skill or grant much autonomy deserves respect and offers a certain dignity. But this is not an Aristotelian idea.

Fourth, curb executive pay. Presumably this will require the cooperation of board members, who seem thus far not amenable to this move. Bazerman and Tenbrunsel (2011, chapter 6) go further: they give evidence that offering bonuses for behavior that is supposed to add value often turns out to be futile or worse, as executives game the system. In fact those schemes tend to undermine executives' ability to concentrate on the success of the firm. Bazerman and Tenbrunsel even give evidence that people will be more cooperative in some areas if they are not compensated for it. They broaden the point by arguing that imposing rules is by no means always an effective way to manage. No virtue ethicist will disagree.

Fifth, make decision-making participative, and encourage rational critical dialogue. Moore would no doubt agree with Lerner and Tetlock (2003, p. 433) that participants should state their views as though to a well informed, truth-seeking audience of people who have not made up their minds. It is indeed hard to see how organizations that are top-down dictatorships can encourage employees to take the organization's mission as a guide to action or a source of pride if they have no ownership of it. There are of course some organizations – the military in battle may be one – in which there can be little scope for extended discussion. But the disadvantages of command and control are well known: there are some dictatorial managers who could improve their performance by listening occasionally, though not all of them will, since they enjoy being dictators. I have argued, and will argue again, for the importance of dialectic in working out the right thing to do. But to believe that dialectic is always sufficient for solving problems of authority and accountability in the workplace is, as Moore would probably agree, to put too much faith in the rationality of managers and employees.

Sixth, trust rather than monitor employees. This seems to presuppose that the other parameters are in place, though it can amount to a self-fulfilling prophecy. In some cases, however, it can be disastrous.

Seventh, encourage group identity. In politics and management there are few issues more critical than finding ways to cause people to support the common good. A compelling mission will help. In some organizations it will be useful to create band-of-brothers cultures within units, though competition and mistrust across unit lines may be an unintended consequence. Creating an Us often entails creating a Them.

Eighth, maintain transparency. This creates and is created by trust, with which it shares some advantages and disadvantages. In some large organizations, however, revealing details of matters such as corporate strategy to all employees would be risky.

Of Moore's recommendations only one has much to do with MacIntyre's views of possible (or impossible) virtues in organizations. There is nothing about the noxious influence of the profit imperative. On the contrary, given what Moore says about the importance of the organization's purpose (i.e., mission), he can argue that profit is a means to accomplishing the purpose, and not an end in itself. That should satisfy MacIntyre, and Aristotle as well.

Taken as a whole, the point of the eight parameters seems to be that an organization succeeds by giving each employee reason to believe that the mission of the organization is worth pursuing and reason to believe that the other employees have the same reason. The eight parameters are best effected together. Some of them cannot easily be done in isolation; others, including the last, can, but it would probably make things worse.

Could an organization like this be internally good but externally bad, by producing bad products or taking advantage of monopoly power, for example? Possibly, but in that case it would be less likely to be able to rally its workforce around its mission.

It would be an understatement to say that none of this is easy, particularly for large organizations in which most employees do not know most other employees. We know that Aristotle believes that the *polis* is the school of virtue, but he is thinking of a city-state that we would not consider large. For reasons to be discussed in Chapter 7, it is easier to create what Moore advocates in small companies or subunits of large ones.

Organizational citizenship behaviors

Moore's ideal organization fosters and is fostered by what are called Organizational Citizenship Behaviors (OCB), a concept recently formulated to describe employees' acting for the common good – or, as we might say, acting to preserve the commons – in the corporation (Sison, 2011). An organization benefits from OCB when its employees go beyond the minimum requirements of their individual jobs and with good will and mutual respect work cooperatively for the success of the enterprise. In MacIntyre's terms, they are engaged in virtuous practices. They are creating social capital, which is good in itself as well as being productive in a competitive market.

Sison uses the notion of OCB in discussing Aristotelian citizenship in organizations. Akerlof (2007) has proposed that economics attend to what he calls "natural norms," which lead employees to contribute more than they strictly must to corporate success. Recall his claim (1982, p. 543) that employees' productivity can be explained by reference to their "sentiment for each other and also for the firm."

As Sison notes, there is a long-lived controversy about the ways in which employees are like citizens of a polis. In discussing the issue, Sison brings in two distinct conceptions of citizenship. One of them is what MacIntyre would call a liberal conception, which emphasizes rights, and in particular freedom from government control. The other, which Sison identifies with Aristotle's notion of full citizenship, requires assuming obligations to the group and generally being civic-minded. It goes well beyond fulfilling a contract, whether a pay-for-performance contract or any other; in fact such a contract presupposes employees are distinct from the organization in a sense that OCB does not contemplate, for a good organizational citizen is supposed to share responsibility for the success of the organization. Such a citizen is a virtuous employee.

One might reasonably say – though Aristotle would not – that the obligation-rich form of citizenship is appropriate for employees and the liberal one for citizens of a state. Néron and Norman (2008, pp. 10f.) note Galston's (1991, pp. 225–7) similar distinction between civic-republican citizenship and liberal citizenship. The former obligates you to take an interest in the community and aim for the common good. The latter permits you to be self-interested. If we could summarize Moore and Sison in a phrase, we would say that the liberal form of citizenship is insufficient for a good organization. From MacIntyre's point of view, liberalism of this sort in either an organization or a state is the enemy. We shall discuss this issue further in Chapter 7.

A difficulty about this kind of organizational citizenship is that one can count on it to benefit the employee only if the organization has the characteristics that Moore predicates of good organizations. If the company is dominated by free riders, cooperators will be at a severe disadvantage. Trusting the untrustworthy and contributing to the exploitative is too virtuous by half, hence a kind of vice.

A problem about loyalty

Many theories of management appear to be aimed at improving corporate performance by designing jobs that essentially involve practices, with goods internal to them. Earlier in this chapter I mentioned trustworthiness, honesty, sensitivity, pride in one's work, loyalty to the group, and unselfishness. Theorists of Total Quality Management, for example, would claim to be encouraging these and similar virtues. Behind many such theories is the notion that managers and employees are working together as loyal and committed members of a team, or even a family, in aid of a corporate mission that animates them all.

One problem with theories of this sort we have already noted. A corporation will be celebrated in the literature for demonstrating the power of this or that arrangement, and then serious problems begin shortly after publication. As Rosenzweig argues, managers are often deluded when they take teamwork and so on to be independent variables. But when we attribute them to successful companies, the halo effect is often at work: success is the true independent variable, and the impression of virtuous solidarity is the result of success. In any case, corporations often find that management innovations work well for a while but then run into unintended and unforeseen consequences. At this point MacIntyre might well argue that Rosenzweig has demonstrated the futility of pseudo-scientific theories of management. But who would argue that cooperation is unproductive or that it does not require trust? Who would argue that free riding is a success factor in an organization? The least we can say is that MacIntyre fails to show that the corporate profit motive is inconsistent with virtue in the corporation.

Unfortunately MacIntyre is not wholly wrong. A great many companies, including those that undertake teamwork based on loyalty and commitment, fail to act on their espoused values. Often they have proved ready to turn to downsizing when it offers advantages. And "Who can blame us?" they might ask. To forgo opportunities for profit as a way of preserving jobs is really a form of welfare. This response presupposes that employees are to be treated primarily as means, and stockholders as ends. That follows from Friedman's principle that the overriding responsibility of management is to make profits for the stockholders. But Friedman does not offer any proof that stockholders should get as much as possible of the margin while employees get only what is needed to keep them from leaving. That the stockholders own the company is a pertinent fact, but not a decisive one. Friedman argues that this is the way to build a strong economy. Hedrick Smith (2012), on the other hand, argues that a strong economy requires a strong middle class, which stockholder capitalism is undermining in America.

Fake loyalty

But worse, as Ciulla (2000, especially chapter 9) says, companies are betraying their employees. Management demands loyalty and commitment and only pretends to offer it in return. As things are, many downsized employees have reason to feel deceived. It is common to blame the competitive pressures of globalization for downsizing and outsourcing, and consequently for employees' stagnating wages despite their increased productivity. But employees' wages have not stagnated in all industrialized countries: in Germany, for example, they have increased along with workers' productivity, as they did in this country for nearly thirty years after World War Two. Since then executives and stockholders have reaped nearly all of the gains from productivity (Ciulla, 2000, especially pp. 155–7; Smith, 2012, chapters 4–6). That this situation is so common in America makes it difficult for employees to have the confidence required to participate in creating the kind of organization that Moore envisions.

It is unrealistic to think of most organizations as families, and dishonest of management to represent them that way. It is possible to make employees members of a team without offering them permanent employment. Employees can think of their jobs as representing opportunities to develop valuable skills, including those that enable them to participate in coherent and complex forms of socially established cooperative human activity according to standards of excellence and to derive great satisfaction from doing so. They can liken themselves to athletes who may be traded to a new team but are expected to mesh with their new teammates and continue to play the game the right way. Jones and Smith are in business for themselves, in a sense, but it does not follow that they should have a narrowly selfish attitude towards their work. It is possible to have an organization that approaches Moore's ideal without promising anyone lifetime employment.

There will be situations in which a measure of loyalty is a necessity. Training an employee may be a significant investment, and there will be little or no return on it if Jones leaves the company and uses his newly acquired skill elsewhere. Or if the training is narrowly applicable, Jones too will see a return on his investment of time only if he keeps his job. In cases of this sort there is reason for the employer to keep Jones on for an extended period, and to give Jones a strong incentive to stay. And of course Jones and the company will have to trust each other if they are to undertake the joint investment.

Leadership

If all or nearly all people were rational in the way economists typically think people are, management would be a nearly impossible task, even with the best possible performance compensation schemes. But in fact some people are reasonable in Rawls's (1993) sense: the reasonable person is motivated to act cooperatively according to mutually acceptable principles. The rational person in this sense is more narrowly self-interested. Reasonable people are typically willing to play by the rules so long as others in the game play by them as well, even when being reasonable conflicts with rationality in the economists' sense. They appreciate and reciprocate others' cooperative behavior rather than exploit it. These are the conditional cooperators that Moore claims constitute about half the typical workforce. In an organization a rational person in the sense we are discussing – not Aristotle's sense – may be a free rider; a reasonable person will not be. The commons is preserved in an organization only if most people are reasonable.

Competitors may be reasonable people. So, for example, I want to succeed; it follows that I want you, my competitor, to fare less well than I do. I am not thereby being unreasonable, because I accept that you want to win too, and I espouse no principle to the contrary. My governing principle is that I am motivated to play by the rules if you do, but I still want to beat you.

To be reasonable in this case is to be motivated by the interests of the organization. Smith may cooperate even if she thinks that she would be better off as a free rider; she may even think that she can get away with being a free rider and serve her own narrowly defined interests or her own notion of correct compensation policy. But however reasonable she is, she will not cooperate as long as she believes that others are not cooperating and that therefore her cooperation would be futile.

That everyone is reasonable is not a sufficient condition of the preservation of the commons, because any individual in the organization may be reasonable and yet doubt that others are as well, and may consequently feel justified in acting selfishly in the belief that to do otherwise is pointless. So the reasonable people must trust the other reasonable people; that is, they must believe that the other people are reasonable. Not only that: they must also believe that the other people trust them. For if I am reasonable and think that you are reasonable but think that you do not think that I am reasonable, I have good reason to believe that you will not cooperate, hence good reason not to cooperate myself.

Cases like this create an assurance problem that cannot always be solved just by punishing free riders. The problem may arise even where employees are not being selfish but instead want to add more than financial value, and to people other than only themselves. They may have different values, or different ideas of how the organization may add value. A strong sense of professionalism is not proof against the problem.

A *third sort of leadership*

This situation calls for a certain sort of leadership. James McGregor Burns (1978) argues that leadership may be transactional or transformational: the former is a matter of getting people with different desires to negotiate and compromise. The latter is a matter of changing people's desires or even their values, so that all those involved willingly aim at the same goals. Burns seems to prefer the latter sort of leadership, which he apparently believes entails getting people to put aside their selfish desires and embrace larger and worthier ideals. But changing people's desires and ideals is difficult, and not obviously a good thing. We may even think that there is something intrusive about doing so. Should managers – or politicians, for that matter – really manage other people's values? We know that this is a controversial issue.

I believe that organizations need a different kind of leadership, a mean between transactional and transformational. This sort of leadership is about creating social capital. It is a matter of thinking of the organization as a commons that must be preserved, on the understanding that preserving the commons is the best way to accommodate the desires and values of the managers in the aggregate. It is a matter of causing managers and employees to take the interests of the organization, or their part of the organization, as reasons for action. This is not transactional leadership. A transactional leader will typically offer compensation and job security in exchange for productivity; but as we know, that deal does not always work very well even if the commitment is kept. In fact it may make people less productive. Nor are we talking about a transformation of people's core values; that is a task beyond most managers.[10] If employees put their personal interests ahead of corporate interests, it will be hard to change their minds. A leader of the sort I have in mind can convince people that their own interests are best served if the organization prospers and that they should take a measure of pride and satisfaction in their cooperative achievements. But there is an issue of credibility: each employee must not only trust the leader but also believe that the other employees do as well.

A leader who values social capital will encourage practices that create internal goods, including not only technical skill but also pride in the quality of one's work, loyalty to the group, unselfishness, trust, trustworthiness, and honesty. But because these internal goods include trust and trustworthiness, employees will believe that their own interests are best served if the organization succeeds, because they will believe that that success will benefit them all, financially and in other ways. They will therefore be motivated to work for the success of the organization, as, I think, in the case of Moore's ideal organization.

This is what MacIntyre says cannot happen in an organization that must make a profit, for financial incentives drive out virtue-related incentives. He is right to this extent: as I have argued more than once, if an organization offers only financial incentives to motivate employees and managers, they will take their work seriously only as a means to their compensation and not as having any intrinsic value or as fulfilling any ethical obligation to the organization. As a result they will tend to work less productively and perhaps even opportunistically.

MacIntyre does not contemplate situations in which external success, including financial success, is the result of employees committing themselves to the success of the organization on the understanding that all employees are doing the same. In that case – far from crowding out the practices that create internal goods – success will reinforce virtuous

---

[10] But Turner *et al.* (2002) found that managers scoring high in moral reasoning
     showed relatively high transformational leadership behaviors.

practices much as a team's victories reinforce teamwork. Nor has he thought, as Newton (1992, p. 359) does, about how employees may develop in their jobs: first they follow instructions; then after a time they act by habit; finally, at least in some kinds of job, they understand the purpose of what they are doing and creatively find new ways to do it. That will probably not happen if the employees think of a job only as a means to compensation.

Moderate optimism

We should not give in to oversimplification or overoptimism. Not all organizations can create or even need much social capital. There are some that require their employees to be creative and to cooperate in ways that make assessment of individual achievement difficult, but some jobs and some organizations are not like that. Even in some organizations that are like that there may be room for slacking and other kinds of free riding that are hard to detect.

Much of this chapter has argued for a certain community of interests between labor and management and among competitors. This is part of the story, but not all of it: labor and management and competitors do not have identical interests, though bargaining in good faith can help preserve the commons. Where their interests are not identical, it would be naïve to try to reach a dialectical resolution of their differences. They are arguing not about the truth but about who gets more, and all parties should understand that. Ciulla is right in warning that talk about everyone being on the same team can be deceptive.

Having argued that employees can create social capital that supports and should therefore be supported by a profit-oriented enterprise, I now undertake to criticize MacIntyre further by proposing that there is room for social capital not only in firms but also in competitive markets.

MacIntyre's case, we should recall, rests on the notion that the purpose of the firm is to make money – that is, enrich the stockholders. But we have seen evidence that the most successful firms aim at a corporate mission that extends beyond profits and achieves profits as a result. Corporate missions typically mention customers, but there is no reason why they should not mention other stakeholders whose purposes a firm must serve in some way if it is to succeed: in particular, employees and suppliers. These stakeholders are not necessarily means to the interest of the stockholders, though they might be if the stockholders had most at stake and at risk in the organization. And that would be the case if a corporation could fire any of its stockholders and confiscate their stock.

Virtues and stakeholder relations

Aristotle would not accept MacIntyre's view that commerce is a zero-sum game. On the contrary, as we noted in Chapter 1, he argues in *NE* V 5 that exchange is a uniting factor in a community. Exchanges happen because people can meet each other's needs, and thus make each other better off through trading justly. This seems to be a view that most businesspeople and most business ethicists would readily accept. But sometimes there are heavy transaction costs, and we look for ways to reduce them.

According to the standard theory of the firm, usually attributed to Coase (1937), organizations exist because they reduce transaction costs relative to market relationships. The latter are sometimes fraught with uncertainty that no contract can eliminate; so the parties must undertake research, negotiation, and other costly means to reduce risk. The relationship may fail because of mutual distrust, to the disadvantage of both parties. By acquiring the supplying firm the buyer can preserve the economies that would otherwise be lost, but it is not always possible. When it is not, social capital becomes important.

Freeman, Harrison, and Wicks (2007) argue that corporations and their stakeholders ought to create win-win situations – just what MacIntyre claims is impossible. For example, a supplier might say to a customer, "My materials costs have exploded and I'll take a huge hit if I have to sell to you for the price in our contract. Can you help me?" If the customer is happy with the supplier's work and trusts the supplier, the response might be, "All right, but I'm assuming that the next time your materials costs are less than you anticipated, you will return the favor." A relationship that allows that kind of flexibility will be better than one that demands sticking to the letter of the contract. (This will not surprise a virtue ethicist.) The latter kind of relationship could put one party or the other out of business and/or enrich some lawyers.[11]

---

[11] See Phillips and Caldwell (2005) for a discussion of supply chain relationships.

This is not to say that there is no place for contracts in the supply chain or elsewhere. MacIntyre, unlike Rawls, dislikes the contractual model of ethics, in part because it presupposes an untenable kind of individualism; but that is no reason to say that there is never any place for contracts. Heugens, Kaptein, and van Oosterhout (2006) take a position between MacIntyre and Rawls: they make much of the importance of free consent in the contracting process (p. 393), but they do believe that contracts are inadequate in some cases, as where the interests of the parties cannot be aligned at all (p. 401). They also suggest that trust plays a crucial role in contracting.

A supplier and a buyer can both gain from a situation in which the supplier dedicates a lot of resources to manufacturing an item that a small number of buyers can use profitably. There is a risk, however: if the supplier or a significant buyer leaves the relationship and no other party takes up the slack, great costs will be forever sunk. Negotiations in matters like this may turn into a lose-lose battle for leverage. Relationships of this sort, and stakeholder relationships generally, will be win-win insofar as the parties are trusting and trustworthy to a significant degree. It is helpful for both parties to have, and be seen to have, the virtues of honesty, loyalty, dedication to quality, and some concern for one another's well-being. They should work out a win-win relationship based on justified trust. This does not preclude hard bargaining, but in many cases each party needs to bargain with the possibility of a long-term relationship in mind.

A kind of friendship

Drake and Schlachter (2008) argue that what they call sustainable collaboration engenders trust, communication, and acting toward common goals. This is, they believe, a special case of what Aristotle calls friendship of utility, a genuine kind of friendship and not mere mutual exploitation. (Aristotle's account of friendship is in *NE* VIII and IX.) They say, correctly, that the attitudes that it engenders not only create long-term advantages but also are good things in themselves. They constitute just the sort of virtuous activity, we might think, that MacIntyre does not expect to find in business.[12]

---

[12] Koehn (1992) too interprets Aristotle as saying in *NE* V 5 that parties to exchanges ought to be bound by something like friendship of utility.

Sustainable collaboration goes beyond information-sharing and may involve manufacturers using their own resources to help improve suppliers' operations and suppliers sending people to work in the manufacturers' factories. There is utility in such relationships, which are relatively stable and long-lasting. But incentive sharing, communication, and trust are goods in themselves, and so resemble the goods of friendship (Drake and Schlachter, 2008, pp. 858–62). This is a persuasive account, though it is not certain that Aristotle's conception of friendship is flexible enough to be pertinent to it.

The same is true of Sommers's (1997) account. On her view, a friendship of utility requires reciprocity not governed or limited by contracts but expected because each trusts the other to honor the nature of the relationship. It requires the parties to be virtuous, and to recognize each other as people with legitimate interests. Each party wants the other's prosperity, and promotes it in the relationship. But this mutual goodwill rests finally on the desire for profit – or at any rate was created by it.

MacIntyre believes that competition undermines the virtues. In the sort of case we are discussing, however, actual and possible competition will usually put pressure on firms not to exploit, but to create social capital with stakeholders in the supply chain and elsewhere. The alternative is to be weighed down by transaction costs. Creating high-quality goods and services at prices determined in competition – or at least not much higher than competitive prices would be – is a way of succeeding that enhances a firm's reputation for trustworthiness and similar virtues.[13] It helps develop social capital with one's stakeholders and rallies employees around the corporate mission. Social capital and profit are mutually supportive; and of course social capital, in addition to preserving the commons, is a good thing in itself.[14]

From Adam Smith onwards, some philosophers have argued that free markets demand such virtues as honesty and dependability; others have argued in the other direction. (See Hirschman, 1982, on this controversy.) I do not claim that these virtues are competitive advantages in every case, still less that most firms have them. But they can

---

[13] Hirschman (1982) credits Simmel (1955) with the insight that the essence of successful competition is doing the best job of benefiting their customers.

[14] But as we have noted, social capital is no guarantee of virtue: think of Albert Speer, think of the Mafia.

be competitive advantages in some cases. MacIntyre has not made his case.

The real pro

Sometimes we use the expression "real pro" to refer to someone who achieves success by doing things right. Carlton Fisk, the highly professional catcher for the Red Sox and the White Sox, understood excellence as well as any player. When he saw the flashy Deion Sanders, an opposing batter, fail to run out a foul ball, he shouted at Sanders to "play the game right," or suffer physical violence from Fisk. Fisk always played hard, and his aggressive play sometimes led to fights with opponents. But he would have said that trying to win showed that he and the players on opposing teams shared an appropriate respect for the game.[15] Other players agreed that Fisk played the game right, and that he was right to confront Sanders, even though by doing so he was helping strengthen Sanders's team, at that time the rival Yankees.[16]

We do not expect competitors in baseball or in business to make particular decisions in the light of the common good, even when they contribute to it in the long run. We do expect that a good outcome will usually emerge from a competitive market in which competitors succeed on the basis of quality and price. Friedman is right in holding that managers of publicly held corporations should not focus primarily on how to help humankind, but we need to add something about the importance of trustworthiness and of at least conditional cooperation, and of the social capital that they help create.

I have suggested that the game of business, like the individual organization, has some of the characteristics of the commons. The stakeholders are better off in the aggregate if they play the game right – that is, if they are all honest and make profits from selling goods and services that add value, rather than tricking other stakeholders. But a businessperson who can act dishonestly and get away with it may do well (externally) if the others are honest. We avoid the tragedy of the

[15] Almost all ballplayers will agree to the rule that you must respect your teammates, your opponents, and the game. (See Turbow and Duca, 2010.)
[16] Manfred von Richthofen, the Red Baron, the greatest of all German fighter pilots in the Great War, killed as many as 80 allied pilots before being killed himself. His body, borne to the grave by allied pallbearers of his rank, was buried amid wreaths in a military ceremony as his enemies' guns fired a salute.

commons insofar as regulation is successful, but we know that that is hard to get right. We strengthen the commons insofar as the stakeholders respect – as opposed to serve – one another's interests, as Adam Smith believed they could and usually did. I do not need to be friends with my competitors, but I must treat them as ends in themselves and not merely as means. That is the sort of competition for which the real pros, the Carlton Fisks of the world, demand the respect of all who participate. That sort of rivalry will lead to prosperity.

Then there are the internal goods. Many successful businesspeople, especially the real pros, enjoy what they do because it teaches and exercises some virtues that, as Aristotle rightly says, make for *eudaimonia*: intelligence emotional and rational; courage; sensitivity; cooperativeness; respect for excellence; patience and, when appropriate, impatience; conscientiousness; thrift; ability to postpone gratification; honesty. Contrary to what MacIntyre believes, fair competition can teach these business virtues and create their internal goods.

That list of virtues is not much different from Adam Smith's, and very close to McCloskey's (2006) list of bourgeois virtues. Rosenzweig (2007) too would buy into this list. Graafland (2009) argues that commerce encourages certain virtues and discourages others. Wells and Graafland (2012) argue that intense competition may be inhospitable to virtue. But businesspeople have an obligation to be virtuous even when the environment, which is indeed influential, does not encourage it.

We find the right sort of market more often in some businesses than in others. In particular, it is hard to see the financial services industry as anything but a zero-sum game. Even if we assume that all investment advisers are honest and competent professionals, every successful investment is someone's opportunity cost. And no sane person would assume that honesty and professionalism prevail among those who create arcane derivatives, as opposed to arcane electronic technologies. There MacIntyre's strictures apply well, and in fact may understate the problem. It is a cause for worry that an increasing number of the ablest college students are taking positions in financial services, where their skills cancel each other out and virtue is not much encouraged.[17]

It was not always that way.

---

[17] Shiller (2012) argues that arcane financial instruments are not bad in themselves, and can be highly beneficial. I do not doubt it, but he has little to say about the effect of highly probable information asymmetries.

An example of corporate virtue and vice

For many years savings and loan institutions earned respectable profits by making mortgage loans and paying modest interest on savings accounts. A good loan officer would lend to people who could pay off the loan. A bad one might lend to someone whose future income was in doubt, or refuse to lend to a qualified applicant who was a woman or a member of some minority group. The mission of the typical savings and loan institution was to support savings and community development, and in so doing the institution would make some money. Think of George Bailey in the Frank Capra film *It's a Wonderful Life*.

Many of the George Baileys of that bygone world were virtuous bankers. They made a loan with care, taking into account not only the financial position of the borrower but also such factors as the quality of the builder's work. They followed the norms of mortgage lenders and passed them on to their successors. They did not pause and ask of every loan whether it would contribute to the community, but they were aware of the contributions that their institutions made, and proud of them. George Bailey himself was unsatisfied with his lot for some time; but in due course he saw what he had done for the community of Bedford Falls and how grateful his fellow townspeople were, and then he realized that he was, as his brother said, the richest man in town.[18]

The George Bailey banker considers the relationship between lender and borrower a win-win situation; each party to the transaction adds value to the other, and from George's point of view his participation in that sort of transaction is a good internal to his job and generates external goods as well. George will not offer a customer an adjustable rate mortgage that might suddenly adjust unaffordably upwards. He will not encourage a customer to buy an expensive house on the questionable assumption that its value will double in a few years. He will not exploit his superior financial expertise. If there proves to be a problem about repayment, George will try to work with the borrower to find a mutually satisfactory alternative. He always wants a win-win situation, and foreclosure is a loss for both parties. He has reason to assume that the borrower, a neighbor in Bedford Falls and perhaps a friend, wants win-win as well.

MacIntyre is right in noting that a contract between willing parties does not guarantee fairness or a win-win outcome, especially when

---

[18] I do not mean to suggest that these arrangements were the best possible ones, but their shortcomings are not explored in the Capra film.

there is asymmetry of information. It is impossible to write a contract that will guarantee that both sides do well no matter what. The deal requires a certain level of mutual trust that the other party is not an opportunist who will take advantage of an unexpected circumstance. Personal acquaintance helps build that trust.

In due course regulations on these institutions were lightened, in part because depositors' opportunities for better interest rates elsewhere threatened to put the institutions out of business. The institutions could also sell their mortgages to Fannie Mae and Freddy Mac or some other entity and make some money that way while doing a lot more lending without taking any undue risk, or so the bankers believed. In two ways, then, the lenders were tempted to make bad loans. Deregulation and the Federal Savings and Loan Insurance Corporation made it easier to do so, and the ability to earn a fee by passing the mortgages and their associated risk on to the next party eliminated the negative incentive. In many cases the loan officers were paid on the basis of the amount of money they pushed out the door; hence they had an incentive to make bad loans, and many of them did, and then passed them along.

These loan officers were often not virtuous. Their institutions had lost their old community-oriented mission and had no new one except to make money – in fact, to make it in ways sometimes antithetical to the old mission. Their lending practices were motivated by their compensation scheme, which gave them an incentive to steer borrowers to unsuitable loans (Morris, 2008, p. 56). Their institution itself was not virtuous, and Aristotle will tell you that personal virtue does not thrive in a bad community. The broader community was not exactly evil, but its combination of deregulation and insurance that created moral hazard, its financial institutions whose structure and strategy were not designed with much foresight, and its spectacular opportunities to indulge greed helped create a toxic brew.[19] There was no place in it for George Bailey and his virtues. It was made for the evil Mr. Potter.

But the current problems are not merely a result of a generation of mortgage lenders being like Mr. Potter. Some major factors are

---

[19] This is not to say that all securitizing is unethical. The problem has been that some have taken it too far. We know that Aristotle would say that there are no principles that tell us exactly how far to take it, and that virtues have something to do with avoiding extremes. Securitizing must be done in the right way, etc.

situational, as Doris would no doubt argue. The lenders do not know the borrowers personally, and they may not live in the same town. They will not worry very much about the prospects of getting the mortgage paid off, since they intend to sell it. Their compensation is often based on sales. The question whether character as well as environmental pressure is a factor in making decisions is a practical one in cases like this. In some situations people do respond to very large financial incentives, and there are few who can set aside their financial interests and act on the basis of the long-term, broad-gauged view. And why should they, if hardly anyone else does? On the other hand we know that, contrary to what Jensen and Meckling (1994) claim, people do not always respond to financial incentives in the same way, and they do sometimes respond to more communal incentives. But in this case as in others, the financial incentives crowded the communal incentives out. Aristotle's view that a virtuous person requires the support of a good community applies to this environment, in which lending as George Bailey did it would be unprofitable, in part because that kind of lending requires a long-gone relationship of care and trust between lender and borrower. Bankers could either forgo large profits and risk the wrath of their stockholders or play the prevailing game of dangerous leverage. They were in a lose-lose situation.

As we have discussed, Aristotle holds that one of the marks of good character is the ability to grasp the essence of an ethical situation. That requires that you see your role correctly. If you are a good doctor, you see your job as promoting the health of patients, but at the same time you may be under pressure to contribute to the bottom line of your health maintenance organization. In such cases the two goals – those of practice and those of the institution, MacIntyre might say – are antithetical, at least in the short run. We can say much the same of a good mortgage lender, like George Bailey. But in the absence of the tradition and the support of the profession, virtue disappears. Then if you are a lender you typically describe your work as *enriching our loan portfolio* rather than *helping Mr. and Mrs. Grossman buy their dream house*. There is nothing intrinsically bad about enriching one's loan portfolio: banks are supposed to make profits. There is indeed something wrong with only ever thinking of the effect of the transaction on the bottom line.

If Friedman and MacIntyre are right in claiming that increasing the bottom line is the ultimate purpose of the firm, then there is little or no room for deliberation about ethics over and above deliberation about profits. If, on the other hand, the manager thinks of his/her job as involving the assessment of the claims of other stakeholders than merely the stockholders – customers, suppliers, and employees especially – then strategic decisions look rather like ethical decisions.[20]

It is worth repeating that I am not claiming that most managers think of stakeholders in this way, or that they are real pros, or even that they aim to create social capital in their organizations. I say only that all that is possible, that it is consistent with corporate profitability, and that it is a good thing. It is not contrary to human nature or to the nature of capitalism.

[20] It is no coincidence that Freeman is at once a strong advocate of stakeholder-oriented management and a strong opponent of the separation thesis, the notion that business decisions and ethical decisions are distinct.

6 | *Teaching virtue in business school*

Teaching ethics

Aristotle claims that building character is a long process requiring the best efforts of one's family and especially one's community. One does not become a good person easily or quickly. If he is right, how can anyone expect to make a business student a good person with one course in one semester? My aim in this chapter is not to discuss the broad question of how to teach business ethics, but to consider why and how to teach character in a business ethics course.

There is something odd about expecting a business ethics course to make students more ethical. We do not expect that a course in accounting will make students want to be accountants: it tells them what accountants do, and it may give them some sense of why that is a good thing. A corporate finance course tells students how to husband and increase corporate financial resources, among other things. It does not make them greedy, except perhaps incidentally.

The objection to that argument is that courses in management, accounting, and finance are supposed to show students ways to increase their own wealth, hence their quality of life, by having a successful career in the field, or in an allied field. That is not true of courses in ethics. Not only do they not make students more ethical, says the objector: they do not increase students' quality of life. But by now we know that this objection is poorly based: ethics is about one's interests, if Aristotle is right.

Even if they cannot mold students' character, business ethics courses have some value if they help students who already want to be ethical businesspeople get better at it. Business ethics courses can raise critical questions about the standard economist's definitions of morally significant concepts (utility, maximization, and rationality, for example) and presuppositions about behavior (egoism and empty utilitarianism, for example) and thus leave room for alternative concepts and presuppositions (about performance incentives, for example). It may thereby reduce the bad behavior that these self-fulfilling presuppositions encourage.

One can also teach well-meaning students some techniques for thinking rationally about what the right thing is, or at least for avoiding some of the pitfalls of facile thinking. Recall that Aristotle considers habituation a crucial process in moral development, but that at a certain point it is necessary to introduce rational reflection. Some social science, presented modestly, is appropriate as well. Organization theorists can teach students some ways of creating organizations that encourage rather than punish doing the right thing, and their lessons belong in a business ethics course.

Focusing on character

All this is worthwhile, but recent corporate scandals may make us hope that business ethics courses of some sort will improve the character even of those future businesspeople who are not clearly predisposed to work and play well with others. I want to claim that a business ethics course can improve students' character by helping them think critically about their values and realize them in practice.

I have argued, following Aristotle, that virtues recommend themselves in a way that principles do not, in part because there are self-regarding, though not narrowly selfish, reasons to be a person of good character. All the same, an ethics course may not much affect you if, after careful consideration, you believe that the most ruthless person is the likely winner in the zero-sum game that business seems to be, and that you want to be that person. Nor can we do a great deal for people incapable of learning to deal with complex situations, or those incapable of doing anything other than what nearly everyone else is doing. (Courses in management no doubt have similar limitations.) Not every student is in such bad ethical condition, however, and a good course can reach the ones who are not.

A good course in business ethics should raise questions about how the students ought to make decisions once they are in business, and in particular about the sort of reason that they should take seriously. Adequate answers to these questions should encourage students to ask themselves what kind of life they want to have.

Controversy

Students know that ethical issues are controversial: we disagree about them, and we disagree about how to resolve our disagreements. Courses in ethics show that philosophers, who seem to think that they have some special knowledge to impart about ethics, have disagreed among themselves for millennia. At the same time, somewhat paradoxically, students and others have strong intuitions about ethical questions, and on occasion emotions to match. We argue, often coherently and sometimes convincingly, about matters of right and wrong. Often, moreover, we do not need to argue, for we have a set of views about specific issues on which we do agree.

One way to resolve this paradox would be to claim that ethical questions really do have right and wrong answers and that in some cases we just have not discovered what they are. Then we might try to find some principles of ethics that perform the same function as the principles of science, or perhaps logic or mathematics, and do it just as well. But I have joined many others in claiming that ethics does not give us algorithms like those familiar to mathematicians, or principles that look at all like scientific laws. If we ignore Aristotle's warning and expect too much of ethics, we shall be disappointed, and our disappointment may lead to unfounded skepticism about the whole ethical enterprise.

Acknowledging that ethics is not scientific may undermine it in the eyes of some, including those who believe that organization theory is a science. But organization theory is not a science, and a class in business ethics would be a good place to show why it is not. Students may be inclined to say that whether Jones is a better person than Smith is subjective, but they should be asked whether they would say the same of the claim that (say) Jones is a better manager than Smith. The fact is, however, that neither claim can be decided by the scientific method, yet both can be true or false and both may yield to evidence.

Corrupting the youth

Almost anyone who teaches ethics has had to deal with the familiar slogan, "Who's to say what's right or wrong?" Most students are not true relativists or nihilists – among other things, they have a lively sense of their own entitlements – but they are skeptical about our ability to make sound ethical judgments. Students may become skeptics because their time in college has led them to question the opinions and values that they have learned from their childhood mentors, especially their parents, and nothing solid has replaced the old certainties that they now doubt.

Some students who enter college come from religious homes and communities in which ethical verities are taught without much examination. Their parents may find, to their discomfort, that their children's time in college has undermined the verities and left a kind of amateur nihilism, or at least an immodest skepticism, in their place.[1] This creates tension in the family, and the faculty gets some of the blame. Parents and other traditionalists are not mollified by the response that the unexamined life is not worth living. They may decide that there is much to be said for religious colleges.

By the time these skeptical students begin to study business intensively, usually in their third year, they are ready to embrace the view that ethics, whatever else it may be, is not a major factor in business. A student may read Adam Smith or Friedman and infer that one can and even should be an egoist, for the Invisible Hand will take care of the equitable production and distribution of goods, if that even matters. Acting in one's own best interests becomes more than a pleasure: it becomes a duty. Students who take *homo economicus* as a model of human motivation may believe that that is how nearly everyone is motivated. Utility is a matter of getting what one wants. Preferences are neither rational nor irrational; rationality is a matter of the efficiency with which a means leads to the satisfaction of some preference. People are egoists, utility maximizers; and if you are for some reason not an egoist, you had better act like one if you want to succeed. Ethics, which is often called altruism, is inefficient and even irresponsible.

Students, and not only they, often assume that any reason you have for doing something is based on self-interest. As we noted in the Introduction, if a counterexample is proposed – Mother Teresa, for instance – the response is that Mother Teresa was actually motivated

---

[1] I know of no reason to claim that college typically makes students less religious. Putnam and Campbell (2010, pp. 276f.) offer a survey that shows that among African American and evangelical Protestants those with a college education attend church more often.

by the glow of pleasure she got from helping poor people. Quite apart from whether there really is any such glow in the hearts of the charitable, the argument renders psychological egoism trivially true: since nothing could count as evidence against it, it is compatible with all states and events and therefore offers no information about the world. In practice, however, students typically identify self-interest with having money. (Why else would anyone go to business school?) Agency theory is the embodiment of this attitude in the management and business ethics literature. The assumption that agency theory describes the motivations of senior managers has a self-fulfilling aspect, since it has led to practices like stock options for senior managers.

It is possible that business ethicists bear some responsibility for this state of affairs. One can teach a fairly enjoyable and well-evaluated ethics course by just provoking arguments among the students. Unless the professor brings the arguments to convincing closure, which is not always easy, students may assume that there are no final answers to ethical questions. Even if Professor Smith believes that there are right or wrong answers and that she has the right ones, the inference that students draw from her failure to convince them that some position is correct, or her stance of neutrality in classroom debates, will reinforce the impression that traditional opinions and values are questionable and that there is nothing solid to replace them, except perhaps the profit motive.

I know of no research showing that ethics courses undermine ethics,[2] but we can see how it might happen. The Socratic method, much favored by those who teach classes in philosophy and other disciplines, may be part of the problem. Let us consider the method by looking at its founder.

The dubious contributions of Socrates

On the most plausible reconstruction of a philosopher who left no written work behind, we can say a number of things about Socrates.[3] First, all his conversations are about ethics. Ethics is about improving one's soul; the best reason for being virtuous is that it makes one's soul

---

[2] But Bazerman and Tenbrunsel (2011, pp. 27f.) present some indirect evidence that this is so.

[3] The greatest influence on my views about Socrates is the work of one of my mentors, the late Gregory Vlastos. See, for example, his *Socratic Studies* (1994).

better and grants a greater measure of *eudaimonia* than does vice. So Socrates' conversations with friends and acquaintances aim at improving their souls and his. Second, the immediate purpose of most of his conversations is to define some virtue: piety, justice, etc. Being able to define each of these virtues is, he thinks, a necessary and sufficient condition of having the virtue in question. You cannot be courageous if you cannot give an unassailable definition of courage. In that sense the unexamined life is not worth living; in fact, the unsuccessfully examined life is not worth much either. This is in part because only a virtuous life can be a good life, so Socrates suggests, but he does not argue the point to any great degree. Third, in the end Socrates' interlocutors can never define the virtue under discussion. Nor is Socrates himself able to define it: he can only destroy the definitions that others propose, and he regularly does so. Finally, Socrates' futile search for virtues suggests that most people who believe that they are virtuous are not.

Socrates was tried and found guilty of corrupting the youth, and in particular of teaching them atheism. Defiant to the end, he claimed that the most appropriate "punishment" would be to give him free meals for life in thanks for his service to Athens, or at worst a small fine. Instead he was executed. The plaintiffs were motivated in large part by political considerations, for Socrates had had some questionable ideas about Athenian democracy and some associates among its enemies. But under the prevailing amnesty he could not be tried for treason, and the charge of corrupting the youth was a substitute. Still, he had made powerful enemies by apparently undermining the traditional values of Athens.

Aristophanes, the greatest of the Greek comic poets, portrays Socrates in *The Clouds* as a sophist: that is, one who teaches students that there is no right or wrong. Sophists, who typically were paid for their services, taught students how to argue for any conclusion that they liked. The Socrates of *The Clouds* helps one of his students "prove" that he ought to beat his father. The historical Socrates taught no such thing, but he probably gave some of his students the impression that there is no sound basis for traditional morality and no known way of demonstrating what is right or wrong.

Socrates might have said that traditional morality has stood us in fairly good stead on the whole, and can continue to do so even as we suggest possible improvements. We know that Aristotle was to say something like that, but Socrates did not. Perhaps he thought that Athenian traditions had led to a democracy that was little better than mob rule, thence to a brutal and unsustainable empire, thence to a bloody and ultimately futile war against Sparta. And in the end, of course, the Athenians killed Socrates. Why should anyone take the ethical judgments of this community seriously?

Socrates' errors

If Socrates encourages skepticism in his conversations, it is in large part because he raises the bar too high. Being able to create a definition of some item by finding what all instances of it have in common may not even be possible. As Wittgenstein argued and Aristotle suggested, words can be meaningful and useful without definitions that are unitary in that way. More to the point, one can surely be pious or loving or courageous without knowing how to define the virtue in question. We might say that in certain difficult cases we make better judgments if we have some clue about the features that make an act brave or reckless or cowardly – that is how we interpreted Aristotle's view in Chapter 4 – but that is not Socrates' view.

Socrates claims that there really are true propositions that set out the necessary and sufficient conditions of certain virtues, and that not knowing these conditions is fatal to ethics, though one is a little better off if one knows, as Socrates does, that one is ignorant. Today moral philosophers are more likely to say that there are no algorithms for discovering right or wrong answers, or even for applying ethical principles on which we can reach consensus. That sort of statement could contribute to corrupting the youth if one claims also that the absence of such algorithms (or clear and unassailable definitions, as in Socrates' case) is fatal to ethics. Most moral philosophers do not make that claim, but some students might draw the inference, especially under the influence of Socrates.

There is something puzzling about this. We have no algorithm for rating American presidents, and we have no way to settle an argument over whether George Washington or Abraham Lincoln was the better president. But we do know that Lincoln was a better president than Warren G. Harding, and only a few students are prepared to waste class time arguing otherwise. It would make sense to us to ask ourselves why we consider Lincoln better than Harding and to identify some criteria on which we make that judgment. Surely we can do the same in the case of ethics.

If the criteria we choose are principles, however, the result may be disappointment and cynicism. I have argued that, even assuming that principles related to utility, justice, and rights are all somehow pertinent to ethical assessment and decision, applying the sometimes competing insights of each sort of principle to complex situations in the real world is difficult and often inconclusive, especially in disputed cases. Think of Deborah. If students believe that ethics ought to be sound in the way logic or geometry or natural science is sound, then they might well infer that there is no fact of the matter in ethics. Making principles central to ethics does not have that implication, but it may leave that impression. Making virtues central does not, since students know that cowardice and dishonesty are real.

The students' well-being

Aristotle does not want to raise the bar of precision in ethics as high as Socrates did, or depict the study of ethics as an abstruse discipline available to only the few anointed ones – professors of moral philosophy, perhaps – who alone can clear the bar. We can make sound ethical judgments, and the wise among us do so regularly and with good reason. Students seldom doubt that some people are more intelligent than others and that it is good to be intelligent, even though most would agree that intelligence is too complex to be measured reliably and validly. Nor do they doubt that some people are braver than others or more honest or more virtuous in some other way. They have all met cowards and liars, whom on the whole they do not respect.

Even though we do often recognize virtue when we see it, however, we might still ask why we have any sort of self-interested reason to be honest or otherwise ethical. Businesspeople have been known to say that this isn't Sunday School, that they are out for number one, and so on. Some businesspeople claim that ethics is good business – a means, they seem to be suggesting, to business success. Those who take ethics seriously will not believe that it is worthwhile to be ethical only if doing so contributes to the bottom line. That thought, I have argued, makes ethics just a branch of strategy. But if it is not a branch of strategy, corporate or personal, what good is it to businesspeople?

To address that question, as we did in Chapter 3, requires students to think about what it is to live well. One reason for saying that Aristotle's form of ethics is particularly suitable for business students is that they do need to think about what it is to live well, in part because many of them confidently assume that they already know.

It would be too much to expect that a business ethics course would convince all students that Aristotle is right in arguing that it is in students' long-term best interests to be ethical – in particular, to be people of good character. It might, however, show some of them that they should ask "What do I want my interests to be?" before they ask "How do I best serve my interests?" It might show them that one can develop one's character and one's interests with an eye on the opportunities and limitations that human nature offers for living well. But even if that is too much to ask, it is not unrealistic to encourage students to consider their values, and to reconsider them. Doing so may help undermine their unreflective assumptions about their interests, particularly about the notion that ethics is opposed to self-interest and the notion that success is a matter of satisfying one's preferences or maximizing something.

Ideally Jones as a student could think of his life as a whole, a story, and work out what will be good for him now and later. If he is rational, he can plan his future (*NE* I 10 1100b34–1101a14, VI 7 1141a27–9; *De Anima* III 10 433b5–10, 11 434a5–10), but not everyone is so rational. But Jones can at least understand that he can have mistaken beliefs about what will turn out to be good for him. Most people are not very good at "affective forecasting," as it is called. Gilbert *et al.* (1998), Loewenstein and Adler (2000), and others offer evidence that you cannot accurately estimate how happy or unhappy some future event, or your future success, will make you. Hence it is not easy to know what sort of life you can enjoy. One can begin to teach Jones and others the necessary self-knowledge by encouraging them to reflect on their facile assumptions about what will make them happy.

This is not to say that business students have bad values. On the whole they do not think of themselves as evil. They are more likely to believe, along the lines of Friedman, that they serve a socially useful purpose in pursuing their economic interests vigorously.[4] There is no

---

[4] Some of them say that in the long run it is a good thing for society that businesspeople act unethically or amorally. That is just a confusion.

reason to believe that they are different from most people who give values any thought: other things being equal, most of them would prefer to be driven by morally good ones (see Jones and Ryan, 2001). Here too, as I argued earlier, virtue language comes more easily to businesspeople and probably to others than does talk of principles: we all like to think of ourselves as wise, mature, rational, and courageous, though occasionally our doing so requires rationalization. So students gain motivation as well as information from learning that, for example, courage is something quite different from acting without restraint in a macho culture.

It is salutary to suggest to students that as rational people they have reason to value integrity, and as sociable people they have reason to value associations. The guidelines implied by these facts, though significant, are broad indeed, as I have argued. Most of us would recognize a greater variety of possibly satisfying lives than does Aristotle. In fact, most of us think that the room for choice among possible lives is itself a good thing, and we have seen reason to believe that Aristotle would not entirely disagree. At the same time we respect the limits on that variety that are implied by the requirements of our nature. As students plan their lives, those who teach them ethics should encourage them to consider their strengths and limitations, their opportunities, and what they can and cannot learn to enjoy. Some of them may indeed turn out to enjoy a life of intense competition and high risk, but it is a mistake to let them thoughtlessly assume ahead of time that whatever they happen to want is possible, or that they will enjoy it if they get it, or that it would be a good thing if they did.

I do not claim that Smith can just decide while she is in business school that she is going to be a certain sort of person with certain preferences. Aristotle, who puts so much emphasis on learning good habits over a long time, would not say so, as we can infer from Chapter 4. Smith must be prepared to cultivate certain preferences and intuitions and the strength of will to put them into practice. But right now she can consider what sort of life she wants to have and why she wants to have it. That consideration can be part of the process – no short-term one – of consciously designing a life of sustainable values and of preferences that are consistent with them. That is better than letting her preferences be determined by the immediate environment into which she places herself without thinking about how it may affect her.

Milgram as cautionary

Nor should Smith assume that she will always act on her values. Students respond to the Milgram experiment in part because they understand one of its primary messages: that one's values can be swept aside with appalling ease by an authority figure. You are not autonomous, the experiment says. Your values do not matter very much. Your character is weak. The lesson, taught by many social scientists, is a harsh one; we do not want to believe that about ourselves. There is reason to hope that, when confronted with it, students who go into business will be able to respond to pressure by recognizing it, taking its possible effects into account, and acting on their values. Former students who have learned about the experiment in a business ethics course testify that they do sometimes think of Milgram when they are in similar situations, and act accordingly. Beaman *et al.* (1978) show that people can be inoculated against crowd-induced culpable indifference by being taught to recognize the crowd's influence and to act appropriately despite it (see Slater, 2004, pp. 109f.).

In Chapter 4 we discussed Haidt's claim, similar to that of Doris and to some degree to that of Kahneman as well, that on the whole people are not motivated by principles or first premises of practical syllogisms, but by shorter-term, more narrowly selfish or clannish preferences. The Milgram experiment seems to be a case in point, especially for the subjects who rationalized their shocking behavior. If students can learn from the Milgram experiment to avoid blind obedience in some cases, we might hope that they could learn how easily they can fall into all kinds of rationalization. On the Aristotelian view, we have a moral responsibility to be guided by first premises that reflect our considered values. It is not clear that students can be taught to do so, but at least they can be encouraged to ask themselves from time to time whether they are rationalizing.

Bazerman and Tenbrunsel (2011, pp. 11–13) seem to agree that students familiar with the experiment are less likely to be taken in by Milgram-like features of the corporate environment, and when they are responsible for that environment they are less likely to make it Milgram-like. In fact they argue that business ethics courses should turn away from considering utilitarianism and deontology and focus on what actually makes people in organizations behave badly or well.

But one focus does not preclude the other, and in any case students need some sense of what counts as living well, which is more than just refraining from shocking someone or, generally, doing something that on reflection seems wrong.

This view presupposes that business students and businesspeople care about their values. Most do, though not in all obvious ways. If you tell a businessperson, "What you just did was unethical," you will probably get a negative reaction. If you say, "You are not a fair-minded person," the reaction may be a bit stronger. If you say, "You are weak and easily manipulated," the response will likely be downright nasty. Most people want to think of themselves as being of strong character, and so may pay insufficient attention to information about the ways in which their character can be overridden or ignored, though many will deny in a particular case that it has happened to them.

We are familiar with the claim that the Milgram experiment shows nothing about character, only that one's behavior and immediate desires are affected by the ambient culture. One's character is a different matter, a harder thing to change and hard to assess as well, even assuming it makes sense to talk about it. On the basis of a number of studies of the impact of corporate culture, Chen, Sawyers, and Williams (1997) echo Aristotle in concluding that ethical behavior depends on the employee's ability to recognize ethical issues, and they go on to say that this ability appears to be a function of corporate culture more than of individual employees' attributes. But I agree with Bazerman and Tenbrunsel that it can also be a function of good teaching ahead of time.

Even one who is willing to countenance a wide variety of sorts of good life will agree that there is something pathetic about living according to values that someone else has implanted in you without your knowledge or consideration. Socrates was right in demanding that his interlocutors examine their own values and try to show that they were at least coherent. He was wrong about how they should be understood and criticized, but right about the need to control and take responsibility for one's values – one's soul, as he put it – to the extent possible. Neither he nor Aristotle would admire anyone who was content to be rich and weak. Nor, so far as we can tell, would most business students.

Ethical vocabulary and framing

Vocabulary is one of the prime vehicles of culture, as Schein (1985) and others have argued. In an organization in which people are called decisive and risk-accepting with approval, the culture may create peer pressure that encourages shortsighted disregard of possible costs. One who acts on impulse will be called strong. One who prefers moderation or consideration of alternatives will be known as a wimp.

If you are a person of good character in Aristotle's sense, you know genuine strength and cowardice when you see it. The ethical manager can help people consider the difference between (say) courage and the readiness to succumb to macho peer pressure, in part by identifying macho behavior by name and saying that it is not courageous and not acceptable. A business ethics course can aid the educational process by helping students become more fluent in the language of character. This may entail raising questions about what they have been taught in economics courses about utility and rationality, and in management courses about effectiveness. Character is not about maximizing. But the problem should not be exaggerated. Students should have learned in courses in organizational behavior that motivation is not simple, and perhaps even that incentive compensation often does not work very well. In any case, we have seen evidence that the language of character is not a foreign language to business students or businesspeople. Keeping character and virtue to the fore in teaching a business ethics course is a good way of connecting with students' intuitions about honor, courage, and respect for fellow-workers and competitors, and a good way of undermining some presuppositions that the students may have acquired in some courses and encouraging those acquired in others.

A good business ethics course can give students practice in framing states and events in ethical terms. That ability needs to be exercised and developed, given a rich language, and sharpened by critical analysis. Even then it may be overridden by social pressure or inattention or anything that causes people to perceive and describe their actions inadequately, particularly if the corporate vocabulary and emotional reaction become their own. If their moral language is impoverished or insufficiently exercised, they may latch on to some other, non-salient description of the situation: "I am helping Dr. Milgram, who knows what he's doing," rather than "I am torturing innocent people." Or, more generally, "I am a loyal employee," rather than "I am a person of such weak character that I'll do anything I'm told to do."

Mother's knee and dialectic

One of the objections to teaching business ethics, or any sort of ethics, to college age or older students is that their ethical views are set in stone long before the course begins and that it is too late to change them. Some of the objectors add that Mother teaches us some lessons that will always stand us in good stead – the Golden Rule, for example. These may be the same people who say that what is taught in management courses is all common sense.[5]

Aristotle's account of how one acquires one's character from community and family over a period of years, discussed in Chapter 4, seems at first look to strengthen the objection. You come to act in certain ways habitually, perhaps in part because Mother offers rewards and punishments. But Aristotle says that the good habits that you learn from Mother are not yet virtues.[6] He demands that at a certain point one's judgments and principles be subjected to rational scrutiny. The set of principles needs to be internally coherent, and it needs to be consistent with one's views on specific matters. A dialectical conversation can force students to compare their principles with their habituated intuitions and see the need for some adjustment on one side or, more likely, both. That is a task for a good ethics course.

It is not something that people usually do for themselves. Most of us are not very rational if we do not have to be; most people are less rational than they believe that they are. A dialectical argument can expose inconsistency between, for example, the principles of equality that I espouse and how I treat women. It is less likely to be able to effect an immediate change in my attitude towards women, but I am more likely to do so if I decide that justice requires me to treat women professionally. And if I get into the habit of doing so, then my attitude may change as well.

In the classroom or in the real world, dialectic or reflective equilibrium should have some appeal for both principle-based and virtue

---

[5] Recall that Costa and MacCrae (1994) argue that character is not well fixed until about age 30. Aristotle would agree with them.
[6] But Mother's nurture is a necessary condition of your becoming virtuous (*NE* X 9 1180a1f.).

ethicists. While the former emphasize principles, virtue ethicists have an interest in judgments – in Aristotle's case, common ones, but those of wise and experienced people especially – about particular situations. Aristotle suggests that virtuous people must trust their intuitions where principles compete or are hard to apply. People of inferior character often do the wrong thing not because they have bad principles, though many do, but because they are unable to apprehend the situation under the right principle, as Aristotle says people of good character do. They may act on a principle that social pressure forces on them, or one that rationalizes their previous behavior. This will happen often when we are in unfamiliar situations or face complex problems. You did not learn from Mother whether to send Deborah to London, and her advice against hurting innocent people might or might not help you deal with situations that resemble the Milgram experiment.

Long experience and the ability to see complex situations from the point of view of professional responsibility enabled some wise old heads at Arthur Andersen to grasp the salient descriptions of the sleazy actions of their auditors and others at Enron (see *Chicago Tribune*, 2002). No doubt they had emotional reactions that supported their view. Unfortunately the winning intuitions were those of people of bad character, who acted on principles having to do with large billings rather than their obligations as certified public accountants. Some of them had long experience, but that clearly is not a sufficient condition of being a real pro.

A course in business ethics helps develop the kind of character that generates morally salient descriptions of complex situations with emotions and motivations to match. It plays the part that dialectic plays in Aristotle's understanding of moral education by encouraging students to engage in critical analysis of their values with an eye to what is coherent and sustainable.

There is no substitute for experience, however. Recall that Aristotle claims (*NE* X 9 1180b7–23) that a good doctor understands a range of illnesses and can handle individual cases best by virtue of his broader scientific knowledge. But the only doctor who is a true expert is one who has experience: without it, that general knowledge is useless. Similarly in politics: experience and understanding of political science are both necessary, but neither by itself is sufficient. So a good course in business ethics offers the next best thing to experience: case studies that sharpen students' ethical perception much as experience does, and help them put it into practice.

Ethics and strategy: the value of case studies[7]

The case study method suits business ethics as it suits strategy. In a typical strategy course the students read a text and then consider case studies that challenge them to apply the principles in the text to a real situation. This is the beginning of the process of developing not only rules but also intuitions about strategy.

Strategy usually involves trade-offs. For example, investing for growth will typically mean lower cash flow. This does not always make decisions easy. Where the market is teeming with opportunity and the strategic business unit (SBU) is stronger than any of its competitors in all important respects, the strategy of reinvesting for growth is obvious. But sometimes a group of weak SBUs can together achieve economies of scale or use slack resources. Even if there were an algorithm indicating the correct strategy on the basis of the available numbers, it is not clear that the value of finding the algorithm would justify its cost. At a certain point the experienced and wise manager must make a partly intuitive decision. Some managers are consistently better than others at knowing which of the many accurate descriptions of a strategic situation is the salient one. Their track record is evidence, though not always conclusive evidence, of their wisdom.

In ethics, similarly, one may have to choose between, say, benevolence and justice. It would seem to be an act of kindness to pay Jones, who is not well off, more than Smith, who does not have a family. On the other hand, Smith is more productive. Here benevolence and justice do not actually conflict, since benevolence, which aims at a mean between extremes, does not require paying Jones or any other employee significantly more than he is worth. Still, the situation requires some sorting out.

Not all cases are so easy, however. Should some form of justice prevail in Deborah's case? Or loyalty to the partners? Or professionalism in some sense? These virtues do seem at first glance to conflict. But Hank is able to find the right action because he has the practical

---

[7] Colle and Werhane (2008, pp. 757f., 761) argue for what is recognizably an Aristotelian approach to ethics training that emphasizes dialectical conversation and case studies. Obviously I agree. Furman (1990, pp. 34f.) also recommends case studies.

wisdom to see that being just to Deborah requires Bell Associates to stand behind her, and that to do so is not an act of disloyalty to the partnership or of unprofessionalism, and he acts accordingly. With the instructor's assistance students can reconstruct Hank's reasoning and learn something about what makes him a person of good character, and they can see the point of his decision. For the students the discussion of the case combines the advantages of experience and dialectic.

Using case studies gives students experience that supports the development of their practical wisdom. They learn the warning signs of rationalization and ethical anesthesia, especially if they also learn about it by reading social psychologists like Haidt. They study cases in which machismo and courage are opposites. So when a former student joins an organization that is an ongoing Milgram experiment, there should be a spark of recognition. Or a student might be in a situation reminiscent of Deborah and Hank Saporsky. In looking at a case and considering what its salient features are, students are developing practical wisdom and thus good character.

Authors of textbooks do not usually alter the principles that they espouse to accommodate the complexities of business. A business with high entry barriers is not always more profitable than one in which growth quickly attracts new competitors, but Michael Porter (1980) does not try to list all of the possible exceptions to his general principles. We do, however, expect a wise strategist to know an exception upon seeing it. Most virtue ethicists acknowledge that there are situations in which (say) lying would be a useful move for all concerned, but most of them would say that one should not lie even then, because it is bad to be a liar. An analogue in strategy would be the advice that an organization should usually stick to doing what it does best even when the organization does business in a suboptimal way but change would be disorienting.

I have noted with approval that Ghoshal and others have criticized business theorists for trying to be natural scientists and thus violating Aristotle's rule that one should not seek more precision than is appropriate to the subject matter. The notion that business is essentially about maximizing something can create a mindset that a business ethics course can barely penetrate. But teaching practical wisdom in management courses would not only help students understand ethics better, it would also make them better managers.[8]

---

[8] Here I agree on the whole with Roca (2008).

What shall I be?

A leading objective of a business ethics course is to help students get better at answering the question, "What shall I do?" The practical wisdom required to put one's values into practice is a necessary but not sufficient condition of an adequate answer to that question. The students need a critical understanding of their actual and possible values. That is to say, they need to get better at answering the question, "What shall I be?" The question asks what dispositions and emotions and interests one should cultivate over time, critically and dialectically.

An Aristotelian would take the view that in business, as anywhere else, a life of integrity is a fulfilling life on which one will be able to look back with satisfaction. Choosing that sort of life is no easy task, however. One cannot readily choose which desires to have: many people are tempted by doughnuts; some are tempted by dishonesty. We can, however, ask students to reflect on what is most important to them and how to protect it. Reading Michael Lewis's *Liar's Poker* (1989), for example, provides an opportunity for this. Does Dash Riprock lead a good life? Is the Human Piranha's approval a good thing? Is selling equities in Dallas inappropriate for anyone with any self-respect? Why? How does Salomon Brothers of that era differ from the Zimbardo experiment? Knowing about Salomon or Zimbardo or Milgram may enable one later to stop and reflect, and to do some moral reasoning rather than rationalization.

There is some encouraging evidence about the possibility of doing that. As we noted earlier, Beaman *et al.* (1978) show that people who are taught certain effects of social pressure will act better thereafter. Nickerson (1994) argues that little of the moral reasoning that is taught in the classroom is transferred, but Lieberman (2000) claims that continued discussion in an appropriate environment – something like what Aristotle would call dialectic in a good *polis* – can make a positive difference. At least we can disabuse the students of the notion that ethics is by its nature opposed to their interests, show how certain virtues are compatible with a good life, and argue that integrity is a necessary condition of it. If most students have fairly good values already, as I suggested earlier most of them do, that should not be impossible.

One would have to be deeply optimistic to suppose that a business ethics course could change a student's character, though it might increase the probability that a student will notice what is at stake in some cases. The Milgram case seems to have that effect. Remember, a person of good character has correct perception. To understand the phenomenon of framing and what affects it, to know how irrational people can be and why, to realize how inaccurate affective forecasting is, to understand how corporate culture can affect even one's higher-order desires – these are possible results of a business ethics course that emphasizes character. If students understand the fragility of character, they have a better chance to preserve it.

Fairly hopeful conclusion: choosing a job and choosing a character

The decisions and experiences of a human life are linked by memory, intention, commitment, and growth, which taken together constitute a character. A human being has the unique and essential capacity to create a life. It is seldom possible to design your entire life at once, but you can create some goals and boundaries on the basis of the sort of person you want to be and think you can enjoy being. A course in business ethics can encourage that process. One important step of it will be to make a decision about the beginning of your career.

Even for those who remember Milgram, corporate culture may be very powerful. By encouraging a certain notion of success, a bad culture can thwart people's ability to reflect on their values and to identify salient characteristics, as it can thwart the strategist's attempt to maintain a long-term perspective and see events from that perspective. But if a strong organizational culture can affect one's character in that way, then the choice of an employer is a most important one. Having been in a certain organization for a while, I may like being the sort of person who enjoys acting ruthlessly, or in some other organization I may become the sort of person who takes satisfaction in maintaining a professional attitude. If Aristotle is right, by acting ruthlessly or professionally I can become that kind of person. For some students, choosing an employer (or a career, for that matter) will in effect be choosing which desires and values to cultivate, hence choosing a character. Choosing an employer can be part of what Elster (1985) calls self-management.[9] Aristotle does not accept that living in the right

---

[9] A mean between the view that character is what counts and the Doris view that it is all about one's environment is the view that a person of good character chooses a good environment.

polis is a sufficient condition of developing a good character, but he does believe that it is a necessary condition.

The instructor can intervene here and help students examine what their values really are at the moment of choice of a job. It is useful to raise questions about why someone would want to pursue a certain sort of career or join a certain sort of firm, and about whether getting a certain job will be as satisfying as one has anticipated. That may help expose the reasons given as incoherent or based on self-ignorance or peer pressure or some other basis for rationalization.

Think of Smith, who is considering entry-level positions as she completes her MBA. She has two options: a job in the finance function of a large firm known for valuing teamwork and personal integrity, or a job in an investment banking house known for its competitive environment and its contempt for its customers. Call them, by way of considerable oversimplification, Google and Salomon Brothers. Maybe she is already the sort of person who will be happy in one of those environments but not the other. Maybe, on the other hand, Smith is wrong in thinking that she could not be happy if she were not winning admiration for making a vast amount of money. Maybe she has bought into the pecking order in her second-year MBA cohort without considering what sort of life in business would satisfy her. She might indeed go with Salomon and come to feel contempt for those who settle for selling equities, or she might take a job in a high-ethics company and come to enjoy it and be quite happy that she did not go with the investment house. But if what Lewis wrote about life at Salomon is still true and the researchers on affective forecasting are right in general, she might achieve success in the investment house but never find it quite satisfying. Like Dash Riprock, she might always be looking for the next fix. But by the time she learns this about herself, she may not be the sort of person who could enjoy life at Google either.

It should be clear by now that I think Smith would have a better life at Google, but that is not for me or any instructor to decide, though it is appropriate to introduce the evidence, cited in Chapter 4, that happiness has much to do with good associations. She might choose a job on the firm conviction that it is a glorious thing to be a pirate king. The instructor should help her think about whether that or any prospective career or prospective life can be compatible with values that will sustain her happiness, and to warn her of the fallibility of affective forecasting. It would also be a good idea to make sure she understands that she will probably have to deal adaptively and creatively with new situations beyond her current understanding, in which piracy may not be a viable strategy.

Other things to think about

Let me end with an Aristotelian admonition: one should not design or assess a business ethics course in a purely results-oriented way. Aristotle holds that the best life of all is one that is dominated by abstract thought (*NE* X 7–8). That is something that one might expect a philosopher to say. But the study of the humanities is important in part because there is something to be said for rationality, subtlety, and creativity of thought for their own sake. A course in business ethics should aim at these internal goods as well as at preparing students for a successful and honorable career in business.

There is reason to believe that the communities of the future will be created by businesses as much as by governments. Like it or not, one who is successful enough to become a leader in business will be making a contribution to a better world or a worse one. Steve Jobs surely did not spend most of his time thinking about how to build a better world, but he seems to have had sufficient imagination to understand the possibility that he was helping create a new notion of community, which would affect people's values and priorities. Few MBA students will go on to be visionaries in the mold of Steve Jobs, but it would be appropriate for them all to understand the impact of business on the shape of future society as well as their own impact on their immediate communities.

In the end you should go into business, or into anything else for that matter, to enrich your life. You do this in part by making money, so that you can afford to do life-enriching things. You also do it by undertaking life-enriching things in the workplace. But it is a mistake, one that Aristotle rightly deplores, to believe that making money in business is intrinsically enriching. So a business ethics course should at least point the way towards thinking about what constitutes living well and, no less important, what does not. In choosing a job Smith is in effect building a foundation for a life, and that is all the more difficult because she should not assume ahead of time that she knows in any detail where she wants to go, or even what she wants her interests to be. On that issue it is important to Smith to make that decision and not have it made for her by someone else. And it would not be a bad idea to make it with something like Aristotelian guidelines in mind.

A course in business ethics can make some contribution to developing this understanding; so can other business courses taught with appropriate perspective; so can courses in history, politics, literature, and other fields that can educate us about character. All of them can and should contribute to the ethical development of businesspeople. Some of them do so by warning us of our weaknesses, such as our ability to rationalize seriously irrational thought and behavior. Great literature in particular sharpens our practical wisdom, deepens our moral imagination, and challenges our parochial ways of dividing the world into those to whom we acknowledge obligations and those whom we see as only means rather than ends in themselves.[10]

Many of today's business students will become citizens of the world, because business is global. They will need to be sophisticated enough for that. In the next and final chapter I argue that Aristotle's ethics, though it is parochial and rigid in some important ways, offers us useful insights as we consider how to deal with ethical issues, and especially ethical disagreement, in global business.

---

[10] One could cite hundreds of sources in making arguments of this sort. A recent and valuable one is Nussbaum (2010). Bragues (2006) advocates studying Aristotle, Kant, and other ethicists rather than the virtue ethics and deontology that are their legacy. Thereby one gets the advantages of reading great literature and contemplating ethics closely.

7 | *Ethical conflict and the global future*

Global commerce involves people who hold a wide range of ethical views. Can these divergent ethical views be sufficiently reconciled to enable those who differ to work together? Have we any good reason to claim that the ethics associated with modern democratic capitalism is superior to more traditional ethics? This final chapter will not fully answer these questions, and it will not even address many other questions about ethics and global business. That would take more than a chapter. What I propose instead is to show that Aristotle has some insights to offer us as we consider global business ethics, even though he shows little interest in global business and has nothing to say about many of the ethical issues that it raises.

Global business may seem to pose especially difficult problems for virtue ethics. Enlightenment thinkers have sought principles that encompass all of humankind; virtue ethicists have been more modest and more parochial. Aristotle's ethics is designed primarily for citizens of a *polis*. It is adaptable to other contexts, but it seems to work best in fairly small groups, where people hold many opinions in common, have emotional ties, and communicate directly. Virtual communities based on radically improved communications cannot substitute for social relationships based on actual acquaintance.[1] Ethics is about Us, and most of the people in the world will be forever Them. Aristotle's parochial views on slavery, women, and businesspeople do nothing to dispel our suspicion that his virtue ethics does not travel well, through time or through space. As business becomes an increasingly global affair, we may think that we should adopt global ethics, with broad principles suitable for addressing the breadth of problems and opinions we face. But that plausible and un-Aristotelian notion is wrong.

---

[1] Dunbar (1992) argues that the size of the neocortex, which has not grown very much in the past quarter million years or so, limits the maximum possible number of stable personal relationships one can have to about 150.

For the foreseeable future the increasingly dominant economic system will be capitalism. Business ethics and business virtues and vices will therefore be similarly prominent, and their effect will be felt well beyond business. The ethics of business is part of a Western culture that, according to Haidt (2012),[2] presupposes a certain view of what ethics is all about. In North America and Western Europe and in many urban centers around the world, most people would say that the purpose of ethics is to benefit individuals and to do so fairly and with due respect for their autonomy. Your autonomous pursuit of what you prefer may be curtailed only when necessary to prevent harm to others or serious harm to you. The traditional view, as Haidt calls it, is based on in-group loyalty, respect for authority, and purity as determined primarily by religion.

As globalization proceeds, multinational corporations will recruit managers and employees from wherever they can find qualified ones, and multicultural workplaces will be a fact of life. So corporations must deal with some different views of ethics, including the traditional view, which is not very hospitable to capitalism. Business ethics as we understand it represents the modern, Western view of what ethics is. As a result of global commerce, traditional ethics is under siege. But it will not quietly go away, and managers in global enterprises must deal with it.

In a conversation with Haidt some years ago I briefly outlined Aristotle's ethical theory. On the basis of that summary Haidt told me that he thought that Aristotle's views put him somewhere between the modern liberal conception of ethics and the traditional one – a mean between two extremes. This struck me as an insightful remark, and I thought about it afterwards for some time and came to believe that it was right, on the whole, and important.[3]

This chapter will consider some ways in which Aristotle can help us as we consider the divergent notions of ethics that the world's cultures have to offer. Despite his lack interest in global commerce and his coolness towards different notions of ethics,[4] Aristotle can assist our

---

[2] Others have made similar points, but I focus on Haidt to emphasize the connection between his views on modern liberal ethics and his (and Doris's and Kahneman's and others') skeptical views on rationality.

[3] Haidt did not elaborate; the elaboration that follows is mine. On the whole it vindicates his statement if it is true; if it is false, he bears no responsibility.

[4] Aristotle cites with approval the poets who said that it was fitting for barbarians to be ruled by Greeks (*Pol* I 2 1252b8).

thinking in three ways. First, it is characteristic of a person of practical wisdom in Aristotle's sense to be flexible and adaptive enough to deal virtuously with situations not covered by familiar principles. So it is practical wisdom that will stand us in good stead as technological progress, especially in communication, creates new issues and globalization unearths competing ways of dealing with them. Second, his substantive view of ethics offers an attractive compromise between the traditional conception and the modern one, of which the extreme form is the Enlightenment view. Third, Aristotle's methodology offers a particular way of reconciling the conceptions: dialectical conversations in *mediating institutions*, such as small organizations or subunits of larger ones, between advocates of differing conceptions of ethics, may resolve enough of the differences that their proponents can coexist and perhaps even reach a consensus on some important matters. This is consistent with Aristotle's view that the (small) *polis* is the school of virtue. We do not become ethical by first learning great principles and then applying them to our lives, and we most easily learn to cooperate with and trust people with whom we associate frequently and closely and to whom we must be responsive.

I shall not argue that the world will eventually embrace Aristotle's views. The spread of capitalism may result in the victory of empty utilitarianism, radical individualism, and all of the other afflictions we have discussed. I have no prediction to make and little to say about how to make it all come out well. I want only to make some suggestions, inspired by Aristotle, about possible ways forward.

Traditional morality

In more traditional societies – Haidt mentions India, where he lived for a time – the cardinal virtues of loyalty, obedience in a hierarchy, and purity lead to a significant emphasis on Us vs. Them, with a tightly-knit Us, and in consequence little attention to individual autonomy.[5] It is the sort of morality that one would expect to find in a tribe that does

---

[5] As Haidt notes, however, cultural conservatives in this country are more likely than liberals to take traditional notions of morality seriously (2012, especially chapters 7 and 8). We also see in the West an ongoing clash between communitarians like MacIntyre and libertarians. Some (e.g., Sen, 1997) have pointed out that certain ancient Asian philosophers sound remarkably modern and liberal, for example in their emphasis on individual rights. But Haidt seems to be thinking of the majority of people in traditional societies today.

not associate with many other tribes, except in hostility or suspicion. We are hard-wired to bond with people similar to us, and such a tribe does little to alter or rationalize the wiring. One thinks of the people of the Hebrew Bible. Their morality does proscribe murder and lies and theft in the ennobling Ten Commandments, but much of what the people are required to do is tied to their unique identity. They are not noticeably tolerant of other tribes. Their respect for authority, often including religious authority, is of a piece with their commitment to the community, which does not hold votes on a range of vital issues or encourage respectful and rational consideration of the opinions of people in other communities. One of the functions of purity is to distinguish themselves from those who are uncircumcised and eat *treyf*.[6]

We see reflections of this moral divide in business. In India, still a traditional society in some places, there is less opposition than in America to managers hiring their relatives even when others are better qualified. The view seems to be that, though profit and growth are important, they should not crowd out all family considerations. In Japan companies have long been more like families. But some American companies have become more familial,[7] while Japanese companies are becoming less so. In any case, we find both of these models and others throughout the world. Which one is most appropriate will depend on many factors, of which tradition is just one.

Traditional morality appears to be largely the invention of powerful men in isolated and highly religious communities. People are expected to do as they are told by their leaders, who claim to derive their legitimate authority from God, whose demands these leaders alone understand and convey to the loyal and obedient people. The demand for purity can serve to control the most intimate and personal aspects of people's lives and thereby create not only a willingness but also a desire to be loyal and obedient. This attitude has some survival value in an embattled community that requires a strong Us. The challenges that face a traditional society are different from what we in the West

---

[6] St. Paul, a virtue ethicist, downplayed the exclusivist aspects of Judaism and sought to make Christianity a universal religion. St. Peter saw Christianity as a part of Judaism.

[7] At least they pretend to be. Recall that Ciulla (2000) shows that American firms espouse something like the family model but in fact follow the market model when they have an opportunity to lay employees off.

normally face. One might say that traditional morality works better for people with traditional lives and institutions.

But that is too facile. Leaving aside the question whether the ancient practices are still functional, it is not enough to say that some practice or principle works better. Denying education to girls "works" for communities dominated by extreme Islamists in that it helps maintain their traditional way of life. But considering how the practice relates to the way of life seems to reveal a utilitarian justification at best, and the utility in question is largely a matter of preference satisfaction.[8] That is to say, the best possible argument for the practice has some limited force but is inadequate for the same reason as is the utilitarian justification for capitalism: as Aristotle would say but for his prejudice against women, not schooling girls fails the test of human flourishing. In any case, as both Aristotle and standard capitalists would say, dictatorship based on religion may offend against citizens' natural propensity to deliberate and choose rationally. How can we hope to speak to those who accept that view of ethics?

Looking for reconciliation

Donaldson and Dunfee (1999) approach the problem of widely differing ethical views by identifying some widely accepted "hypernorms," by which we can judge the soundness of local norms, which differ from one community to another. Communities may have different norms that are equally justifiable; or one community may have justifiable norms and the other not, or both may be wrong. But judging local norms on the basis of hypernorms will not be easy. As we know, principles, whether or not we call them norms, may be hard to apply. Different communities may have different conceptions of justice, of the scope of rights, and of the good life.[9] If there is a hypernorm that rules out some notion of justice, defenders of that notion will argue that the hypernorm is biased in favor of some other conception of morality.

---

[8] Paradoxically, a Western economist might support the practice for that reason.
[9] Hampshire argues (1983, pp. 5f.) that one cannot assess a practice apart from the way of life, whether modern or traditional, that gives it its meaning and value. He is not claiming that we cannot criticize a certain practice or a way of life, only that the criticism must take into account the contribution that the practice makes to the way of life in which it is situated.

If the available hypernorms do not rule out any notions, they are not useful.

I shall next argue, following on Chapter 3, that there is much to be said for capitalism, despite its problems. In fact what there is to be said for it can be attractive even to some traditionalists. On the other hand, capitalism is by no means good in all respects or in all its forms. So I shall note some challenges that capitalist ethics faces, but then go on to argue that Aristotle helps effect a reconciliation between the modern liberal view underlying capitalism and the traditional view with which capitalists must deal.

Capitalist ethics

I have argued that free markets score well with respect to certain forms of utility, justice, and rights. Free market competition is extraordinarily productive. It is just, in the sense that it rewards contributions to the economy, hence to society. It supports autonomy, in the sense that it offers wide ranges of choice of products one can buy and of jobs one can take; and since there is competition for your dollar or your services, your options are favorable. As Maitland (1997), McCloskey (2006), and others have argued, it encourages honesty, industry, and other bourgeois virtues.[10]

But while markets encourage certain bourgeois virtues, they do not guarantee them. On the contrary, markets can also encourage greed, short-term thinking, an Us-Them approach to ethics if any approach at all, dark satanic mills, and the commodification of too many aspects of life. We should be content with the more modest claim that markets can support virtue given the right sort of businessperson and the right sort of government, which must be answerable to the right sort of populace. But more than that, the right sort of people and government can support markets that are productive of goods that we have reason to desire and of virtues that are desirable in themselves. But "can" does not mean "will," and emphatically not "will overnight."

---

[10] But recall that Graafland (2009) and Wells and Graafland (2012) find a complicated picture in the relationship between these virtues and competition.

The standard defense of the free market – that it is ethical from the point of view of utility, rights, and justice – embodies some questionable and characteristically capitalist presuppositions.[11] It takes utility to be preference satisfaction, and I argued in Chapter 3 that it is not. As for rights: a buyer has a right not to buy a product; an employee has a right to resign. But are there no more rights in play? Is there no other recourse for an abused employee? Are negative rights the only ones? The standard defense presupposes that justice is a matter of hiring, paying, and firing on the basis of actual and possible contributions to the success of the organization. But all we can say about that notion of justice is that productivity requires it (a dubious claim in any case), not that it most closely approximates the Platonic Form of Justice. In a small firm, as opposed to IBM, a form of socialism might be quite productive. Would it be unjust? I know of no principle of justice that justifies the judgment that either company is more just than the other.

But there are some areas in which capitalism does seem to serve justice in ways that may come to be attractive even to those who have held more traditional notions of justice.

Justice for women

Justice was done, most of us would say, by Hank Saporsky in the case of Deborah. I have argued that Hank not only understood that gender is a poor basis for discrimination in business but also saw Deborah primarily as a promising young colleague, not primarily as a woman. We know, however, that there are organizations in which Hank Saporsky would not be able to get Deborah sent to London. Some organizations have their homes in national cultures in which a woman's normal place is nothing like what we find, or hope to find, in North America and Western Europe. There a manager who is considered just would not likely support a woman in a situation like this. The manager's intuitions will be unaffected by any feminist sensibility, and if pressed he may offer principles that have to do with a woman's proper place.

---

[11] Let us ignore for the moment the problem that real markets are often uncompetitive, that participants are poorly informed or irrational, that there are externalities – in short, that free markets are as scarce as free lunches.

What can change this attitude? Capitalism has provided some opportunities for women because it has offered compelling incentives for not
discriminating on the basis of gender. In organizations that face serious
competition, as some large companies now do, thanks in part to globalization, discrimination on the basis of anything other than ability to
do a necessary job is an increasingly unaffordable luxury. People who
have claimed that it is fair to give Jones the promotion because he has
earned it by his performance are now under pressure to say the same
about Smith. People who have claimed that Jones is an adult who has
the right to be treated with respect are now more likely to say the same
about Smith. It is costly to do otherwise.

One can, however, set out to make decisions and have attitudes that
are based on talent, fairness, and rights but still retain one's prejudices. We tend to find plausible-sounding principles that justify our
intuitions, which are warped by our prejudices. So, for example, we
search for reasons to say that Smith, unlike Jones, is really not so good
at the job. But however irrational we may be in that respect, economic
pressure often leads to the habit of dealing with women as though they
were one's equals, and that habit can spread beyond business.[12] That
is a point in favor of capitalism.

Insofar as they encourage participants to judge people on the basis
of their contribution to the success of the firm, business considerations
may crowd out other, worse, bases of judgment. Leo Durocher, the
manager of the Brooklyn Dodgers when Jackie Robinson joined the
team in 1947, was a pragmatist rather than a freedom fighter,[13] but
the power of pragmatism is the point of this story. Sensing a possible
revolt against Robinson, Durocher assembled the players and said, "I
don't care if the guy is yellow or black or if he has stripes like a [exple-
tive deleted] zebra." The reason he gave for not caring about race was
that Robinson was an excellent player and would help the team win
and make money for the players and, of course, for Durocher. That
is a narrow basis on which to judge people, but it helps undermine
racial prejudice in favor of persuasive grounds based on the legitimate

---

[12] Kupperman (2005, p. 205) notes that changes in attitudes on matters such as
gender may "radiate out" and affect how we see and describe situations
beyond where the change occurred.

[13] His most famous remark, "Nice guys finish last," was taken out of context,
but it probably did not seriously misrepresent his attitude, which was very
much Us vs. Them.

mission of the organization. He probably did not speak of aiming at the common good, but he did appropriately talk about the success of the team.

Tradition opposed Robinson. Some of his Brooklyn teammates were, as his minor league manager had been, southerners by whom racism was taken for granted, and they were not especially pleased to have him on the team, especially as they had no choice in the matter. What won them over, even more than being told that they had no choice except to leave the team, was that Robinson was not only an excellent player but also a fierce competitor, ready to do anything to support his teammates. For that reason he reached their emotions, and they saw him in a new way. The teammates did not cease to be clannish, but now Robinson was one of the leaders of their clan, and the reported racial attitudes of some of his skeptical teammates changed.

Business can do the same for gender equity. Where it is recognized in a business context, for financial reasons, it will be easier for women to gain the same kind of equal respect elsewhere, as in the family. In some developing countries that are predominantly Muslim, practitioners of microcapitalism face possible resistance from the husbands of women who get the loans and use them to make serious money. The lending officers try to explain the arrangements to the husbands in a way that shows respect for their views and acknowledgment of the importance of their support for their wives. It works fairly well if the profits start flowing,[14] though some religious leaders criticize it.

I have argued that a business that makes money by creating excellent products and services and selling them for competitive prices is, all else equal, a good business – an opinion that unites Friedman and Freeman. Such a business will have good reason to set aside judgments based on gender and race and to hire and promote on the basis of the employees' ability to contribute to their legitimate way of making money. This policy will be attractive to most employees who benefit from it, and it will help socialize them.

It would be a mistake, however, to expect that people with deep-seated traditional views about women will quickly be won over by Smith's competence. Seeing her as a good manager will require seeing her differently, without the blinkers of confirmation bias and other kinds of bias.

---

[14] I heard Mohammad Yunus make this point in a public talk some years ago.

Bribery

Most businesspeople and public servants in the West agree that corruption is a major moral and practical problem. Those who take bribes no doubt disagree. One can argue that bribery is widely accepted,[15] and claim that it is not much more corrupt than the practice of tipping. A cultural relativist might say that to call a practice ethical amounts to no more than to say that it is accepted in a particular culture, and might defend bribery on that basis. But at the very least bribery is an enemy of the good that capitalism does. It diverts money to those who have leverage and away from those who can earn it in competition. It harms those who have a right to expect that their tax dollars will pay for the best possible bridge, not to pay off the best placed briber. It creates a negative-sum game. It undermines markets and cancels out much of what is virtuous about them. Some defenders of bribery argue that police officers and other public servants are paid so little that it is only fair that they supplement their meager income in an informal way. That is at best an argument in favor of paying public servants more. We have reason to hope that the global spread of democratic capitalism will reduce bribery. We shall learn something about justice from understanding why and how bribery, once considered respectable in some quarters, becomes less acceptable. There is no guarantee, however, that capitalism will reduce bribery just because it is the enemy of capitalism. Consider Russia. Consider certain American states.

The Organization for Economic Cooperation and Development has told large, efficient companies that they have the most to lose in the race to the bottom that permitting bribery precipitates. They continue to try to convince developing (and other) countries that their people are much better off if they pay civil servants better and do not let them take bribes or even solicit grease payments. That will work better where the populace actually has a strong voice in affecting practices relating to bribery, as it does not in (say) Saudi Arabia. But large, efficient companies are on the right side of this argument – as they eventually were on the right side of the argument over apartheid in South Africa, and for roughly similar reasons: it was bad for business.

Civil servants open to bribery will have strong intuitions about the appropriateness of the practice and will not shed them easily. If you are a poorly paid civil servant in a developing country, you will not

---

[15] But not, significantly, widely legal.

think yourself dishonest in asking for a grease payment. You need the money, after all, and that is how things are done. In fact, it would be a bit harsh for anyone to call you dishonest. What will probably have to happen is that over time civil servants will get into the habit of following the law and being honest, in part because they will be paid better, and they will take pride in their honesty and be embarrassed if they act otherwise. They will be developing a better understanding of what honesty is. Think of Australia, where there is no tipping. If you try to leave a tip, the server will likely stop you, sometimes with a convincing show of mild indignation.

The growing consensus against bribery suggests that, as globalization proceeds, cultural relativism may continue to be an interesting philosophical issue but a less pressing practical one. Globalization will probably move us towards consensus on bribery because it is bad for business on the whole. So are cruelty and dishonesty in the workplace: these vices reduce commitment, undermine trust, and so create costs. For that reason their survival requires that they not see the light of day; so transparency is their enemy, as therefore is communication, which continues to improve radically as technology does. Similarly, a measure of social capital will probably survive widely, in organizations, supply chains, and elsewhere because, as I argued in Chapter 5, it is good for business on the whole.[16]

There is some uncertainty about what counts as bribery, however, since there are no airtight and unassailable principles defining it. One of the great political issues in this country now is the legitimacy of campaign contributions. Most people agree that it would be immoral to pay voters to vote for a certain candidate, but there are many who see nothing wrong with rich citizens contributing millions of dollars to buy campaign ads to influence those voters and the candidate as well. But freedom of speech is a difficult issue here, in part because communications technology has broadened our notion of speech and raised questions that the old rules cannot easily answer.[17]

---

[16] Whether the guanxi version of social capital is ethically justifiable can be determined in part by whether it spreads or survives or, on the other hand, is anticompetitive and therefore a drag on the economy that cannot be sustained. See Dunfee and Warren (2001).

[17] As it happens, the Supreme Court judges who are most confident of their ability to understand and judge according to the intent of the Founders were the ones who most readily applied the First Amendment to mass political advertising.

Property

Capitalism armed with technology will raise questions about property as well. We have long known that commerce and therefore social progress would be impossible without the institution of property,[18] which Aristotle takes very seriously. He discusses it in *Pol* II 5, and leaves little doubt that he believes, among other things, that one normally takes better care of a property if it is one's own. He goes beyond utilitarian considerations in claiming (*Pol* II 5 1263a29–b14) that private property supports friendship, increases self-love, and encourages virtues like generosity and moderation.

There are some difficult cases, however, even about what counts as property. Suppose you, a product manager in a home products firm, are eating lunch in a restaurant and overhear two of your competitor's product managers, who do not recognize you, talking rather too loudly about their rollout of a new product in your market segment.[19] If you use the information that they have accidentally given you, are you taking fair advantage of a competitor's mistake or stealing intellectual property?

Students usually argue that it is not unethical to use the information: those people should have been more careful, they say. On the other hand, when one day I put the case to two senior executives in a large multinational media company, they both immediately responded that one must approach the competitors and tell them to stop talking about their marketing plan in public. In fact, both claimed to have been in a similar situation. Their reaction was probably affected by their position: they had had long experience trading in information, and they took it seriously as a commodity. They considered the situation with a strong sense of justice: whoever would appropriate that information is stealing property. That seems to be a minority view, but it may gain support as we become more sophisticated about the idea of intellectual property.[20]

---

[18] But much progress has been made in electronic technology by people who can create networks precisely because they do not claim property rights.

[19] I first heard of a case much like this from Tom Dunfee, who used it in teaching at Wharton.

[20] There are other equally difficult issues around property. Consider Friedman's and others' questionable inferences from the claim that a corporation is the property of its stockholders.

In these cases markets support instances of justice: a fair and respectful attitude towards women, honesty in working for what one gets rather than extorting it, and respect for another's property. These are not the only virtues that markets teach us, and they do not come with detailed instructions for application, but they are important and laudable ones.

Problems

This account raises two related problems, however. First, even we who accept the modern liberal notion of ethics face some unresolved issues. We see the problems associated with bribery, but we disagree about practices that resemble bribery in some important respects and may seem inconsistent with democracy. Mass media have complicated our notions of speech and the press, so we should not be surprised if we cannot easily resolve today's questions about political advertising. We consider property a matter of great moral importance, but we are unsure about how to extend it to intellectual property. Our standard conception of property, which after all has not prevailed in all societies throughout history, does not answer certain questions satisfactorily. So we have to ask ourselves what the purposes of the institution of property are, and how we best fulfill those purposes under new conditions. Second, not everyone will accept bourgeois virtues as truly virtuous. From the point of view of traditional ethics, women's equality is not a good thing, and neither the profit motive nor any other utilitarian consideration will always override that point of view.

The first problem is in one important respect amenable to an Aristotelian approach. We have noted that Werhane (1999, p. 93) offers a conception of moral imagination that is useful as we contemplate these new situations: it is the ability to discover and evaluate possibilities not determined by present circumstances, mental models, or principles. This is a fair description of some of what practical wisdom does.

Recall that, as a virtuoso pianist does not just play the notes, a person of good character does not just act according to principles. Practical wisdom, a faculty of the virtuous, is a matter of being able to go on thinking wisely after the rules leave off. We have inadequate rules to guide us as we consider how and why to protect intellectual property.

Determining what counts as theft of intellectual property is more than a matter of applying the principle "Thou shalt not steal" to copyright and patent cases. Deciding how long to extend copyrights and patents requires taking into account considerations that have to do with economics – considerations with which Aristotle is not thoroughly familiar. It takes great practical wisdom to create a system of intellectual property that rewards productivity, maintains fairness (as opposed to widespread monopoly pricing), and otherwise serves the stakeholders appropriately. It takes an appreciation of how context can determine the meaning of a thing or an action, as Aristotle suggests in discussing the mean (at *NE* III 7 1115b17–19 and II 6 1106b16–22), where he emphasizes the definitive roles of time, place, purpose, and so on. It also takes trial and error, whose results will not end all arguments. We may have what appear to be good principles for delineating intellectual property, but then some new technology raises questions that the principles cannot address. The best we can do is to bring practical wisdom to bear on the questions that it raises in the light of our strongest intuitions and our favored principles concerning the purpose of property. That is to say, as we are seeking new guiding (but not precise) principles and new intuitions as well, we shall have to engage in dialectical conversations. Much the same is true of our competing intuitions about bribery.

Werhane and Gorman (2005) bring moral imagination to bear in a sophisticated treatment of some issues in intellectual property. Among other claims, they note that we are not dealing with a simple case of ownership. The development of drugs and other intellectual property is possible only owing to "an interactive networking set of processes and overlapping ideas" (p. 607); hence the pharmaceutical companies have some obligation to share their drugs. How to bring to bear all the right stakeholders in the right way at the right time will require great practical wisdom.

Now to the second problem. It may be possible to convert some traditionalists who see financial and other advantages in capitalism, but bourgeois "virtues" may still not be real virtues at all. To critics like MacIntyre they will look like nothing more than traits that help capitalism – admittedly a productive system – work smoothly and appeal to capitalists old and new. More radical questions come from traditional societies, in which, as Haidt says, there is a different notion of what ethics is all about. These questions arise around the issue of gender equity. Why, a traditionalist might ask, should there even be any female managers, however productive they may be? That is not what women should do.

A virtue approach is appropriate here, and it is compatible with the values of capitalism. Granting women access to positions for which their talents qualify them permits them to reach their potential as rational deliberators and effective agents. A reduction in bribery can encourage pride in contributing to the production of excellent goods and services. The spread of private property can support family and neighborhood values, as Aristotle suggests. The development of intellectual property calls on our practical wisdom to help us answer new questions and act virtuously accordingly.

In these cases involving gender equity, bribery, and property, the virtue in play is justice. This is a virtue that most cultures honor, but they have different conceptions of it. Even within the modern liberal culture we are often unclear about what justice requires in new and complex cases. The person of practical wisdom is creative and flexible enough to address these cases and find ways of putting justice into practice. Precisely because Smith is a practically wise manager, she is open to discussing various possible ways of designing just practices in a wide range of situations.

We know that Aristotle himself would not call the reconciliation of modern and traditional ethics an easy task or suggest that just anyone is up to it, but he offers us some resources for addressing it. One of them is his notion of virtue based on humans as rational and sociable creatures: it is a mean between the modern and the traditional conceptions ethics that should be attractive to both. The other is dialectic. Global enterprise will never resemble the Academy or the Lyceum, but it can make room for and learn from dialectical conversations among people who, though some of their values differ, have some important things in common.

We shall first discuss Aristotle's view as a reconciling mean between ethical extremes, and then turn to the usefulness of dialectic. I do not offer his views as the only or even the best approach to global ethical reconciliation, but they are surprisingly useful, especially considering how parochial Aristotelian virtue ethics may seem.

Differences of degree

Solidarity and hierarchy differ from one community to another in degree. Most of us in Western societies do believe that community is important and that most communities require hierarchies of authority. But unlike people in traditional societies, most of us think that authority in the political sphere comes from the just consent of the governed, and we want to live under the least authority compatible with good order. We take loyalty seriously, but we try to identify its limits on individual autonomy in a way traditionalists do not. We make moral distinctions based on personal and other relations, but we do not necessarily have less respect for those who are at a distance from us: we do not divide the world into Us vs. Them in that way, though we acknowledge special duties to those in our community and especially to our families. We include among Us people who have somewhat different convictions about religion, in part because most of us no longer consider religion the unquestionable and unique basis of morality.

Let us therefore not exaggerate cultural differences. What most people in any culture want is health, a happy and stable family, pleasant neighbors, some spare time for interesting things to do, and enough income to pay for it all. Most people despise cowards, liars, and slackers, though they may invoke different ethical theories or religious beliefs to justify their judgments. As Appiah (2006, pp. 67, 80) says, many of our disagreements are about how to practice values that we share, such as respect for the importance of human life. We all value loyalty and honesty, but we disagree about the rightness of grease payments and whistle blowing. On Appiah's view (pp. 63f.), this is because we honor similar virtues but differ on their priority. Which priority is correct may depend on circumstances that differ from one arena to another. But I believe we also give slightly different accounts of the virtues.

Even a concern for purity, a staple of traditional morality, plays a role in the modern conception. We may think that in general we shall care less about purity as our scientific knowledge of the world increases. Once we know that thorough cooking can prevent trichinosis, we are less likely to believe that God does not want us to eat animals with cloven hooves. Yet in almost every culture there are certain things that most people find disgusting (Appiah, 2006, p. 54). We find the thought of cannibalism disgusting, as does Aristotle (*NE* VII 5 1148b15–20). But what's wrong with eating someone who is already dead? Who gets hurt? Questions like these seem to us to be beside the point. In cases like this it is not wrong to examine our feelings and ask what reason there may be for them, but it is certainly wrong to dismiss those feelings as superstitious. As we know, our emotions can be sources of understanding and of support for our intuitions, and they will not and should not readily go away. In this case they seem to be connected to feelings of profound respect, even reverence, for human beings.[21]

To my knowledge no Enlightenment philosopher or modern businessperson is so radically utilitarian as to accept cannibalism and similar practices, but in today's modern liberal societies Sandel (2012) and others find a related utilitarian tendency to buy and sell things for which there should not be a market, and thus to undermine their actual value in aid of economic efficiency. There is nothing superstitious, Sandel thinks, about forbidding poor women to become pregnant with the intention of selling their children to willing buyers. Calling it an abomination might be a bit excessive, but we can see the point. There is something questionable about paying children to read books, for a reason that sounds Aristotelian: reading ought to be a pleasure in itself, and not merely a means to an end, particularly not to a financial end; yet perhaps it could get children into the habit of reading, as in the case of playing the piano. And as with incentive compensation, payment may undermine better and stronger motives. So while traditional cultures are less likely than are modern ones to apply utilitarian tests, hence less likely to commodify inappropriately, even in modern cultures there is disagreement on this issue, as Sandel illustrates.

Aristotle's ethics as a mean

Recall Haidt's claim that we can see the Aristotelian position as a mean between modern and traditional moralities. At one extreme on the continuum that they occupy is Enlightenment morality, or at least a caricature of it, with its emphasis on abstract universal principles, unanchored individual autonomy, and empty utilitarianism. At the other is dogmatic authority bossing all citizens around for the good (authoritatively defined) of the obedient community.[22] At the mean

---

[21] So Woodruff (2001) would no doubt say.
[22] Nussbaum (2010, p. 53) claims that deference to authority causes disasters in corporations and elsewhere. The disasters surely come about as a result of extreme deference. Refusal to acknowledge authority, the opposite extreme, causes disasters of a different sort.

we might hold that individual well-being and even identity are essentially dependent to a significant degree on one's community and that any autonomy worth having entails being rational about what one prefers. From this Aristotelian position we can reach out to those of traditional morality by saying this: Yes, we understand the importance of community to one's identity; it is legitimate to divide people into Us and Them, to recognize special obligations to family, friends, and fellow citizens, with emotions to match. We must honor good communities sustained by friendships of utility and be prepared to play our appropriate roles in them, for it is in our nature to be dependent upon others. We naturally are and ought to be motivated by the common good. We understand that what looks like autonomy may not be morally justifiable or even beneficial for the agent. We cannot base all of morality on unfettered supply and demand. In particular, we are prepared to support customary practices that represent the special nature and transcendent significance of humankind. All that said, however, human beings are by nature creatures who make morally responsible choices and create lives for themselves.

As we consider the communal virtues of loyalty and respect for authority, we should remember that Aristotle's doctrine of the mean acknowledges the importance of context. So how loyal one should be, how one should treat members of the out-group, and how much power any authority ought to have are issues to be determined by context, for example by the nature of the work to be done. Respect for authority is a high priority in the military and in small warring tribes, less so in business, still less so in academe. Spreading capitalism, whose effects are felt far beyond organizations, will create new contexts in which people will come to see that loyalty and other virtues need to assume new and different degrees and forms. Increasing education, communication, and the intellectual demands of work will probably cause people to become habituated to greater autonomy and greater gender equality, perhaps first in the workplace but eventually elsewhere in people's lives – in the family, for example. But the notion of autonomy that Aristotle sponsors is linked to the good life, which is not the life of the isolated, unconstrained, unsupported, emptily utilitarian individual.

Aristotle's intermediate position gives hope that, despite serious differences, some reconciliation or at least conversation is possible between the traditional conception of morality and the modern one. Dialectic offers a possible way of effecting that reconciliation.

Dialectic

Recall that Aristotle claims that ethics should take common opinions, with special attention to what wise people say, as its starting point, in one sense of the word *arche*. By induction from these opinions and what we have learned from collecting facts about biology and psychology, we may reach principles that explain those opinions. We do not start from nowhere, contrary to Descartes; we start from where we are.

Most of us who study business ethics think of capitalism as the best system available now, and focus on how to make it and its participants more ethical. It is at least conceivable that some other economic system would work even better in important respects, but any argument in favor of another system would carry a burden of plausibility, if not proof. In the spirit of Aristotle, we should think about ethics in this our world and try to sharpen our widely held intuitions, many of which were formed in competitive enterprise, and gather them under principles that we can accept. But the result will not necessarily give the strongest possible support to the form of capitalism common in America. Many people have views about fairness, for example, that represent a challenge to the American form of capitalism. It takes some doing to justify wage stagnation in American companies in which profits and executive compensation are soaring. There are Friedmanite principles that could justify that arrangement, but they conflict with other principles having to do with sharing the results of shared work, and with some people's intuitions.

Over time businesspeople ought to develop a sophisticated set of principles and intuitions that will enable them to make decisions about employment and other issues at the right time under the right circumstances in the right way in dealing with new people under pressure from new stakeholders. Even with all the best possible principles and intuitions, however, they will have no manual telling them what to do in these new situations. But they have never had such a manual.

Intercultural dialectic[23]

Suppose Jones, a western businessperson, speaks with an executive from a more traditional society about incentive compensation. The principle that more productive managers ought to get paid more may seem intuitively fair to the Westerner, but the traditionalist, caring more about solidarity, may object to the practice as divisive. How can this difference be settled? Suppose that the two executives have available some information that shows that in many cases incentive compensation does not have the desired effect, that in particular it does loosen bonds of trust and loyalty. Jones might then reconsider his intuition that fairness requires incentive compensation, since it alters the employees' preferences in a way that undermines their understanding of their work and therefore the intrinsic satisfaction that they derive from it. He might then accept a guiding principle that recognizes a form of justice that is not merely a matter of more pay for more productivity. On the other hand, Jones might object that justice should not be so dependent upon utilitarian considerations: he might say that Smith deserves more because she is more productive. Then the two executives could try to work out a principle that tells us how justice should relate to utility in cases like this.

Particularly in an intercultural context, dialectic should not be confused with negotiation, though the two processes overlap to some degree. The parties to negotiation usually begin with a clear idea of their interests, and of what they want on this occasion. In the case of dialectic one's interests are themselves subject to scrutiny. To redeploy the language of Burns on leadership, discussed in Chapter 5, we can think of negotiation as transactional, whereas dialectic has an aspect of the transformational. In the case of gender equity, for example, the goal is not to reach a mutually satisfactory or unsatisfactory compromise but to change the attitude of one or both parties towards women. That change may require rethinking some deeply held religious or ideological convictions.[24]

---

[23] Whether dialectic or reflective equilibrium can claim neutrality across cultural boundaries is controversial. See Norman (2002) for a moderately optimistic view. But neutrality is not an absolute necessity.

[24] McCracken and Shaw (1995, p. 307) claim that negotiation in the real world may be about not only the apparent substantive issues but also the terms of negotiation. Behind the parties' differing positions may lie differences in values

Sometimes a dialectical conversation will reveal important intuitions that may be obscure to both parties. Bribery looks like a straightforward matter of paying someone with leverage rather than counting on the quality and price of one's product or service to gain a competitive advantage, but the situation may be more complicated than that. How then can we explain the refusal of a Nigerian executive or public official to accept a bribe proffered by an American company while accepting the same bribe if it is the Nigerians who first propose it (Tsalikis and Wachukwu, 2000)? Perhaps the answer lies in what the Nigerians consider exploitation.

Consider a conversation with a Chinese traditionalist. Can we talk usefully about whether a businessperson ought to be a gentleman in the Confucian sense? I think we can. It is striking that Confucius, something of a virtue ethicist himself (see Chan, 2007), offers a conception of a gentleman that looks very much like Aristotle's conception of a person of good character – trustworthy and trusting, among other things. Aristotle and some Jane Austen characters might believe that a businessman is by definition not a gentleman. But given the facts of our world, we might be able to persuade them and Confucians as well that a businessperson can be a gentleman, or even a lady, and that the apparent tension between gentlemanliness and professionalism can be resolved by dialectical deliberation.

In some cases the advance of capitalism has rendered traditional views nearly irrelevant. It is unlikely that North American and European businesspeople will encounter many Confucians among their Chinese counterparts, as capitalism has overtaken older ideologies, including communism. (Not entirely, perhaps: it is doubtful that liberal individualism thrives in China, though it may grow as capitalism does.) But a traditionalist might argue that some traditional values worth keeping have been lost, particularly since the regime has not asked its subjects whether they would prefer living under capitalism.

Executives in multinational enterprises can try to deal with competing moral traditions by ignoring them and simply telling everyone what to do, and never mind their values. But if the values of the organization are a rallying point essential to the success of the enterprise, the executive would be better advised to create a dialectical

and attitudes. But negotiation does not normally address these greater issues directly with a view to reconciling them. Perhaps it sometimes should.

conversation that considers people's intuitions and principles in aid of reaching some practicable consensus on business issues with ethical implications, along with respect for more peripheral differences of opinion. Mere habits of acting in the valued ways, reinforced by rewards and punishments, are not yet virtues and therefore may not survive critical reflection and will likely be brought to bear in a mechanical way that is neither creative nor practically wise. Worse yet, a peremptory management style may encourage nothing more than the habit of working productively only while closely watched, or the habit of gaming the incentive compensation system.

Yet there is much to be said for changing habits. It can lead to changing prevailing intuitions, an essential component of dialectical progress, or at any rate of getting to a useful consensus. So, to consider gender prejudice once again, some men must begin to have different intuitions about women as they get into the habit of dealing with them. Here we can say, following Aristotle, that habit plays a role in developing people's intuitions, and that emotional change is part of the development of intuitions. Eventually some men will stop reacting resentfully to being required to report to Smith and begin to see her as a manager, not as a pushy feminist – or words to that effect. At this point it will be easier to discuss a hiring and promotion policy explicitly based on gender neutrality. But since Smith will initially face prejudicial judgments of the quality of her work, it will be important for her to do very well and to make visible contributions to the success of the firm. As the negative emotion fades, many of those who report to her will come to feel comfortable about it, and will not care whether she is male or female or has stripes like a zebra. At that point they will be ready to think about why gender equity is morally required.

Limits of dialectic

Dialectic begins with not only some common beliefs and intuitions of the participants but also some guiding presuppositions. Those who engage in it must commit to a level of rationality and intellectual honesty that may come naturally to us but does not come easily. It would be a good thing if ethicists made it their business to orchestrate conversations under the conditions set out by Lerner and Tetlock (2003), mentioned in Chapter 4. As I suggested there, if Smith is a good manager she can convey to subordinates that she cares about the issue under discussion, that she cannot be fooled about the pertinent facts, and that her mind is open and undecided. All this conveys a commitment to rationality, but more. Smith is signaling that she respects her subordinates' views and cares about their interests and that she believes that they are intellectually honest people motivated by the prospect of the organization's success. She is also willing to forgo the pleasure of ordering people around.[25] And as with virtuous citizens in a good *polis*, people in the organization need to agree that they are aiming at the success of the whole enterprise rather than at determining who is stronger.

We should not assume that dialectic by itself will get us to moral truth, as we should not believe that democracy assures us of a good government, or that a perfectly competitive market will benefit all participants fairly, or that the Original Position assures us of justice. I have argued that no system or structure or process by itself is proof against knavery. Fort (1999, pp. 402f.), seeing this problem, argues that there must be something transcendent, perhaps religious, guiding the dialectical conversation. Aristotle relies on the possibility of the participants' rationality, which he thinks is in some way akin to the divine, as we noted in Chapter 2. His model is the virtuous citizen in the good *polis*: that citizen participates in politics with a view to making the *polis* just, not with a view to getting the most of whatever he or his interest group wants. So only the virtuous can participate in political argument in the right way. There is no guarantee that the good *polis* itself will make its citizens virtuous in that way: its support is a necessary but not sufficient condition of the justice of the citizenry. But Aristotle consistently opposes the notion that citizens are disposed by nature to act selfishly rather than for the common good. No doubt he would say the same about employees.

But what have we proved if we reach a point at which there is a consensus on intuitions and principles within a capitalist system that dominates the world? Is it not possible to arrive at a bad consensus, one that takes insufficient account of intuitions we once had? Suppose that over time we grow accustomed to the practice of selling children where there is a willing buyer and a willing seller and the child would be better off. It might change our attitude towards children: we might

---

[25] Woodruff (2001, p. 27) argues that meetings are often rituals that confirm our solidarity in spite of our differences.

lose some of the *eudaimonia* associated with parenting. But it might happen without our regretting it, as we would not regret the loss of the sense of family honor that leads family members to kill a straying daughter. We might then embrace certain utilitarian principles about children. How do we know, when we reach a consensus, that we have made progress?

In the real world there is little chance that dialectic will lead us to anything like a complete consensus, not least because conditions are always changing and raising new problems for our old principles and intuitions. Consensus might otherwise be stultifying; dissenting voices play an important positive role, for reasons that have been familiar at least since Mill.[26] In any case, even the greatest possible consensus in business will not be the last word. While gender equity in firms may lead to gender equity in families or vice versa, the priorities of firms and the priorities of families are very different, and conversations within them will differ as well. They will have their different versions of the virtues, and different virtues will be prominent. So excessive commodification of humans, for example, may serve the interests of businesses, and some individuals as well, but there will be resistance to it from most families and from critics who study them, and serious conversations will ensue.

One of the reasons why dialectical conversations are so important is that today a typical person is a member of many different tribes. As Putnam (2000) has argued, certain important associative ties in our society have been weakened, but most of us live in a workplace, a nuclear family, perhaps an extended family, a neighborhood, a circle of friends, a religious body. We can criticize the values of any one of these groups from the point of view of another. So, for example, this multiple membership will help us avoid the crude way in which traditional morality may encourage us to divide the world into Us and Them. Insofar as modern life puts us into a variety of groups that we can consider Us, it encourages us to reflect on how much loyalty we owe to whom and why. To do so is not to abandon the virtue of loyalty or

---

[26] Eastman and Santoro (2003) argue that what they call "value diversity" reduces the influence of group interests, at least weak ones, and thereby increases the aggregate welfare of the primary stakeholders of an organization. How their notion of value diversity relates to Aristotle's views is a complicated story, but they make an interesting case for their sort of diversity, which might be found in a multinational workplace.

the pleasures of association that every sociable animal ought to enjoy, but to think critically about why loyalty is important, what justifies you in being loyal to me, how and why loyalty can degenerate into chauvinism, and how our strong intuitions about loyalty may conflict with justice when our family, friends, and colleagues deserve justice. In this way our multiple memberships help equip us to undertake dialectical conversations.[27]

Dialectic and human development

Arguably Aristotle is too optimistic in holding that humans naturally are and ought to be rational and sociable: dialectic demands mutual respect and understanding and the belief that the other party is intellectually honest to a degree beyond what Haidt, Kahneman, and Doris would allow. Even the willingness to enter a dialectical conversation and to make the commitment to rationality and sociability that it entails is not one that everyone, especially among traditionalists, is willing to make. Dialectic is difficult even for those who are willing to try it: we tend to make bad moves, like misdescribing our intuitions and tailoring our principles to them.

Recall, however, that Aristotle emphatically does not say that we are born rational or sociable. We have the potential to achieve both, and thus virtue, but we do so only if we acquire first the right habits and then the ability to reflect on what we ought to be and do. But Aristotle does not believe that everyone eventually gets to that natural point of finding *eudaimonia* in ties of family, friendship, and citizenship. He knows about weakness of will, perversion, cannibalism, and other forms of evil, though nature does not aim at these things. He offers no reason to believe that dialectical conversations will spring up spontaneously. No doubt they require some preparation. That is one of the functions of leadership.

There is some evidence of progress by way of nature. Over time humankind has acquired an increasingly sophisticated level of sociability; that is a good thing. According to some evolutionary scientists,[28]

---

[27] Think of a conservative legislator who has a gay son. The disconnect between principle and intuition in this case should make the legislator more thoughtful, at least on the obvious issue.

[28] For example, Bowles and Gintis (2011). Their view is not unanimously shared, however. Group selection is a contested issue.

certain social skills and institutions have survival value. Community solidarity, trust, and cooperation may keep the community going. In many cases this bonding takes the form of suspicion and hostility towards those outside one's group. That tendency survives today, as a kind of genetic habit, and it can sometimes stand us in good stead and sometimes lead to bigotry. But at our best we have acquired not only the habits of the group but the ability to reason about them and about the right relationship with insiders and outsiders.

Since, as Aristotle says, we are not gods, our most rational deliberations are fallible, and we must be modest in deliberating as well as attentive to a range of intuitions. We cannot always predict which institutions and arrangements will contribute to the good life. We sometimes find out the hard way, and sometimes we do not find out at all, but our shared satisfaction with some arrangements and not others may improve our principles and our intuitions. In the meantime we must sometimes compromise, and hope we learn something from the results of doing so.

Lessons of business ethics

Most business students understand that they are likely to work in the global arena, hence with people outside their culture. They will see the point of finding ways to engage them, to achieve consensus with them if possible. They will have little difficulty understanding dialectic if, as is probable, it occurs naturally in the classroom.

Consider how you might lead a discussion about the overheard marketing plan. You ask the students whether they believe that one should never steal another person's property except in the most extreme circumstances. They agree. Then you tell them the story, and ask them whether they should listen to the conversation and use the information. Yes, they say. You ask them why. They say it is not stealing; the talkers should have been more careful. Then you ask them whether they would feel obligated to return a wallet carelessly dropped in their lap. Yes, they would. You ask how the two cases differ. They answer, in effect, that the wallet is a tangible piece of property, and that keeping it is stealing. You ask them whether they would like to revise their principle that one should not steal another's property; would they narrow it to tangible property? And if so, why? Is there no such thing as stealing intellectual property? What about stealing a patented process left lying around? Do they now want to revise their original intuition that it is all right to listen to the conversation?

Dialectic is particularly useful in a case like this, in which a change in a traditional institution – property can be an elusive sort of thing, and copyright and other standard measures for protecting it do not offer satisfactory accounts in all cases – leaves us wondering what to do in this situation. I am claiming that technological progress and globalization are creating new situations like this one, many of them more complex.

As I argued earlier, the students' original intuition would probably differ if they had acquired the habit of taking intellectual property very seriously. That habituation might have had some emotional support as well: they might be repulsed by anyone who would steal that information, as the executives of the communications firm were. In that case their intuition would fit their espoused principle; in fact, the espoused principle would be embedded in their intuition. But no matter how experienced they are, they must understand that they will face some problems that do not look like anything they know now. So, having worked out how important intellectual property is, they may have to argue about whether a pharmaceutical company has a moral right to protect its patent on a profitable retroviral drug when thousands of people who cannot afford it are dying of AIDS.

The manager's own values

Learning to manage in situations of serious disagreements about values requires learning to manage yourself, with an eye on the integrity of your life. If you are a person of good character, you will commit yourself to a life in which you enjoy being honest, courageous, and benevolent in undertaking the tasks that are part of being a good citizen, a good spouse, a good parent, a good friend, and a good worker (employee, manager, or professional). So you will play a number of roles in a number of associations, and you will have some choice about the roles you will play, depending on the course you decide your life will take and the projects that will be part of that course. But it would be a mistake to suppose that engaging people with different values and priorities requires you to change your own. An integrated life gives you a place to stand and enables you to bring some values to your participation in dialectic.

Consider an especially prominent role, that of the citizen. Aristotle regards it as the obligation of a virtuous person to be a participant in creating and maintaining a just community. You may run for office, but that is not necessary. It would be fair to add that you can be a good citizen without necessarily being a conservative or a liberal, so long as you are not so extreme that you cannot understand how any rational person could disagree with your position. In your participation in government you will maintain your integrity while seeking effective solutions to political problems not described in detail in any textbook. If you are considering compromising, or extending or decreasing the reach of government, or mounting strong opposition to the most powerful officials, you must do it at the right time, in the right way, about the right things, with the right kind of involvement of the right people and for the right purposes. That is not a matter of incoherence in your values. It is a crucial feature of virtue: adaptation to time, place, relations, and other features of the particular situation. If you are a virtuous person, one who regularly hits the mean, you have a character that is strong enough to be flexible and adaptive in the absence of rules to tell you exactly what to do – a situation to which you have become accustomed – and you have justified confidence in your intuitions and emotions. This is never easy in the absence of algorithms to guide you. If you do not have a firm grip on the values and commitments that make your life a purposeful whole, it will be impossible. You will pursue short-term objectives; you will make decisions on the basis of pressure, irrelevant sentiments, your narrowly selfish interests and biases.

Much the same can be said of a good manager who participates in creating an effective and ethical organization. Your good character does not tell you exactly what to do in most complex situations, and certainly not in situations that, owing to radical changes in the environment, are unlike any you have seen before. It does demand that you make your significant decisions at the right time, in the right way, about the right things, with the right kind of involvement of the right people and for the right purposes. If you have only rules and habits to go by, you will be lost in complex situations and you will be unable to come to any kind of useful understanding with people who have different rules. If you are not guided by a clear sense of what is important to you, you will make irrational decisions, and you will be a terrible leader.

Suppose that you value individual autonomy and justice based on equality, and that the organization that you represent does as well. Suppose that you are dealing with people new to your organization, people whose culture emphasizes obedience and solidarity. You will not make much progress by arguing that your principles are right and theirs wrong. On the other hand, if you have a sense of what is important to you, you can confidently enter into a serious conversation. You may find that you and your interlocutors can agree that, for example, there are times and places and kinds of work and ways to grant more or less autonomy of certain kinds to certain employees but not others. Then, keeping in mind that a primary purpose of the conversation is to create an effective organization that has its employees' respect and loyalty (i.e., the right kind of loyalty on the right subjects for the right reasons), you and your more traditionally oriented partners may come to some agreements on specific issues related to autonomy without compromising your core values. You will have achieved a mean between individual autonomy and the good of the corporation.

These specific agreements may eventually lead to some principles that will guide your thinking as you work out further issues. You may also arrive at some principles that cause you to take a second look at some of your specific agreements. Dialectic may take you that far; it will probably not take you to contemplation of universal principles. But that is not necessary in an organizational context, or in most others for that matter. In any case, no principle will be useful without the help of a great deal of practical wisdom in working out how to apply it (and when, and with whom, and for what purpose, and so on).

Purity again

Though purity is not a notion that we usually associate with Aristotle, he does suggest a kind of purity, even godliness, when he discusses theoretical study in *NE* X 7–8. Because we are rational beings, we are capable of purely theoretical thinking. No nonhuman animal can do this. And just as the theoretical thinking that Aristotle has in mind is not about the changing world of matter and form, the part of the soul responsible for theorizing is immaterial – untainted, we might say (*De Anima* III 4 429a24–6). Philosophizing in this way is the highest form of human *eudaimonia*. Like other virtues, it is good and desirable in itself; unlike most other virtuous activities, it does not also lead to some definitive result, such as the safety of the *polis*. The rationality that is active in theorizing is the divine element in us. We are not gods, Aristotle concedes here as elsewhere; that is a point of great importance to the Greeks, who deplore *hubris*. But we should live according to this divine element insofar as possible, and then we shall have as much *eudaimonia* as possible. Precisely how this pure theorizing relates to the rest of one's life and its concerns is not altogether clear, but Aristotle says (X 8 1179a22–4) that one who nurtures one's understanding[29] and acts according to it is beloved by the gods.

There is an element of religious reverence in Aristotle's story about pure rationality. Though Aristotle is not given to flights of Platonic poetry, his words on rationality faintly echo Plato's claim, in the *Phaedrus* and elsewhere, that the truth that philosophy seeks is divine and that apprehending it is like having a mystical experience.[30] Aristotelian rationality, even in its unadulterated condition, is not seen as a kind of purity in most traditional religions, but it does represent a transcendent element of ethics that is not prominent in the modern ethics that MacIntyre criticizes, the sort of ethics that recognizes no form of goodness or happiness that goes beyond human desire. So Aristotle occupies a mean between modern utilitarianism and traditional purism.

He does observe that humans are capable of growth and improvement in rationality, and he infers that the slavish life of one who does as ordered – a kind of life often found in commerce, he thinks – is not a worthy life for a human being. We might interpret him as saying that one's life should not be for sale. This may remind us of Sandel's argument that a commercial society sometimes encourages us to sell inappropriate wares.[31] An unsubtle form of utilitarianism might applaud any bargain between consenting adults as a win-win situation. Aristotle, no unsubtle utilitarian, believes that a certain level of material prosperity is necessary for *eudaimonia*, but he does not acknowledge that a capitalist economy is the one most likely to provide that prosperity, hence the best opportunity to extend one's human capacities,

---

[29] The Greek word is *nous*, which is crucial to our ability to see actions and situations as they truly are. Recall the discussion in Chapter 2, and *NE* III 5 1114a32–b3 and VII 3 1147a18–35.

[30] See Woodruff (2001, pp. 100f.) on Plato, but not on Aristotle.

[31] Aristotle considers lending money at interest inappropriate (*Pol* I 10 1258b2–8). He says at *NE* V 5 1133b14f. that everything has a price, but I think he is referring to goods normally exchanged in a market.

including rationality. With some prompting and some understanding of large-scale capitalism he might agree to a form of economy that finds a mean, a way of creating widespread prosperity without encouraging undue commodification, which in any case may be the result of desperation created by poverty. Commodifying nothing is no better than commodifying everything.

One of the great dangers of capitalism is that it can lead to the commodification of oneself. That is what has happened when a businessperson works ever-longer hours to make more than enough money to buy more stuff than a reasonable person could want. Such a person has weakness of will about wealth (*NE* VII 4 1147b33), Aristotle says. This attitude afflicts some but by no means all successful executives, and the attitude sometimes trickles down through the organization. It is at least conceivable that hyperactive American executives who associate and converse with their counterparts in – let us say – Denmark will reflect on their lives and begin to ask themselves whether getting and spending at that level are essential to well-being.[32] There is no reason to believe that all dialectical conversations will finally vindicate the view that happiness is a matter of preference satisfaction. In fact that is especially unlikely to happen where the conversation includes people who take religion or the common good seriously, or people who think that money is a means rather than an end.

Combining rationality and sociability

One way of distinguishing the modern conception of morality from the traditional one is to say that the former is about rationality and the latter is about sociability. And of course on Aristotle's view, a mean between extremes, morality is about both. The extremes are deadly. We learn about sociability without rationality from considering Milgram, Zimbardo, and Asch. We learn about rationality without sociability from considering Phineas Gage.

Kahneman, Doris, and Haidt appear to see a struggle between rationality and sociability, with sociability winning. Aristotle takes a different view of this question. He argues that rationality shapes our

---

[32] Skidelsky (2009) would advocate this kind of conversation, which would make some executives ask themselves why they sacrifice leisure for money that they do not need.

sociability, including our "hivish"[33] habits: we are not mere members of a *polis*, we are participants striving for justice. If he is right, then we can have social capital and perhaps even virtuous business. But Aristotle's view is aspirational. Getting Us–Them just right is difficult, even for those who want to attempt it. What we need, I believe, is a modern liberal morality that has learned something from Aristotle.

Recall that Aristotle thinks that at its highest level human sociability is infused with rationality and that a rational person chooses objectives that recognize humankind's sociable nature. To oversimplify slightly, at its extreme modern morality builds on a kind of rationality that fails to factor in sociability, and traditional morality is about a kind of sociability that fails to factor in rationality. If that is true, then Aristotle not only represents a compromise between them, he represents an improvement, as the mean is better than either extreme (as usual, he would say). The superiority of his point of view lies in his understanding that, contrary to the claims of certain Enlightenment philosophers and their modern followers in economics and elsewhere, it is rational to be sociable. Rationality is not about means to any old end, and narrow selfishness is not a good end for a human being. Our education, primarily the work of our community, begins by creating habits and intuitions; then we rationally reflect on these, and in the process develop some principles and real virtues that recognize our sociable nature and give us some guidance about what constitutes a good life.

Haidt sees his own views falling somewhere between modern and traditional, but he is not quite where Aristotle is. He believes that we are hivish and that we ought to recognize it. He believes that in this respect the traditional/conservative conception is closer to the mark than liberal individualism. This is a judgment about how we are. Perhaps in some sense we ought to be less hivish, but we are dependent creatures who need the hive. But Haidt doubts that humans are very rational, even when they believe they are deliberating rationally. Aristotle contemplates hivishness that is compatible with rationality, even essential to it. Haidt does not. He claims that, to adapt Melville on Claggart, our conscience is press secretary to our will.

Aristotle does not believe any more than Haidt does that most people are capable of a high level of rationality; he holds that some lack the

---

[33] Haidt (2012, especially chapter 10) uses the word not in a pejorative way.

strength of will to act rationally. But two things he does believe. First, that enough people are sufficiently rational that it makes sense to invoke reasons (sometimes, to be sure, not very good ones) to explain our behavior and that of others. We do, after all, form intentions and act on them. So you look for the car keys because you want to drive over to pick up Philip at the school to which you sent him because you want him to have a good education. This seems straightforward enough. You might also have another drink and then call the school and send a message that Philip should walk home in the rain because the exercise will do him good. You can think that way, and actually believe that you are concerned about Philip's health. You probably do that sort of thing more often than you realize, and so do many others. But it does not follow that we should abandon rational explanations.

The second thing that Aristotle believes is that rational thought and action are natural human ends – in themselves, that is, apart from their good results. It is therefore a good thing to think and act rationally. Nowadays we do not talk very much about natural human ends, but we have little respect for those who live a slavish or pointless life. And we do know that there is something deeply attractive about rational thought. If Haidt himself had tried to persuade his readers to accept his views about the fragility of rationality by offering emotional appeals or financial incentives, he would have failed, and he would not have enjoyed the attempt.

Aristotle believes that at least some people are sufficiently rational to be capable of participating in dialectic. He probably does not include most businesspeople in that group. But we can and should introduce dialectical argument at least in business ethics courses. In organizations it will be more difficult, perhaps even inappropriate in some cases. But a manager can try to create a culture of respect for a range of ethical views, including ones based on religion. Rather than encouraging people to be silent about ethics and religion, the manager can initiate respectful conversations about people's intuitions and the principles by which they frame the world. That will make it a bit easier for the company to swim in foreign waters, and even in some domestic ones.

Mediating institutions and religious diversity

Whatever we may think of the relationship between purity and religion, we know that many traditionalists, including some conservatives in Western societies, claim to base their ethical views on religion. Here we seem to have disagreements that cannot be resolved, in part because religious disputes by their nature tend not to be amenable to rational argument beyond a certain point. We might think it impossible to persuade a Buddhist to take business ethics seriously. Its principles and virtues could hardly appeal to someone who rejects the world as being in some way fundamentally unsatisfying. But in fact there are writings about Buddhist business ethics.[34] We should find this no more surprising than that Christians embrace business despite the Biblical injunctions against wealth and working for a living, and its support of socialism in the early Christian community. It is doubtful that many successful Asian businesspeople spend much time worrying about whether the Buddha would approve of their work. But the tendency of religious people to adjust their faith to meet the demands of business does not make it any easier to argue about what they infer from that faith.

The mediating institution as the school for virtue

Fort (2001, 2008) offers a promising way of thinking about religious and other ideological differences within organizations.[35] He finds evidence (2008, pp. 50ff.) that small groups are the best breeding ground for the virtues.[36] In particular, an organization, or a smaller unit in an organization, may be a place in which employees learn virtues that contribute to cooperation and help build social capital. There one may develop habits through rewards and punishments, then reflect on them and their purpose, and then develop one's own way of acting virtuously. This is not a task for individuals acting alone. Employees must work together in developing the values of the organization (2008,

---

[34] See, for example, Numkanisorn (2002) in *The Chulalongkorn Journal of Buddhist Studies*.

[35] A decade ago Weaver and Agle (2002) undertook a preliminary investigation of the effects of religion in the workplace and found a host of conceptual barriers to investigation that have not since been overcome, so far as I know. It does seem safe to say, however, that there are not serious religious differences over whether one ought to be honest, diligent, courageous, and supportive of one's fellow employees and the company.

[36] It seems unlikely that virtual communities, united by social media, will become places in which dialectic will lead to ethical consensus, but they could encourage understanding.

pp. 48f., 115). As I suggested earlier, the peremptory organization creates not virtues but only habits, and not necessarily useful ones.

Fort (especially in 1999, pp. 427–9) quite properly rejects the
notion that we become ethical by embracing principles that unite
all humankind, or even a nation. We need mediating institutions
that provide people with a sense of community. Small organizations
or subunits may teach us dependence and thereby interdependence.
They may encourage us towards emotional solidarity (pp. 402f). We
learn accountability by seeing and dealing with the consequences of
our actions. We learn compromise and consensus in aid of shared
goals, most obviously corporate success. All this comes naturally to
us, because our brains are wired that way.

Aristotle agrees about the importance of the small group – in particular, the small *polis*. That is where fellow citizens shape your habits,
which lead to the virtues appropriate to citizenship, if all goes well.
That is where you learn to participate in government, and to be motivated to create a just *polis* rather than to favor yourself or your coali-
tion. As we know, Aristotle has in mind citizens who have significant
leisure time. Today, for better or worse, many people spend so much
time at work that it or part of it becomes their primary mediating
institution (Fort, 1999, p. 434).

Diversity

But whereas Aristotle wants a significant degree of uniformity in the
best *polis* (*Pol* IV 11 1295b23–5 and *NE* IX 6 1167b2–9), Fort (2001,
p. 35) argues that an organization should be a ground on which people of diverse political views, faiths, and ethnic backgrounds can meet
and cooperate. In an organization like this, people are training to deal
with diversity and learning lessons applicable beyond the limits of the
organization.[37] But how is this possible?

It is at least necessary. To succeed in global commerce, an organization must deal effectively with stakeholders that do not all share
its values. How can a company with American values communicate
effectively with Muslim stakeholders in the Middle East? How can
American capitalism plant a flag in such alien soil? Dialectic will take

---

[37] As Shaw (1995) notes, diversity is a crucial issue for business ethics, more
important than for other sorts of professional ethics.

some time, assuming it can get started. Fort's answer is that insofar as
a company is a mediating institution, employees can develop a sense of
Us despite some areas of diversity in employees' ideologies. Disunity
and toxicity are not hallmarks of an effective company; differences
will not go away and must be accommodated. The goal is to create a
sense of solidarity and focus on the corporate mission that renders the
differences harmless.

This does not sound easy,[38] but Fort (2001, pp. 168ff.) argues that
companies can accommodate religiously diverse workforces primarily
by showing that they are willing to listen to all voices. We sometimes
despise people of other religions or ethnicities without having a close
acquaintance with what they believe, except that they despise us too,
on roughly the same grounds. But Fort (2008, p. 111) points out that
what appear to be religious differences are often something else. The
"troubles' in Northern Ireland were not primarily about religious doctrine. Evangelical and liberal Protestants invoke the same Bible. Perhaps what is at stake as much as anything else is respect. It is easy to
see how people in traditional societies might feel that executives and
employees in large Western firms do not respect them or their values,
particularly their religious ones, and how they might develop coun-
tercontempt and defensive rigidity about their own religion and thus
confirm the Westerners' stereotype of them as superstitious primitives.
On the other hand, as Fort claims (2001, p. 171), you are unlikely to
be angry with anyone who is making a sincere effort to understand
your faith.

Getting to respectful dialectic

Assuming this can be done at all, it will be a gradual process. If you are
unaccustomed to the notion that a Muslim can be a trusted colleague,
you may at first think of the new hire as an odd and prickly fellow, perhaps typical of Muslims. (Recall the discussion of how we see people,
in Chapter 2.) Meanwhile he is wary of you because you are Jewish.
But you must deal with him on business issues and aim at common
goals, and as a result you may come to respect him as a professional
and think of him as Ibrahim rather than as The Muslim. That is a step,

---

[38] Managing diversity is challenging, according to many scholars of the topic. See,
for example, Ely and Thomas (2001) and Jehn, Northcraft, and Neale (1999).

but only one step, towards thinking of all Muslim professionals that way. William Sloane Coffin used to tell the story of a southern university football team that had finally recruited its first African American in the 1950s. During a hard-fought game an African American on the other team illegally blocked that player. A white player on the southern team raced over to one of the officials and shouted, "You see what that [racial slur] done to our colored guy?"[39]

Once that happens, you will begin to discover that you and I (the Muslim or woman) have much in common, beginning with ethical intuitions about particular cases. From this it is possible, though not inevitable, that dialectic will develop. Agreement on these cases can be the basis for discussion of other cases and of principles, such as principles that relate to loyalty. So can disagreement. The more we have both come to understand our interdependence and have learned to focus on the common good of the organization, the more likely it is that we will respect each other. This mutual respect will give you confidence that you can defend your views on the basis of reasons that I will listen to. In so doing so you will also presuppose that I am rational, in particular that on the whole what you find reasonable I too will find reasonable.

Pinker (2011, especially pp. 647–50; cited in Gutting, 2011) argues that the very willingness to accept reasoned argument is a large step towards moral reconciliation and thus reduction of hostility and thus progress towards a less warlike world. His view of the place of rationality in ethics is controversial – Aristotle would probably not accept it – but it is of great importance to try to be reasonable and to understand others as also trying to be reasonable. We are all familiar with the frequency and futility of *ad hominem* arguments.

Suppose, for example, that Jones blows the whistle on his boss. You admire Jones for it; I do not. You say that Jones acted on the basis of honesty and the long-term best interests of the organization. I say that Jones was disloyal. We understand each other; that is important. I know that honesty is a virtue; you know that loyalty is a virtue.[40] We might test our views about how to combine honesty and loyalty by considering other possible cases about which we have similar intuitions

[39] The story also shows the important role of emotion in changing intuitions.
[40] Recall Appiah (2006, pp. 67, 80): we may honor similar virtues but differ on their priority – and, I would add, on what sort of account we give of them.

and seeing whether they presuppose anything about the two virtues and how they relate. "Well, what if Jones saw his boss stealing an expensive computer?" "Well, what if Jones's boss couldn't trust him?" By this process we improve our practical wisdom, and we may find more useful principles and have more reliable intuitions.

That this kind of conversation could involve two people raised as Western liberals should make us more rather than less optimistic about dialogue concerning religious differences, which Fort claims must be part of the mediating process. To learn about a religion different from one's own is not to accept its truth but to understand it: you come to see how a rational person might accept it. Along the way you might have to consider some of the questionable aspects of your own, the sort of thing you dismiss in the case of your own religion but focus on in others. What are Jews and Christians to make of Psalm 137, often set to music by devout Christian composers? Verse 9, in the King James Version, addresses the Babylonians: "Happy shall he be, that taketh and dasheth thy little ones against the stones." You can see why Muslims, especially Iraqis, might not admire the sentiment.

Beyond the organization

In due course a company that finds unity in diversity, that is respect-fully open to discussing new points of view, is better able to provide a bridge to Them, outside the organization.[41] Not all of Them will be amenable; some will have few intuitions in common with us. The Mus-lims who carried on lethal riots for days after blaming the United States for a crudely insulting movie about their Prophet and those who called for the execution of a British teacher whose pupils called a classroom pet "Muhammad" are not promising partners in dialogue. Nor can we expect the Americans who believe that their President is an African-born Muslim to join a rational conversation. But we can see the point of multinational businesses trying to be mediators for their employees and many of their closest stakeholders, and we can hope that their policies of respectful tolerance will spread much as other forms of their influence spread.

---

[41] In the words of Putnam (2000), bonding capital leads to bridging capital, or so one hopes.

We can hope that changing economic and political conditions will lead an increasing number of ideological participants in mediating institutions to develop new intuitions and principles, much as Christianity itself adapted to capitalism, in part by ignoring some of the plain words of the Gospels, much as China adapted to the demands and rewards of capitalism, which have trumped Marxism. Both Muslim and Christian versions of fundamentalism continue to thrive even among some who have been exposed to Western values and are technologically and economically sophisticated, but we have reason to believe that their antipathies are not based on actual doctrinal differences. If so, better communication may help reduce the Us–Them attitude on both sides – or at least put it on a more rational basis, so that one thinks of the new colleague as "our colored guy" and then, we may hope, goes on from there. The organization's financial success will be a big help.

Despite the many ways in which Aristotle's *polis* differs from a modern company competing globally, there is this important similarity: virtue begins in a small community. That community may be a company or a unit of a company. A company has to make a profit, but MacIntyre is wrong in believing that that requirement always crowds out virtue. What does present a problem is that Aristotle contemplates a *polis* that is culturally homogeneous, and I am arguing that dialectic offers some hope in a culturally heterogeneous setting. We nevertheless have reason to be hopeful, because people who share an interest in being employed in a multinational company probably have enough in common to be able to undertake rational dialogue. I think Appiah is right in saying that people in different cultures respect the same virtues, though not always the same versions of them.

Conclusion

I began this chapter by stating that Aristotle had three insights that could be useful in thinking about global business. First, practical wisdom is a matter of flexibly and creatively addressing new situations for which there are no rules. It is not a matter of identifying and following the right universal rules. If you and I are committed to justice, we may need to work out just what justice calls for in a certain complicated situation. (And Appiah says we both care about justice.) Second,

Aristotle's virtue ethics, a middle way between traditional communitarianism and modern individualism, is hospitable to both the importance of community and the need for individuals to create their own lives rationally. Third, dialectic can lead to ethical consensus. In the context of international business, these three views come together when companies or their units are communities in which people who are virtuous and therefore adaptive can have dialectical conversations about how to deal with ethical issues and about what kind of community they want to be.

I do not claim that this is the best possible approach to ethics in the context of global business. It is an Aristotelian approach, and I believe there is something to be said for it.

Both Appiah (2006, p. 152) and Haidt (2012, p. 307) quote Edmund Burke:

> ... to love the little platoon we belong to in society, is the first principle (the germ as it were) of public affections. It is the first link in the series by which we proceed toward a love to our country and to mankind.

Burke is right in saying that we must proceed towards an ethical world by starting where we are, in our little platoon, with its own version of the virtues and its own differences that must be reconciled. He does not suggest that its virtues can be spread unchanged. It may not have occurred to Burke that we are members simultaneously of many platoons, and he probably did not have units of organizations in mind when he thought of platoons. But he is clearly and correctly saying that we progress from our small communities by developing a sense of Us and then expanding its scope to a wise tolerance of and communication with Them. We do not start with universally applicable principles or conceptions of virtues that apply in all local situations. If we are able to sustain a fairly high level of rationality, we shall probably find that we can compare our intuitions and principles with those of others and arrive at new and mutually acceptable intuitions and principles which we can adapt or alter to fit new but recognizable versions of our old virtues.

Global enterprise is an extraordinary challenge for the Aristotelian view, because it requires a measure of social capital, respect, and understanding difficult to achieve in heterogeneous collections of people, as opposed to the small and homogeneous communities – not very large platoons – that form the context of Aristotle's work on ethics and politics. Following Fort and others I have suggested that global virtue may be possible but that it must start in the right sort of place. We learn virtue in small communities, where we do not contemplate all humankind. Aristotle is right about that.

There is no system or structure that will guarantee a virtuous state or a virtuous organization. Democracy, free markets, dialectic, and other excellent things will not work in the absence of virtuous participants. We noted earlier that Fort (1999, pp. 402f.) argues that we require some substantive and even transcendent morality. Aristotle believes that we require good character and the kind of practical wisdom found in extraordinary managerial and political skill. This is a human condition, not transcendent, but Aristotle suggests that there is something divine about it. If Haidt and the others are right, we lack the kind of rationality that will create organizations and institutions productive and hospitable to virtue. Our sociability, inadequately linked to rationality, sees Them almost everywhere. We might add that there is a problem of circularity: while there is no form of community that can guarantee virtue, we cannot have virtue without a good community.

Human progress depends upon people becoming more rationally sociable. If we accept group selection and Pinker's optimism about rationality, we may believe that that is slowly happening. What Aristotle says about our prospects is that that is the way nature tends, but not that it is therefore inevitable. A strong teleologist will hold that in the fullness of time flourishing will spread. Aristotle gives little sign of believing that: he surely knows that many people do not flourish. We accept teleological explanations of human behavior, but it does not follow that we shall achieve that towards which nature tends.

It is important that human beings are at least capable of rationality along with sociability, and that therefore they are capable of creating good states and even a good international order. This is a bit more optimistic than saying that, for example, humankind is fallen and evil and cannot succeed in creating a good life without the grace of God. The problem is that we simply are not as rational as we ought to be, nor as sociable for that matter. But we can hope to find some imperfect and temporary consensus on principles and intuitions. We can hope that our principles and intuitions will be sufficiently similar that we can tolerate and cooperate and where necessary discuss our differences and see whether we can narrow them and, as new occasions arise, eliminate them. Getting to precisely applicable universal principles is not necessary for moral progress and not possible. Burke does not claim that we can do it. Significantly, he mentions love. Whether or not he meant to be taken literally, he does seem to be making the quite correct point that the necessary project of relating Them properly to Us is, as Aristotle said, in part a matter of emotional binding. But Burke, the great conservative, surely understood how long and difficult will be "the series by which we proceed."

Bibliography

Abdolmohammadi, M., and M. F. Reeves. 2003. "Does Group Reasoning Improve Ethical Reasoning?" *Business and Society Review*, 108, 127–37.

Adler, P., and S. Kwon. 2002. "Social Capital: Prospects for a New Concept." *Academy of Management Review*, 27, 17–40.

Akerlof, G. 1982. "Labor Contracts as Partial Gift Exchange." *Quarterly Journal of Economics*, 97, 543–69.

———. 2007. "The Missing Motivation in Macroeconomics." Presidential Address. Nashville, TN: American Economic Association.

Allen, W. 2006. "Our Schizophrenic Conception of the Business Corporation". In *Professional Responsibility*, 35–47. NYU Stern, Course Book.

Alzola, M. 2008. "Character and Environment: The Status of Virtues in Organizations." *Journal of Business Ethics*, 78, 343–57.

———. 2011. "The Reconciliation Project: Separation and Integration in Business Ethics Research." *Journal of Business Ethics*, 99, 19–36.

———. 2012. "The Possibility of Virtue." *Business Ethics Quarterly*, 22, 377–404.

Annas, J. 2011. *Intelligent Virtue*. New York: Oxford University Press.

Anscombe, G. 1957. *Intention*. Oxford: Basil Blackwell.

———. 1997. "Modern Moral Philosophy." In R. Crisp and M. Slote (Eds.), *Virtue Ethics*, 26–44. New York: Oxford University Press.

Appiah, K. A. 2006. *Cosmopolitanism: Ethics in a World of Strangers*. New York: W. W. Norton.

Aristotle. 1894. *Ethica Nicomachea*. Edited by I. Bywater. Oxford: Clarendon Press.

———. 1907. *De Anima*. Edited by R. D. Hicks. Cambridge: Cambridge University Press.

———. 1957. *Politica*. Edited by W. D. Ross. Oxford: Clarendon Press.

———. 1962. *The Politics of Aristotle*. Translated by E. Barker. New York: Oxford University Press.

———. 1999. *Nicomachean Ethics*, 2nd edition. Translated by T. H. Irwin. Indianapolis: Hackett Publishing Company.

Asch, S. 1955. "Studies of Independence and Conformity: A Minority of One against a Unanimous Majority." *Psychological Monographs*, 70.9, Whole No. 416.

Audi, R. 1989. *Practical Reasoning*. New York: Routledge.

———. 1997. *Moral Knowledge and Ethical Character*. New York: Oxford University Press.

——— 2012. "Virtue Ethics as a Resource in Business." *Business Ethics Quarterly*, 22, 273–91.

Baumeister, R., and J. Tierney. 2011. *Willpower: Discovering the Greatest Human Strength*. New York: Penguin Press.

Bazerman, M., and A. Tenbrunsel. 2011. *Blind Spots: Why We Fail to Do What's Right and What to Do about It*. Princeton: Princeton University Press.

Beabout, G. 2012. "Management as a Domain-Relative Practice that Requires and Develops Practical Wisdom." *Business Ethics Quarterly*, 22, 405–32.

Beadle, R., and K. Knight. 2012. "Virtue and Meaningful Work." *Business Ethics Quarterly*, 22, 433–50.

Beaman, A., P. Barnes, B. Klentz, and B. McQuirk. 1978. "Increasing Helping Rates Through Information Dissemination: Teaching Pays." *The Personality and Social Psychology Bulletin*, 4, 406–11.

Belk, R. 1985. "Materialism: Trait Aspects of Living in the Material World." *Journal of Consumer Research*, 12, 265–80.

Berkowitz, P. 1999. *Virtue and the Making of Modern Liberalism*. Princeton: Princeton University Press.

Bertland, A. 2009. "Virtue Ethics in Business and the Capabilities Approach." *Journal of Business Ethics*, 84, 25–32.

Blasi, A. 1999. "Emotions and Moral Motivation." *Journal for the Theory of Social Behavior*, 29, 1–19.

Boatright, J. 1995. "Aristotle Meets Wall Street: The Case for Virtue Ethics in Business." A review of *Ethics and Excellence: Cooperation and Integrity in Business*, by Robert C. Solomon. *Business Ethics Quarterly*, 5, 353–9.

Bowles, S., and H. Gintis. 2011. *A Cooperative Species: Human Reciprocity and its Evolution*. Princeton: Princeton University Press.

Bragues, G. 2006. "Seek the Good Life, Not Money: The Aristotelian Approach to Business Ethics." *Journal of Business Ethics*, 67, 341–57.

Burke, J. 1985. "Speech to the Advertising Council." In W. M. Hoffman and J. M. Moore (Eds.), *Management of Values: The Ethical Difference in Corporate Policy and Performance*, 451–6. New York: McGraw-Hill Book Company.

Burns, J. 1978. *Leadership*. New York: Harper and Row.

Calkins, M., and P. Werhane. 1998. "Adam Smith, Aristotle, and the Virtues of Commerce." *The Journal of Value Inquiry*, 32, 43–60.

Carroll, A. 1981. *Business and Society: Managing Corporate Social Performance*. Boston: Little, Brown.

Cartwright, N. 1983. *How the Laws of Physics Lie*. New York: Oxford University Press.

Chaiken, S., R. Giner-Sorolla, and S. Chen. 1996. "Beyond Accuracy: Defense and Impression Motives in Heuristic and Systematic Information Processing." In P. M. Gollwitzer and J. A. Bargh (Eds.), *The Psychology of Action: Linking Cognition and Motivation to Behavior*, 553–78. New York: Guilford Press.

Chan, G. 2007. "The Relevance and Value of Confucianism in Contemporary Business Ethics." *Journal of Business Ethics*, 77, 347–60.

Chen, A., R. Sawyers, and P. Williams. 1997. "Reinforcing Ethical Decision Making through Corporate Culture." *Journal of Business Ethics*, 16, 855–65.

Chicago Tribune 2002. "Tribune Special Report: A Final Accounting." September 1–4.

Ciulla, J. 2000. *The Working Life: The Promise and Betrayal of Modern Work*. New York: Three Rivers Press.

Claassen, R. 2012. Review of *Why Some Things Should Not Be For Sale: The Moral Limits of Markets*, by Debra Satz. *Business Ethics Quarterly*, 22, 585–97.

Cleckley, H. 1988. *The Mask of Sanity*, 5th edition. St. Louis: C. V. Mosby.

Coase, R. 1937. "The Nature of the Firm." *Economica*, 4, 386–405.

Colle, S., and P. Werhane. 2008. "Moral Motivation Across Ethical Theories: What Can We Learn for Designing Corporate Ethics Programs?" *Journal of Business Ethics*, 81, 751–64.

Collins, J. 2001. *Good to Great: Why Some Companies Make the Leap . . . and Others Don't*. New York: HarperBusiness.

———, and J. Porras. 2002. *Built to Last: Successful Habits of Visionary Companies*. New York: HarperCollins.

Costa, P., and R. MacCrae. 1994. "Stability and Change in Personality from Adolescence through Adulthood." In C. Halvorson, G. Kohnstamm, and R. Martin (Eds.), *The Developing Structure of Temperament and Personality from Infancy to Adulthood*, 139–50. Hillsdale, NJ: Erlbaum.

Crary, A. 2007. *Beyond Moral Judgment*. Cambridge, MA: Harvard University Press.

Damasio, A. 1994. *Descartes' Error: Emotion, Reason, and the Human Brain*. New York: Putnam.

Daniels, N. 1979. "Wide Reflective Equilibrium and Theory Acceptance in Ethics." *Journal of Philosophy*, 76, 256–82.

Darley, J. 1996. "How Organizations Socialize Individuals into Evildoing." In D. Messick and A. Tenbrunsel (Eds.), *Codes of Conduct: Behavioral Research into Business Ethics*, 13–43. New York: Russell Sage Foundation

Davidson, D. 2001. *Essays on Actions and Events*, 2nd edition. New York: Oxford University Press.

DeSousa, R. 1987. *The Rationality of Emotion*. Cambridge: MIT Press.

Donaldson, L. 2005. "For Positive Management Theories While Retaining Science: Reply to Ghoshal." *Academy of Management Learning and Education*, 4, 109–13.

Donaldson, T., and T. Dunfee. 1999. *Ties that Bind: A Social Contracts Approach to Business Ethics*. Boston: Harvard Business Press.

Doris, J. 2002. *Lack of Character: Personality and Moral Behavior*. New York: Cambridge University Press.

Drake, M., and J. Schlachter. 2008. "A Virtue-Ethics Analysis of Supply Chain Collaboration." *Journal of Business Ethics*, 82, 851–64.

Duhigg, C. 2012. *The Power of Habit: Why We Do What We Do in Life and Business*. New York: Random House.

Dunbar, R. 1992. "Neocortex Size as a Constraint on Group Size in Primates." *Journal of Human Evolution*, 22, 469–93.

Dunfee, T., and D. Warren. 2001. "Is Guanxi Ethical? A Normative Analysis of Doing Business in China." *Journal of Business Ethics*, 32, 191–204.

Dyck, B., and R. Kleysen. 2001. "Aristotle's Virtues and Management Thought: An Empirical Exploration of an Integrative Pedagogy." *Business Ethics Quarterly*, 11, 561–74.

Eastman, W., and M. Santoro. 2003. "The Importance of Value Diversity in Corporate Life." *Business Ethics Quarterly*, 13, 433–52.

Elster, J. 1985. *Sour Grapes: Studies in the Subversion of Rationality*. New York: Cambridge University Press.

———. 1998. "Emotions and Economic Theory." *Journal of Economic Literature*, 36, 47–74.

Ely, R., and D. Thomas. 2001. "Cultural Diversity at Work: The Effects of Diversity Perspectives on Work Group Processes and Outcomes." *Administrative Science Quarterly*, 46, 229–73.

Festinger, L. 1957. *A Theory of Cognitive Dissonance*. Stanford: Stanford University Press.

Foot, P. 1997. "Virtues and Vices." In R. Crisp and M. Slote (Eds.), *Virtue Ethics*, 163–77. New York: Oxford University Press.

Fort, T. 1999. "The *First Man* and the *Company Man*: The Common Good, Transcendence, and Mediating Institutions." *American Business Law Journal*, 36, 391–435.

———. 2001. *Ethics and Governance: Business as Mediating Institution*. New York: Oxford University Press.

———. 2008. *Prophets, Profits, and Peace: The Positive Role of Business in Promoting Religious Tolerance*. New Haven: Yale University Press.

Fox, D. 1985. "Psychology, Ideology, Utopia, and the Commons." *American Psychologist*, 40, 48–58.

Frank, R. 1988. *Passions within Reason: The Strategic Role of the Emotions*. New York: W. W. Norton & Company.

———. 2004. *What Price the Moral High Ground? Ethical Dilemmas in Competitive Environments*. Princeton: Princeton University Press.

———, T. Gilovich, and D. Regan. 1993. "Does Studying Economics Inhibit Cooperation?" *Journal of Economic Perspectives*, 7, 159–71.

Frankfurt, H. 1981. "Freedom of the Will and the Concept of a Person." In G. Watson (Ed.), *Free Will*, 81–95. New York: Oxford University Press.

Freeman, R. E. 1994. "The Politics of Stakeholder Theory: Some Future Directions." *Business Ethics Quarterly*, 4, 409–21.

———, J. Harrison, and A. Wicks. 2007. *Managing for Stakeholders: Survival, Reputation, and Success*. New Haven: Yale University Press.

Friedman, M. 1970. "The Social Responsibility of Business is to Increase its Profits." *New York Times Magazine*, September 13.

Fritzsche, D. 1991. "A Model of Decision-Making Incorporating Ethical Values." *Journal of Business Ethics*, 10, 841–52.

———. 2000. "Ethical Climates and the Ethical Dimension of Decision Making." *Journal of Business Ethics*, 24, 125–40.

Furman, F. 1990. "Teaching Business Ethics: Questioning the Assumptions, Seeking New Directions." *Journal of Business Ethics*, 9, 31–8.

Galston, W. 1991. *Liberal Purposes: Goods, Virtues, and Diversity in the Liberal State*. New York: Cambridge University Press.

Geertz, C. 1983. *Local Knowledge: Further Essays in Interpretive Anthropology*. New York: Basic Books.

Ghoshal, S. 2005. "Bad Management Theories are Destroying Good Management Practices. *Academy of Management Learning and Education*, 4, 75–91.

Gilbert, D. 2006. *Stumbling on Happiness*. New York: Knopf.

———, E. Pinel, T. Wilson, S. Blumberg, and T. Wheatley. 1998. "Immune Neglect: A Source of Durability Bias in Affective Forecasting." *Journal of Personality and Social Psychology*, 25, 617–38.

Giovanola, B. 2009. "Re-Thinking the Ethical and Anthropological Foundation of Economics and Business: Human Richness and Capabilities Enhancement." *Journal of Business Ethics*, 88, 431–44.

Gladwell, M. 2005. *Blink: The Power of Thinking Without Thinking*. New York: Back Bay Books (Little, Brown).

Gould, S. 1995. "The Buddhist Perspective on Business Ethics: Experiential Exercises for Exploration and Practice." *Journal of Business Ethics*, 14, 63–70.

Graafland, J. 2009. "Do Markets Crowd Out Virtues? An Aristotelian Framework." *Journal of Business Ethics*, 91, 1–19.

Gutting, G. 2011. "Pinker on Reason and Morality." *New York Times* (electronic edition), October 26, 2011.

Haidt, J. 2001. "The Emotional Dog and its Rational Tail: A Social Intuitionist Approach to Moral Judgment." *Psychological Review*, 108, 814–34.

———. 2006. *The Happiness Hypothesis*. New York: Basic Books.

———. 2012. *The Righteous Mind: Why Good People are Divided by Politics and Religion*. New York: Pantheon Books.

Hambrick, D. 2005. "Just How Bad Are Our Theories? A Response to Ghoshal." *Academy of Management Learning and Education*, 4, 104–7.

Hampshire, S. 1983. *Morality and Conflict*. Cambridge: Harvard University Press.

Hardin, G. 1968. "The Tragedy of the Commons." *Science*, 162, 1243–8.

Hare, R. D. 1993. *Without Conscience: The Disturbing World of the Psychopaths among Us*. New York: Simon and Schuster.

Hare, R. M. 1952. *The Language of Morals*. Oxford: Oxford University Press.

Harman, G. 2003. "No Character or Personality." *Business Ethics Quarterly*, 13, 87–94.

Hartman, E. 1977. *Substance, Body, and Soul: Aristotelian Investigations*. Princeton: Princeton University Press.

———. 1994. "The Commons and the Moral Organization." *Business Ethics Quarterly*, 4, 253–69.

———. 1996. *Organizational Ethics and the Good Life*. New York: Oxford University Press.

———. 1998. "The Role of Character in Business Ethics." *Business Ethics Quarterly*, 8, 547–59.

———. 2001. "An Aristotelian Approach to Moral Imagination." *Professional Ethics*, 8, 58–77.

———. 2006. "Can We Teach Character? An Aristotelian Answer." *Academy of Management Learning and Education*, 5, 68–81.

Hausman, D. 2012. *Preference, Value, Choice, and Welfare*. New York: Cambridge University Press.

Heath, J. 2009. "The Uses and Abuses of Agency Theory." *Business Ethics Quarterly*, 19, 497–528.

Heugens, P., M. Kaptein, and J. van Oosterhout. 2006. "The Ethics of the Node versus the Ethics of the Dyad? Reconciling Virtue Ethics and Contractualism." *Organization Studies*, 27, 391–411.

Hirschman, A. 1982. "Rival Interpretations of Market Society: Civilizing, Destructive, or Feeble?" *Journal of Economic Literature*, 20, 1463–84.

Horvath, C. 1995. "MacIntyre's Critique of Business." *Business Ethics Quarterly*, 5, 499–532.

Hursthouse, R. 1999. *On Virtue Ethics*. New York: Oxford University Press.

Irwin, T. 1988. *Aristotle's First Principles*. New York: Oxford University Press.

Jackson, K. 2012. *Virtuosity in Business: Invisible Law Guiding the Invisible Hand*. Philadelphia: University of Pennsylvania Press.

Jehn, K., G. Northcraft, and M. Neale. 1999. "Why Differences Make a Difference: A Field Study of Diversity, Conflict and Performance in Workgroups." *Administrative Science Quarterly*, 44, 741–63.

Jensen, M. 2010. "Value Maximization, Stakeholder Theory, and the Corporate Objective Function." *Journal of Applied Corporate Finance*, 22, 32–42.

———, and W. Meckling. 1976. "Theory of the Firm: Managerial Behaviour, Agency Costs, and Ownership Structure." *Journal of Financial Economics*, 3, 305–60.

———, ———. 1994. "The Nature of Man." *Journal of Applied Corporate Finance*, 72 (Summer), 4–19.

Johnson, M. 1993. *Moral Imagination: Implications of Cognitive Science for Ethics*. Chicago: University of Chicago Press.

Johnson and Johnson. 1943. *Credo*. New Brunswick, NJ: Johnson and Johnson.

Jones, S., and K. Hiltebeitel. 1995. "Organizational Influence in a Model of the Moral Decision Process of Accountants." *Journal of Business Ethics*, 14, 417–31.

Jones, T., and L. Ryan. 2001. "The Effect of Organizational Forces on Individual Morality: Judgment, Moral Approbation, and Behavior." In J. Dienhart, D. Moberg, and R. Duska (Eds.), *The Next Phase of Business Ethics: Integrating Psychology and Ethics*, 285–300. New York: Elsevier Science.

Jos, P., and M. Tompkins. 2004. "The Accountability Paradox in an Age of Reinvention: The Perennial Problem of Preserving Character and Judgment." *Administration and Society*, 36, 255–81.

Kahneman, D. 2011. *Thinking, Fast and Slow*. New York: Farrar, Straus and Giroux.

———, and A. Tversky (Eds.). 2000. *Choices, Values, and Frames*. New York: Cambridge University Press.

Kant, I. 1981. *Grounding for the Metaphysics of Morals*. Translated by J. Ellington. Indianapolis: Hackett Publishing Company.

Kasser, T., and R. Ryan. 1996. "Further Examining the American Dream: Differential Correlates of Intrinsic and Extrinsic Goals." *Personality and Social Psychology Bulletin*, 22, 280–7.

Klein, S. 1995. "An Aristotelian Approach to Ethical Corporate Leadership." *Business and Professional Ethics Journal*, 14, 3–23.

———. 1998. "Emotions and Practical Reasoning: Implications for Business Ethics." *Business and Professional Ethics Journal*, 17, 3–29.

Koehn, D. 1992. "Toward an Ethic of Exchange." *Business Ethics Quarterly*, 2, 341–55.

———. 1995. "A Role for Virtue Ethics in the Analysis of Business Practice. *Business Ethics Quarterly*, 5, 533–9.

———. 1998. "Virtue Ethics, the Firm, and Moral Psychology." *Business Ethics Quarterly*, 8, 497–513.

Kohlberg, L. 1981. *Essays on Moral Development. Volume I: The Philosophy of Moral Development*. New York: Harper and Row.

Kraut, R. 1989. *Aristotle on the Human Good*. Princeton: Princeton University Press.

Kupperman, J. 1991. *Character*. New York: Oxford University Press.

———. 2005. "How Not to Educate Character." In D. Lapsley and F. C. Power (Eds.), *Character Psychology and Character Education*, 201–17. Notre Dame, IN: University of Notre Dame Press.

LeBar, M. 2009. "Virtue Ethics and Deontic Constraints." *Ethics*, 119, 642–71.

Lerner, J., and P. Tetlock. 2003. "Bridging Individual, Interpersonal, and Institutional Approaches to Judgment and Decision Making: The Impact of Accountability on Cognitive Bias." In S. Schneider and J. Shanteau (Eds.), *Emerging Perspectives on Judgment and Decision Research*, 431–57. New York: Cambridge University Press.

Lewis, M. 1989. *Liar's Poker: Rising through the Wreckage on Wall Street*. New York: W. W. Norton.

Lieberman, M. D. 2000. "Intuition: A Social Cognitive Neuroscience Approach." *Psychological Bulletin*, 126, 109–37.

Loewenstein, G., and D. Adler. 2000. "A Bias in the Prediction of Tastes." In D. Kahneman and A. Tversky (Eds.), *Choices, Values, and Frames*, 726–34. New York: Cambridge University Press.

Luban, D. 2003. "Integrity: Its Causes and Cures." *Fordham Law Review*, 72, 279–310.

MacIntyre, A. 1985. *After Virtue*, 2nd edition. Notre Dame: University of Notre Dame Press.

Maitland, I. 1997. "Virtuous Markets: The Market as School of the Virtues." *Business Ethics Quarterly*, 7, 17–31.

Martin, M. 2006. *From Morality to Mental Health: Virtue and Vice in a Therapeutic Culture*. New York: Oxford University Press.

Maslow, A. 1987. *Motivation and Personality*, 3rd edition. New York: Harper and Row.

Matson, W. 2001. "Unfair to Justice." *Modern Age*, 372–278.

McCabe, D., and L. Trevino. 1995. "Cheating among Business Students: A Challenge for Business Leaders and Educators." *Journal of Management Education*, 19, 205–18.

McCloskey, D. 2006. *The Bourgeois Virtues: Ethics for an Age of Commerce*. Chicago: University of Chicago Press.

McCracken, J., and B. Shaw. 1995. "Virtue Ethics and Contractarianism: Towards a Reconciliation." *Business Ethics Quarterly*, 5, 297–312.

McDowell, J. 1997. "Virtue and Reason." In R. Crisp and M. Slote (Eds.), *Virtue Ethics*, 141–62. New York: Oxford University Press.

McKinnon, C. 2005. "Character Possession and Human Flourishing." In D. Lapsley and F. Power (Eds.), *Character Psychology and Character Education*, 36–66. Notre Dame, IN: University of Notre Dame Press.

Melé, D. 2003. "The Challenge of Humanistic Management." *Journal of Business Ethics*, 44, 77–88.

Melville, H. 2001. *Billy Budd, Sailor*. Chicago: University of Chicago Press.

Merck. 2011. http://www.merck.com/responsibility/access/access-feature-mectizan.html.

Messick, D. 1998. "Social Categories and Business Ethics." In R. E. Freeman (Ed.), *Business, Science, and Ethics*, 149–72, Ruffin Series No. 1. *Business Ethics Quarterly* (Special Issue).

Metcalfe, J., and W. Mischel. 1999. "A Hot–Cool System Analysis of Delay of Gratification: Dynamics of Willpower." *Psychological Review*, 106, 3–19.

Milgram, S. 1974. *Obedience to Authority: An Experimental View*. New York: Harper and Row.

Miller, F. 1995. *Nature, Justice, and Rights in Aristotle's Politics*. New York: Oxford University Press.

Moberg, D. 1999. "The Big Five and Organizational Virtue." *Business Ethics Quarterly*, 9, 245–72.

_____. 2006. "Ethics Blind Spots in Organizations: How Systematic Errors in Person Perception Undermine Moral Agency." *Organization Studies,* 27, 413–28.

_____, and M. Seabright. 2000. "The Development of Moral Imagination." *Business Ethics Quarterly,* 10, 845–84.

Moore, G. 2002. "On the Implications of the Practice–Institution Distinction: MacIntyre and the Application of Modern Virtue Ethics to Business." *Business Ethics Quarterly,* 12, 19–32.

_____. 2005a. "Corporate Character: Modern Virtue Ethics and the Virtuous Corporation." *Business Ethics Quarterly,* 15, 659–85.

_____. 2005b. "Humanizing Business: A Modern Virtue Ethics Approach." *Business Ethics Quarterly,* 15, 237–55.

_____. 2008. "Re-imagining the Morality of Management: A Modern Virtue Ethics Approach." *Business Ethics Quarterly,* 18, 483–511.

_____. 2009. "Virtue Ethics and Business Organizations." In J. Smith (Ed.), *Normative Theory and Business Ethics,* 35–59. New York: Rowman and Littlefield.

_____. 2012. "The Virtue of Governance, the Governance of Virtue." *Business Ethics Quarterly,* 22, 293–318.

_____, and R. Beadle. 2006. "In Search of Organizational Virtue in Business: Agents, Goods, Practices, Institutions and Environments." *Organization Studies,* 27, 369–89.

Morris, C. 2008. *The Trillion Dollar Meltdown: Easy Money, High Rollers, and the Great Credit Crash.* New York: Public Affairs.

Néron, P., and W. Norman. 2008. "Citizenship, Inc." *Business Ethics Quarterly,* 18, 1–26.

Newton, L. 1992. "Virtue and Role: Reflections on the Social Nature of Morality." *Business Ethics Quarterly,* 2, 357–65.

Nickerson, R. 1994. "The Teaching of Thinking and Problem Solving." In R. Sternberg (Ed.), *Thinking and Problem Solving,* 409–49. San Diego: Academic Press.

Nielsen, R. 2001. "Can Ethical Character be Stimulated and Enabled: An Action-Learning Approach to Teaching and Learning Organization Ethics." In J. Dienhart, D. Moberg, and R. Duska (Eds.), *The Next Phase of Business Ethics: Integrating Psychology and Ethics,* 51–77. New York: Elsevier Science.

Norman, W. 2002. "Inevitable and Unacceptable? Methodological Rawlsianism in Anglo-American Political Philosophy." *Political Studies,* 46, 276–94.

Numkanisorn, S. 2002. "Business and Buddhist Ethics." *The Chulalongkorn Journal of Buddhist Studies,* 1, 39–58.

Nussbaum, M. 1990. "Finely Aware and Richly Responsible: Literature and the Moral Imagination." In *Love's Knowledge: Essays on Philosophy and Literature*, 148–67. New York: Oxford University Press.

———. 2010. *Not for Profit: Why Democracy Needs the Humanities*. Princeton: Princeton University Press.

Ostrom, E., and T. K. Ahn. 2009. "The Meaning of Social Capital and its Link to Collective Action." In G. Svendsen and G. L. Svendsen (Eds.), *Handbook of Social Capital: The Troika of Sociology, Political Science and Economics*, 17–35. Northampton, MA: Edward Elgar Publishing.

Owen, G. 1960. "Logic and Metaphysics in Some Earlier Works of Aristotle." In I. During and G. Owen (Eds.), *Plato and Aristotle in the Mid-Fourth Century*, 163–90. Goeteborg: Almquist and Wiksell.

———. 1986. "Tithenai ta phainomena." In M. Nussbaum (Ed.), *Science and Dialectic*, 239–51. Ithaca, NY: Cornell University Press.

Paine, L. 1991. "Ethics as Character Development: Reflections on the Objective of Ethics Education." In R. Freeman (Ed.), *Business Ethics: The State of the Art*. 67–86. New York: Oxford University Press.

Pastoriza, D., M. Arino, and J. Ricart. 2007. "Ethical Managerial Behaviour as an Antecedent of Organizational Social Capital." *Journal of Business Ethics*, 78, 329–41.

Peters, T., and R. Waterman. 1982. *In Search of Excellence*. New York: Harper and Row.

Pfeffer, J. 1982. *Organizations and Organization Theory*. Boston: Pitman.

———. 2005. "Why Do Bad Management Theories Persist? A Comment on Ghoshal." *Academy of Management Learning and Education*, 4, 96–100.

Phillips, R., and C. Caldwell. 2005. "Value Chain Responsibility: A Farewell to Arm's Length." *Business and Society Review*, 110, 345–70.

Pinker, S. 2011. *The Better Angels of our Nature: Why Violence has Declined*. New York: Viking.

Pizarro, D., and P. Bloom. 2003. "The Intelligence of Moral Intuitions: Comment on Haidt." *Psychological Review*, 110, 193–6.

Porter, M. 1980. *Competitive Strategy: Techniques for Analyzing Industries and Competitors*. New York: Free Press.

Prior, W. 2001. "Eudaimonism." *Journal of Value Inquiry*, 35, 325–42.

Putnam, H. 2002. *The Collapse of the Fact/Value Dichotomy and Other Essays*. Cambridge: Harvard University Press.

Putnam, R. 2000. *Bowling Alone: The Collapse and Revival of American Community*. New York: Simon and Schuster.

————, and D. Campbell. 2010. *American Grace: How Religion Divides and Unites Us*. New York: Simon and Schuster.

Quine, W. 1980. *From a Logical Point of View*, 2nd edition. Cambridge, MA: Harvard University Press.

Rabin, M. 1998. "Psychology and Economics." *Journal of Economic Literature*, 36, 11–46.

Rawls, J. 1971. *A Theory of Justice*. Cambridge: Harvard University Press.

————. 1993. *Political Liberalism*. New York: Columbia University Press.

Roca, E. 2008. "Introducing Practical Wisdom in Business Schools." *Journal of Business Ethics*, 82, 607–20.

Rosenzweig, P. 2007. *The Halo Effect... and the Eight Other Business Delusions that Deceive Managers*. New York: Free Press.

Ross, L., and R. Nisbet. 1991. *The Person and the Situation: Perspectives of Social Psychology*. New York: McGraw-Hill.

Ross, W. D. 1930. *The Right and the Good*. New York: Oxford University Press.

Russell, D. 2009. *Practical Intelligence and the Virtues*. Oxford: Clarendon Press.

Salmieri, G. 2009. "Aristotle's Non-'Dialectical' Methodology in the Nicomachean Ethics." *Ancient Philosophy*, 29, 311–35.

Sandel, M. 2012. *What Money Can't Buy: The Moral Limits of Markets*. New York: Farrar, Straus and Giroux.

Schein, E. H. 1985. *Organizational Culture and Leadership*. San Francisco: Jossey-Bass.

Sen, A. 1987. *On Ethics and Economics*. New York: Basil Blackwell.

————. 1997. "Human Rights and Asian Values." *New Republic*, July 14–21. https://www.mtholyoke.edu/acad/intrel/sen.htm.

————. 2009. *The Idea of Justice*. Cambridge, MA: The Belknap Press.

————, and B. Williams (Eds.), 1982. *Utilitarianism and Beyond*. New York: Cambridge University Press.

Sennett, R. 1998. *The Corrosion of Character: The Transformation of Work in Modern Capitalism*. New York: W. W. Norton & Company.

Shaw, B. 1995. "Virtues for a Postmodern World." *Business Ethics Quarterly*, 5, 843–63.

Shiller, R. 2012. *Finance and the Good Society*. Princeton: Princeton University Press.

Shoda, Y., W. Mischel, and P. Peake. 1990. "Predicting Adolescent Cognitive and Self-regulatory Competencies from Pre-school Delay of Gratification: Identifying Diagnostic Conditions." *Developmental Psychology*, 26, 978–86.

Simmel, G. 1955. *Conflict and the Web of Group Affiliations*. Trans. By K. H. Wolfe. Glencoe, IL: The Free Press.

Simon, H. 1954. "A Behavioral Theory of Rational Choice." *Quarterly Journal of Economics*, 69, 99–118.

Sims, R., and T. Keon. 1999. "Determinants of Ethical Decision Making: The Relationship of the Perceived Organizational Environment." *Journal of Business Ethics*, 19, 393–401.

Sison, A. 2003. *The Moral Capital of Leaders: Why Ethics Matters.* Northampton, MA: Edward Elgar.

————. 2008. *Corporate Governance and Ethics: An Aristotelian Perspective.* Northampton, MA: Edward Elgar.

————. 2011. "Aristotelian Citizenship and Corporate Citizenship: Who is a Citizen of the Corporate Polis?" *Journal of Business Ethics*, 100, 3–9.

————, and J. Fontrodona. 2012. "The Common Good of the Firm in the Aristotelian-Thomistic Tradition." *Business Ethics Quarterly*, 22, 211–46.

Skidelsky, E. 2009. "Capitalism and the Good Life." In S. Gregg and J. Stoner (Eds.), *Profit, Prudence, and Virtue: Essays in Ethics, Business and Management*, 242–53. Exeter, UK: Imprint Academic.

Skinner, B. 1972. *Beyond Freedom and Dignity.* New York: Bantam Vintage.

Slater, L. 2004. *Opening Skinner's Box: Great Psychological Experiments of the Twentieth Century.* New York: W. W. Norton.

Slote, M. 1983. *Goods and Virtues.* New York: Oxford University Press.

————. 1992 *From Morality to Virtue.* New York: Oxford University Press.

————. 2001. *Morals from Motives.* New York: Oxford University Press.

Smith, H. 2012. *Who Stole the American Dream?* New York: Random House.

Solomon, R. 1992. *Ethics and Excellence: Cooperation and Integrity in Business.* New York: Oxford University Press.

Sommers, M. C. 1997. "Useful Friendships: A Foundation for Business Ethics." *Journal of Business Ethics,* 16, 1453–8.

Stark, A. 1993. "What's the Matter with Business Ethics?" *Harvard Business Review*, 71, 38–48.

Sundman, P. 2000. "The Good Manager – A Moral Manager?" *Journal of Business Ethics*, 27, 247–54.

Toulmin, S. 1990. *Cosmopolis: The Hidden Agenda of Modernity.* Chicago: University of Chicago Press.

Trevino, L. K. 1986. "Ethical Decision Making in Organizations: A Person-Situation Interactionist Model." *Academy of Management Review*, 11, 607–17.

————, K. Butterfield, and D. McCabe. 2001. "The Ethical Context in Organizations: Influences on Employee Attitudes and Behaviors." In J. Dienhart, D. Moberg, and R. Duska (Eds.), *The Next Phase of Business*

Ethics: Integrating Psychology and Ethics, 301–37. New York: Elsevier Science.

Trist, E., and K. Bamforth. 1951. "Some Social and Psychological Consequences of the Longwall Method of Coal Getting." *Human Relations*, 4, 3–38.

Tsalikis, J., and O. Wachukwu. 2000. "A Comparison of Nigerian to American Views of Bribery and Extortion in International Commerce." *Journal of Business Ethics*, 10, 85–98.

Tsoukas, H., and S. Cummings. 1997. "Marginalization and Recovery: The Emergence of Aristotelian Themes in Organization Studies." *Organization Studies*, 18, 655–83.

Turbow, J., with M. Duca. 2010. *The Baseball Codes: Beanballs, Sign Stealing, and Bench-Clearing Brawls: The Unwritten Rules of America's Pastime*. New York: Pantheon Books.

Turner, N., J. Barling, O. Epitropaki, V. Butcher, and C. Milner. 2002. "Transformational Leadership and Moral Reasoning." *Journal of Applied* Psychology, 87, 304–11.

Tversky, A., and D. Kahneman. 1981. "The Framing of Decisions and the Psychology of Choice." *Science*, 211, 453–8.

Vidaver-Cohen, D. 1997. "Moral Imagination in Organizational Problem-Solving: An Institutional Perspective." *Business Ethics Quarterly*, 7, 1–26.

———. 2001. "Motivational Appeal in Normative Theories of Enterprise." In J. Dienhart, D. Moberg, and R. Duska (Eds.), *The Next Phase of Business Ethics: Integrating Psychology and Ethics*, 3–26. New York: Elsevier Science.

Vlastos, G. 1994. *Socratic Studies*. New York: Cambridge University Press.

Walton, C. 2001. "Character and Integrity in Organizations: The Civilization of the Workplace." *Business and Professional Ethics Journal*, 20, 105–28.

Weaver, G. 2006. "Virtue in Organizations: Moral Identity as a Foundation for Moral Agency." *Organization Studies*, 27, 341–68.

———, and B. Agle. 2002. "Religiosity and Ethical Behavior in Organizations: A Symbolic Interactionist Perspective." *Academy of Management Review*, 27, 77–97.

Weick, K. 1969. *The Social Psychology of Organizing*. Reading, MA: Addison-Wesley.

———, K. Sutcliffe, and D. Obstfeld. 2005. "Organizing and the Process of Sensemaking." *Organization Science*, 16, 409–21.

Wells, T., and J. Graafland. 2012. "Adam Smith's Bourgeois Virtues in Competition." *Business Ethics Quarterly*, 22, 319–50.

Werhane, P. 1991. *Adam Smith and his Legacy for Modern Capitalism*. New York: Oxford University Press.

———. 1999. *Moral Imagination and Management Decision-making*. New York: Oxford University Press.

———, and M. Gorman. 2005. "Intellectual Property Rights, Moral Imagination, and Access to Life-enhancing Drugs." *Business Ethics Quarterly*, 15, 595–613.

———, L. Hartman, D. Moberg, E. Englehardt, M. Pritchard, and B. Parmar. 2011. "Social Constructivism, Mental Models, and Problems of Obedience." *Journal of Business Ethics*, 100, 103–18.

Whetstone, J. 2003. "The Language of Managerial Excellence: Virtues as Understood and Applied." *Journal of Business Ethics*, 44, 343–57.

Williams, B. 1981. *Moral Luck*. New York: Cambridge University Press.

———. 1985. *Ethics and the Limits of Philosophy*. Cambridge: Harvard University Press.

Williamson, O. 1975. *Markets and Hierarchies: Analysis and Anti-trust Implications*. New York: Free Press.

Winter, S. 1971. "Satisficing, Selection, and the Innovative Remnant." *Quarterly Journal of Economics*, 85, 237–61.

Woodruff, P. 2001. *Reverence: Renewing a Forgotten Virtue*. New York: Oxford University Press.

Zimbardo, P. 2007. *The Lucifer Effect: Understanding How Good People Turn Evil*. New York: Random House.

Index

Printed in the United States
by Baker & Taylor Publisher Services